MW00887692

Amazing Wildlife

True Stories About Wild Animals
Who Demonstrated Intelligence,
Adaptability, Friendship, Compassion,
and Individuality

Judy Hoy

Scientist, Biologist, Naturalist,
and Wildlife Rehabilitator

DISCLAIMER

No information contained herein is intended as medical or veterinary advice for humans or animals, nor is it intended to be a training manual for wildlife rehabilitators. The electrolytes and cell salts, uses of which are mentioned in stories in this book, are not in any way considered drugs and are readily available to anyone. Everyone should be aware that handling wild animals can be dangerous to both the handler and the animal without appropriate knowledge and equipment. Also, regulations regarding caring for wildlife may vary greatly in each state in the United States. Every country has their own laws regarding wildlife. In all cases of handling and/or caring for wild or domestic animals, advice from relevant government officials and medical or care providers with appropriate licenses and permits is recommended before any action is taken. The author and publisher are not responsible for any adverse effects or consequences resulting from the use of any ideas or activities included in this *Amazing Wildlife* book.

Cover photo by Eugene Beckes

Printed by CreateSpace, an Amazon.com Company

DEDICATION

This book is dedicated to my husband Bob, who cheerfully helped with feeding, cleaning, and providing endless support during the nearly 50 years I have been a wildlife rehabilitator; and to Bob's brother, Jack Hoy, who provided funding to get this book published.

I would also like to dedicate the book to my sister Pam, her husband, Bob, and my dear friends Adele Lewis and Mary Gossi, who greatly care, as Bob and I do, for all of Earth's amazing wildlife.

And to all our animal friends who helped me learn to recognize their intelligence, abilities, and especially the compassion and love they share with others, thank you.

Finally, I would like to recognize Dr. Irene Pepperberg and her amazing African Grey Parrots, especially my hero Alex, for their extensive research. Alex and Dr. Pepperberg proved that behavior I observed in animals, especially birds, was not my imagination, as was often suggested. Alex showed the world, including the scientific world, that birds really do think and reason, learn to speak and/or understand human language, communicate intelligently, and are extremely empathic.

CONTENTS

SECTION FOUR: MORE WILD MAMMAL FRIENDS

SECTION FIVE: CLEVER CORVIDS

SECTION SIX: FASCINATING BIRD BEHAVIOR

SECTION SEVEN: INTERESTING OBSERVATIONS

**Nature provides us
with beautiful images
few pause to enjoy.**

The Bald Eagle (*Haliaeetus leucocephalus*) nearly went extinct when DDT was being used, causing their eggshells to be soft and break so no young were hatched. Since DDT was banned in 1972, the eagle populations returned but, in some areas, both Bald Eagles and Golden Eagles are again in decline. Photo by Diane Hoy.

ABOUT THE AUTHOR

By Pamela Hallock Muller

Judy was born on January 3, 1940. She was a scrawny baby, looking something like the wrinkled baby birds she would one day foster. But she was strong and determined to thrive; her parents were proud of their firstborn. She was Daddy's girl, following him around his South Dakota prairie ranch from the time she could walk or cling to a horse's back.

Judy connected with animals very early. The ranch dog's name, Buff, was her first word, to the chagrin of her parents; Buff was her best friend until he died. Her younger years were busy ones, exploring the wide-open South Dakota grasslands on her Dad's horse Nifty, another of her best friends. When she was 11 years old, she got her very own horse, Flicka, Nifty's sister, named after the filly in the book *My Friend Flicka*. Flicka was mostly Thoroughbred, so loved to run. After Judy broke her to ride, they would go for miles over the Dakota prairies. Judy also helped with the many outside chores like bringing in the milk cows, milking them by hand, feeding orphaned calves, pigs, baby chicks, and other animals, weeding the garden, watching over her two younger brothers, and eventually, two sisters who were much younger, and of course helping her mother with household chores.

Often when Judy was quite young, she helped her mother and the neighbor ladies with cleaning vegetables and making dinner for the men who were working livestock or some other project. As they worked, she would describe to the women what her animal friends could do. She told them about tests she did to find how smart her horse friends were and described the tricks the chickens, dog, and horses easily learned to do. Judy told them the animals could obviously think. The neighbor ladies always insisted animals could not think because they did everything by instinct. Judy believed the animals, not the ladies, and never stopped observing the intelligent behavior of the animals for whom she cared.

School was interesting and a place to read books, lots of books. But Judy's favorite classrooms were the barnyard filled with animals and birds, and the prairie with all the wondrous wild birds and small mammals, reptiles, and amphibians who lived in the beautiful native grasses and forbs, in themselves fascinating subjects for study. She wanted to know the names of everything. Her favorite wild animals were the ones everyone else hated, the feisty little badgers, the dog-like coyotes, and the beautiful spotted skunks. Judy was a perfectionist who liked to draw. It was a teacher through whom she learned to observe detail – the kind of detail that escapes most others, even trained scientists. Her eye for detail contributed to her artistic talents; drawing developed her powers of observation.

She watched the Meadowlarks, Bobolinks, and Lark Buntings taking food to their young, marveled at the graceful Red-tailed Hawks hanging in the wind high in the blue sky, and listened to the Great Horned Owl pair calling to each other in the cottonwoods by Antelope Creek. She admired and learned the names of the lovely flowers that swayed in the wind on the South Dakota plains, from the tiny Scarlet Globemallow to the tall Showy Milkweed. Later in life she learned the Latin names for the grasses and flowers.

Judy's horizons and expectations were consistent with those of '50s teens. She needed to get scholarships to go to college, to be a nurse like her mother, so she was studious and hard working. She would have liked to study paleontology, botany, or become a veterinarian, but everyone said these careers were not appropriate for a girl. Lack of money also dictated a more practical career. She dutifully went to nurses' training after two years of college. To help pay for her training, she worked at St. Luke's Hospital nursery in Denver, Colorado, for six months, changing hundreds of diapers and making baby formula. She found that a previous injury to her left knee made it too painful to be standing or walking for eight hours a day, as a nurse must do, so she switched to elementary education.

Judy earned her degree with majors in Science and Elementary Education in 1963. Her family moved to western Montana that summer, so her first goal after they settled into their new home in Missoula, Montana, was to find a teaching position. She was offered a job teaching fourth grade at Russell Elementary School in Missoula.

After a year in Missoula, a friend who was also a teacher introduced her to her life mate. Bob Hoy was working his way through the University of Montana Forestry program to earn a degree in Wildlife Conservation. Bob too was a prairie child, from Nebraska, where he lived on a farm and had also milked cows. Bob loved the mountains, so his goal was to be a game warden for the State of Montana. Prior to graduating in spring 1965, he worked one summer for the U. S. Forest Service near Rabbit Ears Pass,

Colorado, one summer in the Bob Marshall Wilderness, Montana, and another summer as a seasonal park ranger in Glacier National Park.

Judy's elementary school job was over on June 4, 1966, and they were married that evening. After their honeymoon, they left for Bob's first assignment in Malta, Montana. Winters on the Highline were challenging, with well over 100 miles per hour winds and temperatures below zero for weeks at a time.

The prairies near Malta were even more expansive than those of South Dakota where Judy had grown up. As in South Dakota, there were fossils and artifacts scattered in the gravels and sands between the bunch grasses and sagebrush, and many new species of wildlife of all kinds to watch and admire. She wrote her first scientific papers when she discovered and documented several significant Native American sites for the Montana Archaeological Society. Bob shared her passion for fossils and their fossil collections grew.

Judy began to care for the occasional orphan coyote, antelope or other young animals who were brought to them because Bob was the local Game Warden. And she continued to teach, this time a fifth grade class in the Malta Elementary School.

After three years, Bob was transferred back to the mountains he loved, where he began working out of the Missoula District Office of the Montana Department of Fish, Wildlife and Parks. He and Judy bought a piece of property near the Clark Fork River just east of East Missoula and built a home. Judy found a teaching position in a Missoula elementary school and continued to delight youngsters by teaching the wonders of the natural world, as well as the required curriculum.

After moving back to Western Montana, Judy set up a fund to which people could donate to help pay for food and medical bills for wildlife and began to rehabilitate more of them. She received mostly birds, a few mammals, and an occasional reptile for care. Wildlife rehabbers attempt to make injured wildlife well and release them to continue their wild lives. They also raise orphaned or kidnapped young birds and mammals, attempt to teach them how to survive in the wild, and release them. After release, the rehabber may continue to feed the youngsters until they learn to find food by themselves. This phase of rehabilitation can take anywhere from a few days to months, depending upon what the mammal or bird has to learn in order to survive on their own.

Most young animals who had to have round the clock care came in summer when Judy was free from teaching responsibilities. She learned how to take care of the various animals by consulting with veterinarians, game farmers, falconers, by reading books or by trial and error. The most important things she learned were from the animals themselves; the critters let her know what they preferred and if they were not content with what she provided.

In 1975, Judy quit teaching to pursue her wildlife art and do rehabilitation full time. That year, she received a small, dark-eyed owl, the first fledgling Flammulated Owl ever reported in Montana. In subsequent years, several more flams were brought to Judy for care. She began what turned into a ten-year crusade to have Flammulated Owls recognized as a nesting Montana species and to get them placed on the Forest Service's Species of Special Concern list. She wanted them to be considered in forest management plans, so their specialized habitat would be preserved. Interestingly, it was a woman biologist, who placed the small owls on the list of Species of Special Concern. Another woman biologist was hired to find where flams were nesting and new nesting sites were identified. The Forest Service now considers the owls' needs in their forest management plans.

In 1979, Bob was assigned to work as the Game Warden for Ravalli County, Montana. He and Judy sold their home in Missoula and purchased 52 acres along Willoughby Creek in the irrigated drylands southeast of Stevensville, Montana, on the east side of the Bitterroot Valley. The historic Bitterroot River valley is located east of the granitic peaks of the forested Idaho batholith, which thrust skyward to the west, the Bitterroot Mountains. The Selway-Bitterroot Wilderness incorporates these mountains and their valleys. The gentle, rounded metamorphic Sapphire Range serves as the eastern boundary of Ravalli County. The Bitterroot River flows north through the Bitterroot Valley between the two mountain ranges to its confluence with the Clark Fork of the Columbia River near Missoula.

Bob and Judy built their log home overlooking Willoughby Creek in the middle of what would become their 100-acre property, after purchasing several parcels of land to the north of the creek bordering the original 52 acres. The riparian area along the creek and the bluff to the north of the creek are home to a huge diversity of native plants, mosses, amphibians, reptiles, birds, and mammals. The property was placed under Nature Conservancy protection after Judy found a globally endangered plant that had never before been found in Montana. The Hoys wanted to ensure that the rare plants and mosses would be protected and that the birds and other animals would always have a home.

A 1930's era homestead on the west end of their property had an old house and several outbuildings. The rooms of these buildings were modified to house raptors (birds of prey, including eagles, hawks, and owls) and other birds or to serve as flight rooms where young birds could practice flying. These rooms and several wire pens provided temporary home for hundreds of injured or orphaned animals beginning in 1980. They called their place The Bitterroot Wildlife Rehabilitation Center, and Judy began training other rehabbers and coordinating rehab activities in Western Montana. She was given permission to use the Bitterroot Audubon Society to umbrella the fund for western Montana rehabbers and called it the Bitterroot Audubon Wildlife Rehab Fund. Several other western Montana rehabbers are subpermittees Judy trained. Together they have cared for 100-200 birds and many mammals each year for over 25 years.

Through trial and error, suggestions from friends, and observing the actions of the animals, Judy developed treatments for the variety of injuries and illnesses she and her subpermittees confronted among the different species of birds and mammals who were brought to them. While Bob was a game warden, Judy and Bob were given special permission to care for game animals, at least temporarily, until they could be relocated to zoos or to the Wildlife Rehab Facility in Helena, Montana.

Judy also kept several healthy birds, who were flightless due to wing injuries, for use in educational presentations about wild birds and wildlife ecology to schools, churches, civic clubs, and other organizations. Judy also became increasingly involved in educating the public about wildlife and threats to the western Montana environment. She built a network of contacts in the news media, in academia, among health professionals and in government agencies. She also kept detailed records on a variety of kinds of observations. She recorded many first records for Ravalli County of butterflies, plants, and mosses, as well as several first state records. She kept records each year of all butterflies she and Bob saw and when they were first and last seen, reporting the data to a butterfly expert, Steve Kohler, who is writing a book on Montana butterflies. The same type of report was sent to the Montana Natural Heritage Program concerning amphibians, reptiles, and birds seen each year.

In recognition of her contributions as both a wildlife rehabilitator and community educator, in June 1994, Patrick J. Graham, then Director of the Montana Department of Fish, Wildlife and Parks presented Judy with a framed letter of commendation that read:

"Dear Judy:

"It takes a special gift of dedication and kindness to care for orphaned and injured wildlife. Since 1968, you have shared that gift, perhaps more than anyone else in Montana, with unselfish dedication."

"Caring for and rehabilitating over 2,400 birds, mammals and reptiles is a significant contribution to the conservation of our wild resources. As important has been your work in educating families, school classes and adult groups. You have greatly magnified your impact by passing on your knowledge and dedication, training over 35 other rehabilitators to care for wildlife."

"On behalf of Montana's wildlife, its citizens, and the department, I thank you for sharing your kindness and dedication."

"Sincerely, Patrick J. Graham, Director."

Since receiving that commendation, Judy, with Bob's help, has cared for several thousand more birds and mammals. Bob retired from working for Montana Department of Fish, Wildlife and Parks in 2000. Bob has been a coauthor on two studies concerning health issues on wildlife and Judy has been a coauthor on those two studies and two more recent studies concerning health issues in humans and wildlife.

In 2017, Judy published her first book, *Changing Faces: The Consequences of Exposure to Gene and Thyroid Disrupting Toxins*. It is available through Amazon in print (with photos) and e-book versions. Any birth defects or health issues on animals and humans referred to in *Amazing Wildlife* are discussed in detail in *Changing Faces* and reported in the studies she coauthored.

**Rehabbers know that
bird in a bush is better
than bird in the hand.**

REFERENCES

Excellent books about animal intelligence are listed here. All are available from Amazon and in bookstores and libraries, unless otherwise specified.

Listening to Animals by Adele Lewis Coon, 2015.

Link to multiple studies done by Irene Pepperberg with African Grey Parrots, including Alex. <http://alexfoundation.org/about/dr-irene-pepperberg/>

The Shark Sessions by Ila France Porcher, 2015.

MERLIN | The Mind of a Sea Turtle by Ila France Porcher, 2017.

The True Nature of Sharks by Ila France Porcher, 2017.

Koko Love! Conversations with a Signing Gorilla by Francine Patterson, 1999, and many other fascinating books about Koko, another of my animal heros.

Mind of the Raven by Bernd Heinrich, 1999.

Bird Brains: The Intelligence of Crows, Ravens, Magpies, and Jays by Candace Savage, 1997.

"Hierarchical summer habitat selection by the North American porcupine in western Montana" by Katie Ann Mally, 2008. https://scholarworks.umt.edu/etd/516/

The following are references for the studies concerning birth defects and health issues in animals in which Judy Hoy was a co-author, and the link to the book *Changing Faces* by Judy Hoy which discusses those issues and the causes. The hundreds of references in the studies collectively provide thousands of references to more studies concerning the effects of environmental toxins.

Changing Faces: The Consequences of Exposure to Gene and Thyroid Disrupting Toxins by Judy Hoy, 2017.

Hoy JA, Hoy RD, Seba D, Kerstetter TH (2002) Genital Abnormalities in White-tailed Deer (Odocoileus virginianus) in West central Montana: Pesticide Exposure as a Possible Cause. *Journal of Environmental Biology* 23:189-97.

Hoy JA, Haas GT, Hoy RD, Hallock P (2011) Observations of Brachygnathia Superior in Wild Ruminants in Western Montana, USA. *Wildlife Biology in Practice Journal* 7(2): 15-29.

Hoy J, Swanson N and Seneff S. The High Cost of Pesticides: Human and Animal Diseases. *Journal of Poultry, Fish and Wildlife Sciences.* 2015; 3:132. doi:10.4172/2375-446X.1000132

Swanson N, Hoy J, Seneff S (2016) Evidence that Glyphosate is a Causative Agent in Chronic Sub-clinical Metabolic Acidosis and Mitochondrial Dysfunction. *International Journal of Human Nutrition and Functional Medicine.* 4. 9.

SECTION ONE: COMMUNICATING WITH OTHER ANIMALS

Winter weary doves
coo seductively, coaxing
a reluctant spring.

CHAPTER 1
UP, UP, AND AWAY

In 1979, my husband Bob, a game warden for the Montana Department of Fish, Wildlife and Parks (MDFWP), was assigned the north half of Ravalli County, Montana, as his area to patrol. In anticipation of this assignment, we had purchased 52 acres of land on the east side of the Bitterroot Valley, on the south edge of Willoughby Creek. During summer 1979, we began building a log home on the north side of the property overlooking the creek. By spring 1980, the man we contracted to build the log frame of the house had completed his part of the job. We had also finished most of the basement rooms, so we lived in them while continuing the final work on the main floor.

That summer, an MDFWP warden brought me a beautiful adult male American Kestrel (*Falco sparverius*). A family had found the small falcon on the ground with a broken wing, taken him home, and kept him as a pet. They were moving out of state but couldn't take the kestrel with them because it is illegal to transport wild birds across state lines. It is also illegal to keep protected wild birds as pets, as they had been doing. In Montana that includes all wild birds except Rock Pigeon, Eurasian Collared Dove, European Starling, and House Sparrow.

While the kestrel was in their possession, they kept him tethered to a perch with a leather strap, called a jess, around one leg. Jesses are attached to the legs of birds by falconers to control them and prevent them from flying away. It was fortunate the kestrel had not sprained or damaged his leg when struggling against the strap or trying to fly. It is totally unacceptable to jess a falcon or any other raptor (bird of prey) by one leg. To avoid injury, both legs must be fitted with straps that are even in length. Besides being held by only one leg, the strap on this bird was extremely tight, another taboo when tethering a raptor.

15

As soon as I received him, I carefully cut the strap from his leg. For a few days, I kept him in a large cardboard box with a branch through the sides for a perch, and a plastic window on one side to provide light. Bob and I quickly finished the inside walls of a room in our basement. After we covered the floor with plastic topped with newspapers and added perches and branches, the kestrel had his own room where he could practice flying to strengthen his wing. We also built a small stand for his water pan and food, mainly grasshoppers and mice. He could fly short distances, but because the broken bone had not healed quite straight, his right wing didn't flap in a normal, smooth manner. I hoped his flying free in the room would help the wing regain its full motion.

This was the first American Kestrel I had received for care, so I didn't know what to expect. I named him Jasper because of the beautiful reddish-brown color of his back and tail. He had the contrasting blue-gray wings characteristic of male American Kestrels. Females' wings are reddish brown with black bars, similar to the coloring on the back of both sexes. As a result of the difference in wing color, the gender of kestrels is easily distinguished as soon as the tips of their wing feathers begin showing at the end of the pinfeathers on hatchlings. American Kestrels belong to the falcon family. In other falcon species, males and females are similar in color.

I made snap-on jesses for Jasper so he could not escape when I took him outside for exercise, easily unsnapped to release him in his room. Tying the jesses to a lightweight cord allowed Jasper to fly fairly long distances from my fist to post tops or fence rails. Then I could walk to him while rolling the cord, pick him up, and let him fly again. His wings improved with the increased exercise, but he wasn't flying well enough to release by the time the weather turned cool that fall.

I continued to take Jasper outside to fly on nice days. When I was painting pictures in my studio, which I often did in winter, I let Jasper sit beside me on a perch to keep me company. Much of his time in the studio was spent near the large picture window, watching birds flying around outside in the front yard. When there were no birds to see, he sat quietly on the perch watching me paint. I tethered his jesses to the perch in case something startled him; I didn't want him to fly into the window and injure himself. He acted tame with me, allowing me to walk right up to him when he was free in the flight room, pick him up, attach his jesses, and carry him on my hand, all without protest of any kind.

16

Because Jasper was a wild bird when originally found, I didn't know he would begin to consider me his mate. By spring, I found that is exactly what had happened. Whenever I went into his room to feed him, take him out for exercise or just visit with him, he began bowing to me and vocalizing in an amorous way. After several days of trying to seduce me with his courtship behavior, he began flying directly to my head to deposit semen on my hair every time I entered his room. I had heard of hatchling birds imprinting to this extent on their human caretakers but not wild-caught adults. The biggest problem with Jasper's amorous behavior was, after deciding to take me for his mate, he considered Bob his rival. Whenever Jasper saw Bob, he screamed his amazingly loud kestrel alarm call the whole time Bob was within his view. Kestrel alarm calls in close quarters can be extremely hard on the ears.

Since Jasper was the first falcon I had received for care and my falconry book didn't mention sexual imprinting, I consulted a falconer friend about Jasper's strange behavior. He said wild-caught female falcons often sexually imprint on their handlers. He was not surprised a male would do so with a female human.

I had hoped to release Jasper in the spring, but his stiff wing still didn't work well enough for me to be confident he could catch prey consistently and survive on his own. That summer, I received a young female kestrel for care. As soon as she was old enough to fly well, I put her with Jasper in the flight room, thinking he might like a companion of his own kind, but he immediately attacked her. I quickly removed her, placing her in a large flight room in an old house at the west end of our land. It had been built in 1939 or '40 as part of a homestead. Before we acquired the house, the last people to own it had kept turkeys in it. A great deal of cleaning and some repair and remodeling of rooms were necessary before it was suitable for wild birds.

After about three weeks, the young female had built up her flight muscles in the large room. I caught and released grasshoppers there so she had live prey on which to practice her hunting skills. On a beautiful, sunny morning, I was happy to release her, one of the most rewarding aspects of wildlife rehabilitation. She circled while climbing to reach a high altitude, where she soared around for some time before flying back down to land in a tall pine on the edge of our property. She remained on our land for more than two weeks. Nearly every time I saw her, she was eating a large grasshopper she had caught. Grasshoppers being plentiful here, she had good hunting. When she wasn't eating, she practiced her

Jasper sitting on his perch with both legs jessed soon after I received him.

flight skills or hovered over the field looking for prey. Kestrels are able to hang in place while looking at the ground to spot insects or small rodents. Since I was a child growing up on the prairies of South Dakota, I have enjoyed watching them soar and hover.

That fall, I received an injured adult female kestrel I named Aggie. After she recovered, I put her with Jasper to see if he might like an older female. As with the other one, Jasper immediately began to attack her, causing her to try to get away from him. It seemed the only older female he had eyes for was me. That was cause for concern because his preference for a human mate might interfere with his successfully mating with a female kestrel in the wild. I quickly removed her from his room, afraid he might injure her. After Aggie had spent slightly over two weeks in the large flight room to build up her muscles, I released her. She immediately flew high over our field, making a couple large circles as if to determine where she was. Then she flew swiftly off to the south-southwest. I never saw her again.

Jasper spent another winter keeping me company while I created wildlife paintings, one of which was of Jasper. Nearly every day I took him out to practice flying, except when the wind was blowing hard. By the next spring, he could fly perfectly. The only evidence he had been injured was that the right wingtip was slightly higher than that of the uninjured left wing when they were folded against his body.

Early that spring, I received another adult female kestrel who had hit a window, bruising her flight muscles. Not having any serious injuries, she fully recovered in only a few days. I put her in the large flight room in the old house to make sure she could fly normally and to keep her flight muscles in condition. She was a big female and very aggressive. I called her Feisty and thought she might be big and tough enough to knock some sense into Jasper's head. I put him in the room with her, hoping for love at first sight. Although it was mating season, he immediately flew toward her with the intention of attacking, just as he had with the other females. She didn't try to escape from him as the others had. Instead, she stood her ground, whacking at him with her wings or sharp talons every time he tried to attack her. Feisty was not at all aggressive toward Jasper but stood her ground and defended herself when he attacked her. By the next day, Jasper was totally smitten with Feisty. Most amazing, he acted wilder than she did when I went into the room to feed them. He screamed his loudest alarm calls when he saw me, as if I were a predator to be feared. He seemed to no longer remember he had considered me his oversized mate for two years. I have to admit my feelings were a bit hurt by his sudden and total rejection, but having an actual female kestrel as a mate would contribute greatly to Jasper's successful return to life in the wild.

I let the two "love birds" become well acquainted and honeymoon together for several days. On a beautiful spring afternoon, after they had both eaten their fill of mice, I released them together. Feisty flew to a tall cottonwood tree and sat there looking around, as if to become familiar with her new surroundings. Jasper kept flying, circling up and up in ever-widening rings. He caught an updraft and was soon just a small spot high in the azure sky. I lay on my back in the grass to watch him through my binoculars. He was celebrating his ability to fly free by playing back and forth in the air currents. After nearly 30 minutes of soaring in circles and loops so high it made me dizzy to watch him, I began to wonder if he was ever going to return to Earth. Suddenly, he folded his wings in a steep dive, coming nearly straight down. When he reached tree level in the middle of our hay field, he pulled up and glided over to the large cottonwoods, landing on the branch beside Feisty.

A slight twinge of jealousy was quickly overpowered by my extreme satisfaction of finally seeing Jasper fly happy and free after three years in captivity. During the next week, I saw the pair soaring together in the updraft above the ridge top or hovering over the hayfield, looking for prey. Then one day they were gone. Feisty likely took Jasper to her previous nest site or vice versa. Neither of them had come from our land.

A few days after Jasper and Feisty left, our resident kestrel pairs returned to set up housekeeping in the kestrel houses we had placed on each side of our hay field. I have been privileged to watch them raise their young each year since moving here. Because Jasper and Feisty didn't remain to nest on our land, I don't know whether they successfully raised a family. Since then, whenever I see a kestrel or hear their alarm call, I think of Jasper, my amorous kestrel friend, and my day is instantly brighter.

Colorful kestrel
hovers over the meadow;
red kite without string.

CHAPTER 2
CHICKLETTE

After I released Jasper, his room in our basement didn't remain empty for long. A few weeks later that spring I received a single hatchling Gray Partridge (*Perdix perdix*). He became separated from his family when they were crossing a county road on Sunset Bench, not far from where we live. The rest of the partridge family flew when a car passed them, leaving one little hatchling who wasn't yet able to fly. He may have been the last to hatch in the clutch of eggs and so was younger than the others. Both parents remain with and care for hatchlings in Gray Partridge families, with the chicks beginning to fly at about 14 days old.

When the parent birds and their other young ones flew together out of sight, the person whose car frightened them was afraid to leave this one alone by the side of the road, thinking he would be caught by a predator or die of cold that night. The woman stopped her car and was able to catch the little bird because he ran down into the tall grass in the ditch. Fortunately, she could see where he was moving the grass as he tried to push through it. The young partridge was unable to run fast enough through the thick stems to escape. She picked him up and brought him to me, knowing I take care of injured and orphaned wildlife.

Gray Partridges were introduced in the United States from Europe and brought to western Montana for hunting many years ago (long before I moved to Montana from South Dakota), similar to what was done with Ring-necked Pheasants. Partridges are pretty little game birds, rather plump with short, rounded wings and tail. They are also quite wary, making them a popular bird to hunt. In the 1970s and '80s, hunters in the United States were reported to be killing an estimated 500,000 to 600,000 Gray Partridge per year. That number of dead partridges is difficult to envision, as I never saw one in the prairie regions of South Dakota where our ranch was, although we had large numbers of Ring-necked Pheasant. After moving to Montana in 1963, I occasionally saw small coveys of Gray Partridge but have not seen more than a total of 200 to 300 in nearly 40 years of living and birding in Montana.

Gray Partridges prefer to live in a cool, moderately dry climate, making the east side of the Bitterroot Valley perfect habitat for them, with its pastures, grain fields, and brushy draws. Their preferred foods are grains, grass seeds, and insects, so they spend much of their day in pastures or grain fields and, in winter, the stubble left after grain is harvested. In the first 25 years we lived in the Bitterroot Valley, we occasionally saw coveys of Gray Partridge on our land. The populations have declined significantly in Ravalli County in recent years, likely because much of their preferred habitat has been developed into subdivisions. Besides habitat destruction, many cats and dogs run free in subdivisions, cats being especially deadly.

Those factors aren't conducive to successful reproduction by small, ground-nesting game birds or songbirds. The Montana state bird, Western Meadowlark, has declined significantly, and it has been over 10 years since we have seen a Gray Partridge on our land. There are still a few small coveys living on top of Sunset Bench directly to the north of our land, where the little partridge I named Chicklette was originally found. They may travel through our land without us seeing them, but in spring the males have loud courting calls, a sound we haven't heard for many years.

For the first week after receiving him, I kept Chicklette in a large aquarium with a screen top. I put a ticking clock wrapped in a rag in the enclosure to keep him company. There was a heat lamp at one end for warmth and to furnish light so he could eat whenever he became hungry. Chicks have no trouble sleeping with a light on; being able to eat whenever he wanted, day or night, helped him grow rapidly.

While Chicklette was in the aquarium, I began modifying Jasper's room in our basement to accommodate a partridge. I had already removed all newspapers from the floor and rolled up the plastic after Jasper's release, so needed to again prepare the room for a bird. The plastic was actually for covering the floor while painting but worked well for protecting it from bird droppings, too. I also cut off the sides of a large cardboard box so it was about two inches deep; filling it with clean soil gave the partridge chick a place to take dirt baths. I covered the only window in the room with clear plastic to prevent Chicklette from flying into the glass. Within a week, he was able to fly, but for some reason I couldn't determine, he hardly ever did. After placing two large tree branches (blown off our trees in windstorms) in the room to provide perches, everything was ready. I placed a dish each of mealworms, game bird starter, and water on the floor and released him in the room.

Chicklette had been quite cooperative and tame when in the aquarium and remained unafraid of me after he was free in the larger area. He came to eat mealworms from my hand when I called him, and wanted to go with me when I walked out the door. As soon as I was sure he would stay with me, I let him follow me out of his room through the basement door to the lawn outside, where he caught insects. When he was old enough, we went to the hayfield, just past the lawn and orchard, where there were more grasshoppers and leafhoppers. He never roamed far from me and always came to me when I called his name. That was somewhat surprising to me because he had been with his family for nearly two weeks after hatching, so couldn't have imprinted on me as hatchlings do. He chirped fairly often while feeding and I chirped back. When he had eaten his fill, I called his name and he followed me back to his room.

After two weeks in his room, Chicklette was nearly full-grown, adept at catching insects and finding and eating any grass seed he liked. I hoped a covey of partridge would come through so he could join them. I was a bit concerned because he didn't seem to want to fly and always ran or walked, even though I could find nothing wrong with his wings. He could flap them both and flew up onto branches in his room, but when he was outside with me, he didn't fly up into trees. Because Chicklette never flew away, I always put him back into his room for the night to keep him safe.

When winter came, he seemed content to stay in his warm room. If I led him out the door when there was snow on the ground, he just stood there in the snow as if to say, "There are no insects out here and the seeds are covered with snow, so what are we doing in the cold?" He indicated by his actions that he didn't particularly like snow or cold, so I stopped taking him out while there was snow on the ground. He seemed satisfied to stay in his room, eating, sleeping, and taking dust baths. I often sat in his room with him when I read a book or magazine. He would fly up onto my knee and sit there contentedly.

When spring came, being a full-grown adult, Chicklette began making the loud courting calls distinctive of males of that species. As soon as the snow melted in February, I again had him follow me through the basement door to run around the yard in the sun. On cold and snowy days, I left him in his room. As soon as it was actually spring and the grass was growing, I let him stay out all day. I was usually working outside in the garden and yard, so could keep an eye on him. He came to me when I called him and I only put him in his room at night or if I had to go somewhere during the day.

One day in May, a nature photographer and his wife, also a photographer, came to visit. He focused on wildlife; she preferred taking pictures of people. He wanted to photograph the birds and other wildlife who live on our land. She had a camera also but appeared to let him take the lead with the wildlife. I asked if they were interested in photographing a Gray Partridge. Chicklette was foraging on the edge of our yard, so I took them out to see him. The man began taking photos of him as he captured insects living in the fast-growing, bright green grass or pecked in the dirt looking for insects and seeds. He occasionally stopped to give his loud courting call.

Because a Gray Partridge is comparatively small and close to the ground, the man decided to lie on his stomach to take eye level photos. Chicklette soon became intrigued by the clicking of the camera shutter, as the man took picture after picture, in rapid succession. The little partridge stretched as tall as he could, staring in the direction of the unusual sound. He made a loud courting call, ran over to the man, jumped up onto his rump, and stood there calling several times in a row. The woman began taking photos of Chicklette on her husband's backside, trying hard not to laugh so she could hold the camera still. The look on the man's face was hilarious, but to his credit he didn't move a muscle, letting his wife take a whole series of photos of Chicklette making his courting call while standing tall on her husband's tush. I have no idea what they did with those photos because, though a Gray Partridge trying to attract females while standing on a person was highly unusual and quite humorous, it wasn't exactly calendar or nature magazine photo material.

Eventually Chicklette decided to hop down and look for insects just a few feet from where the man lay on the ground. The photographer was able to take a large number of close-up photos. I especially liked the ones the man took when Chicklette stretched to full height and gave his courtship call. Both photographers said Chicklette was an interesting bird and were surprised a Gray Partridge would hop on top of a human to make his courtship calls. Chicklette likely thought the camera clicking was the chirping of a female partridge and used the man's body like a downed log from which to call.

Three weeks after his photo session, Chicklette heard a group of Gray Partridge as they foraged through the creek bottom below our house. He was catching insects at the edge of our yard just above the creek. The covey was mostly females, and he wasted no time running quickly down the hill to join them. That was the last time I saw Chicklette. He left with the covey and didn't come back. Beginning in late afternoon, I occasionally called for him until dark, but there was no response. I hoped he took one of the female partridges as his mate, or more likely, she would have had to accept him as her mate. She had to teach him many new things, such as how to huddle with the covey under soft snow for warmth during winter nights and to be wary of humans. Chicklette had learned to communicate well with me, so he should have easily learned to communicate with his mate and the others in the covey.

**Clever animals
learn from their friends new ways to
survive all seasons.**

The young of wild grazing animals like bison need to quickly learn from their mother and their family how to survive harsh winters in northern United States.

Common Redpolls (*Carduelis flammea*) are small finches with tiny cone-shaped bills. They nest in the arctic regions and winter in Canada and northern states. They can often be found throughout Montana in the winter months, spending much of their time in thick bushes or brush, calling to each other continuously while feeding. Communication between the members of their quite large flocks is important for redpolls. Photo by Eugene Beckes.

CHAPTER 3
SWIFTY'S SIGN LANGUAGE

In 1982, the fourth year we lived in the Bitterroot Valley, a woman found a fully feathered, newly fledged White-throated Swift (*Aeronautes saxatalis*) lying on the sidewalk on Main Street in Victor, Montana. The small bird was alive but unable to fly, so the woman brought it to me to rehabilitate. I couldn't find anything broken, but it was unable to flap either wing. Examination showed the bones were not formed quite normally in the shoulders, resulting in a permanent disability. Such birth defects were fairly common in young birds I received for care between 1982 and 1985. I never knew for certain the gender of the little bird I named Swifty, as both sexes of White-throated Swifts look exactly alike. However, since environmental toxins that cause birth defects more often affect female animals, it was quite likely she was a female.

I hadn't previously had the privilege of caring for a White-throated Swift, so at first was unsure exactly what to feed her. The only suitable food I had were mealworms and any houseflies I could catch. Fortunately, Swifty liked both, especially mealworms, of which I had plenty. Whenever I needed more, I ordered 10,000 at a time from a company in California that raises them. They were easy to obtain and keep, and perfect to feed the insect-eating birds I received for care.

Rather than having to go all the way to the bird room to feed Swifty every 15 minutes, I let her hang from the edge of my pocket under the sweatshirt I always wore over a long-sleeved shirt that buttoned up the front. All of my long-sleeved shirts have pockets, so I put Swifty in the left one, taking the little bird with me when I was away from the house. In the right pocket, I carried a small plastic sack containing her mealworms.

Swifty quickly learned to wiggle and twitter when she wanted to eliminate. I took her out to perch on my finger while she dropped her feces into a tissue if we were inside or onto the ground if we were outside. When she was hungry, she made a slightly different twittering chirp so I took her out to feed her mealworms. She usually ate only two or three insects at a time, so feedings were frequent. When she finished eating, she usually expelled a dropping, even if she had done so before she ate. After letting her look around for a while, I put her back in my pocket. Swifts cling to rock walls, chimneys, and other rough surfaces, so Swifty had no trouble hanging on to the edge of my pocket. She acted like she enjoyed going with me. If I was going to be away from the house for more than an hour on a trip in the car, I took a small jar of water and a medicine dropper with which to drip water into her mouth when she wanted a drink.

She especially liked it when I took her out of my pocket to sit on my finger while we were outside in our yard. She watched the other birds flying around and twittered to them. She always talked to the swallows when they flew overhead catching insects. White-throated Swifts are one of the fastest birds in the United States. If Swifty had not been handicapped with abnormal shoulder bones, she would have been able to dash around the sky even faster than the swallows, easily catching small insects.

For two years, Swifty went almost everywhere I went during the day. I took her to educational talks I presented with unreleasable birds. She was so small and pretty, everyone thought she was absolutely adorable. Children were enthralled by the tiny black and white bird who appeared like a magic trick from under my sweatshirt. It was necessary to take Swifty with me when I went to town or other places because she had to eat frequently. No one ever knew she was in my pocket unless I took her out to feed her or let her eliminate, which I didn't do in public places. If Swifty wiggled to indicate she needed something when we were inside, I immediately went outside to see what she wanted. Swifty taught me to understand her sign language of wiggles and twitters, so we communicated very well.

At night, Swifty hung from a soft cloth draped over a thin board propped in an aquarium. It had a screen cover, so she couldn't crawl out and get lost. Birds well fed during the day don't eat at night. After a last feeding of mealworms, I put Swifty's feet on the soft cloth. She gripped it with her sharp little toenails, tucked her head under her wing, and slept until morning.

One day a little over two years after Swifty came to me for care, she twittered to be taken out of my pocket. As so many times before, I set her on my finger. This time she pointed her bill up at an odd angle and suddenly stopped breathing. Just like that she was gone. It appeared to be heart failure, which is common with animals who have birth defects.

After Swifty came to me for care in summer 1982, I received several other animals to raise who were born with malformations. One was a pretty white-tailed deer fawn with unusual coloring. Besides being mostly white with reddish spots, an unusual color for a deer fawn, she had crooked legs when she was born. She couldn't be released in the wild so the Montana Department of Fish, Wildlife and Parks sent her to a zoo in Red Lodge, Montana. We had splinted her legs to straighten them, so she could run and walk normally by the time she was taken to the zoo. Sadly, when she was only one year old, she died suddenly of heart failure. A necropsy showed she had been born with an enlarged heart.

Caring for Swifty taught me a great deal about swifts and even more about communicating with birds. In all the years I have rehabilitated birds, I have received two injured adult White-throated Swifts but no other fledglings. That may be because most of the White-throated Swifts in our area live in the larger canyons of the Bitterroot Mountains on the west side of the valley. These swifts usually nest in rock crevasses in the canyon cliffs. Any of the fledglings who get into trouble are unlikely to be found by anyone. They simply die when they fall to the bottom of the cliff and/or are eaten by predators. Swifty must have been hatched and raised in a crack or some kind of opening in the bricks or boards of a building in Victor. Because she couldn't fly when it was time for Swifty to leave the nest, she fell onto the sidewalk, where she was found by the kind woman who brought her to me.

Being exposed to car exhaust, pesticides, smoke, dust, and other chemical pollutants on a city street may have contributed to Swifty having malformed bones and a damaged heart. However, two extensively used pesticides at that time, an herbicide, 2,4,5-T, and an insecticide, endrin, were my top suspects for causing her malformations and those in other young animals I received between 1980 and 1985. I came to this conclusion because the specific birth defects that occurred in the early 1980s were never again present on any newborns brought to me for care after those toxins were banned by the Environmental Protection Agency in spring 1985. Also, the roan fawn with the same defects as Swifty, and all the other wildlife newborns I received for care at that time with similar birth defects, were not born in a town.

Everyone who met Swifty agreed she was an amazing little bird. They could also see she had trained her caregiver well. Best of all, she taught me to quickly decipher what birds are trying to communicate to me. That has served me well in caring for the thousands of birds I have received in the years since. Even after 45 years of rehabilitating wildlife, Swifty is still one of my most memorable patients and one of my favorites.

29

**Peregrine Falcon
may be fastest raptor, but
swifts must fly faster.**

A young Peregrine Falcon (*Falco peregrinus*) showing the distinct dark patches on the sides of the face. Surprisingly, Peregrine Falcons and other falcons were found to be more closely related to parrots than to other birds, including hawks and eagles.

CHAPTER 4
RAISING CRANE

In 1985, after I was taught bird communication by Jasper and Swifty, a family who lived many miles southeast of us near the town of Wisdom, Montana, found a newly hatched Greater Sandhill Crane (*Grus canadensis*) chick. They didn't know what to do with it or how to care for it. After they had it for a day, they called to ask if they could bring it here. I was delighted to have the opportunity to raise a hatchling Sandhill Crane. I have long been known for "raising cane," but this was the first time I was privileged to raise a crane.

It would have been much better for the chick if the people who found it had been able to return it to its parents. However, they explained on the phone that, after much searching, they were unable to locate any adult cranes. With no other options, they drove the 90 miles from Wisdom to our place, arriving in mid-afternoon with the little chick tucked in a blanket in a cardboard box.

Fortunately, newly hatched chicks have at least two days' supply of yoke in their digestive system. This provides nourishment to keep them alive until they are strong enough to begin foraging for insects. The crane chick was clearly hungry after two and a half days. It began eating mealworms and game bird starter as soon as I placed it into the large box I had prepared for it. I suspended a heat lamp from the center of a straight branch poked through holes near the top of the box to provide necessary warmth. Food and water were located at one end; the other contained a nest of hay under the heat lamp. After the chick had eaten its fill, it went to the hay nest, sat down, and promptly went to sleep.

Newly hatched birds who can walk and run soon after hatching are called precocious hatchlings. When it wasn't sleeping under the heat lamp, the little crane spent its time running around the large box or eating. I never knew whether the chick was male or female, but for some reason, she seemed feminine to me. I named her Sing, because she vocalized the soft call a baby crane makes most of the time she was awake. Sounding somewhat like a short song, the call is normally used by chicks to let their parents know where they are while foraging for insects in tall grass. Parents also make soft calls in response, keeping the family together.

Newly hatched cranes are fairly tall, looking a bit like a turkey chick but with a longer neck, long legs, and a much larger bill. The large bill gives them a prehistoric appearance. I called Sing my little dinosaur.

Sing grew fast, eating as many mealworms, topped off by Purina Game Bird Startina®, as she wanted all day and all night. The heat lamp was always on to keep her warm, allowing Sing to eat and nap at will 24 hours a day, because it was never dark. Consequently, she grew so fast it wasn't long before I had to find a larger box.

Each morning, as soon as the temperature was warm enough to bring grasshoppers, leaf hoppers, and other insects up onto leaves and grass stems to sun themselves, I took Sing out for a walk to practice finding food. Precocious hatchlings instinctively know they are supposed to catch and eat small moving objects, such as insects, worms, spiders, and amphibians. Like all youngsters, they need practice to become proficient at this and all the other things they must do to survive and thrive. A basic requirement for a crane chick is to quickly become a good insect hunter. Sing's legs were already fairly long, so she had no trouble following me around through tall grass and weeds, watching all the while for small moving objects. With plenty of practice every day, it wasn't long before Sing was an expert at catching her favorite grasshoppers and leafhoppers, as well as other insects she determined to be edible. Occasionally, when she caught something she didn't like, she shook her head, throwing the unpleasant-tasting bug some distance away.

When Sing had grown to the size of a large chicken, I let her run free in the yard during the day. To keep her safe when we had to leave, I put her in a predator-proof pen with plenty of food and water. At dusk, if Sing was out of sight foraging or exploring the alfalfa field, I called her name and she came running. She followed me into the garage, where I had placed a thick nest of hay on the floor for her bed. Any soiled hay was replaced with clean hay each day. For a baby bird, she had large droppings. Sing went directly to her hay bed and sat down. As soon as I closed the garage door and turned off the light, she tucked her head under her wing and went to sleep. Sing had grown beautiful grey-brown feathers that kept her warm, so she no longer needed a heat lamp. I left the lights off in the garage, allowing her to sleep all night. Her food and water were not far from her hay nest.

Light began coming through the garage windows at about 5:00 a.m. so Sing could see to get a drink and eat her breakfast before I got up. By the time I let her out at 6:30, she had eaten her fill of game bird starter and

32

was eager for a day of exploring outside. Sing spent most of the time roaming the yard and the edges of the hay field in front of our house, searching for insects to gobble down. She came back to the garage whenever she wanted starter, a drink of water or to nap on her bed of hay.

By the time Sing was a month old, she had grown quite tall, with the long neck and legs characteristic of adult cranes. Her wing feathers were two-thirds out of the sheath that covers them as they grow. Sing could run quite fast, racing with me when I ran or running behind me when I drove my four-wheeler down the road. She opened her wings for balance as she ran, and soon was able to glide for short distances. Eventually, when her flight feathers were completely grown, she learned to flap her wings to gain altitude. Going up to between 50 and 100 feet, Sing would flap and glide in circles over the hay field. She quickly became proficient at flying, but her landings required practice. She hadn't yet learned the adult method of stopping and hovering before drifting straight down to stand on the ground. Her forward motion often caused her to tip frontward. Using the point of her bill to prevent falling, she demonstrated a classic three-point landing. She liked to fly beside me as I drove down the long driveway on the four-wheeler. I always stopped well before reaching the main road, so Sing could land safely next to me. A two-wire power line runs along the west side of our property perpendicular to the road. I didn't want Sing to fly anywhere near those electrical wires, at least until she had learned to control her flight better.

Having spent much of her time foraging alone as she grew up, Sing had become quite independent. By the time she was fully-grown, she could fly wherever she wanted to go, although she still often walked. The alfalfa and grass in our hay field were taller than Sing. She spent a lot of time there catching grasshoppers, of which there were plenty, raiding vole nests for babies, and digging out earthworms and cutworms with her sharp bill. She swallowed all those tasty morsels whole, along with whatever else she could find that looked edible. She usually came when she was called, but began ignoring me when I called her for bed, preferring the tall grass of the hay field to her nest in the garage. I was concerned our resident foxes, transient coyotes, or the neighbors' deer-chasing dogs might kill or injure her. But it was her choice and, once she sat down to go to sleep, my finding her in the tall grass of the hay field was as likely as finding a needle in a haystack.

When Bob's mother and father, Evelyn and Bus, came to visit us from Nebraska, Sing quickly made it clear that she liked Bus. When he went outside, Sing came from wherever she was to greet him and follow him around. He was quite flattered, saying she was a very special bird. I teased him about being a grandfather to a crane. She had grown to full height by then. If she stretched a bit, her head came to about waist high on Bus. Sing had been doing crane dances with me since her flight feathers had grown long enough to lift her off the ground. I showed Bus how she responded when I flapped my arms and did a little jump. Unlike our clumsy jumps, Sing's dance steps were pure grace and beauty. It was an amazing sight to see my father-in-law and a young bird doing the crane dance together.

I don't know whether Sing was exceptional in her behavior or if she was like all other crane chicks. She did behave differently in many ways from what I've read in books about human-raised cranes. For one thing, she didn't appear to be actually "imprinted" on humans, even though she was raised by us and had no other crane companions until she reached adulthood. She exhibited intelligent and independent behavior, learning to find food and take care of herself, eventually spending both days and nights in our field. She only came back to the house occasionally to eat game bird starter and get a drink of water. She enjoyed being with us when we worked in the yard or garden but seemed content with foraging alone when we were not around.

Sing appeared to understand many of the English words I said to her. She came when her name was called or when I said, "Come here." Even when she was little, when I said, "Let's go!" she ran through the garage door ahead of me, racing as fast as her spindly legs would carry her. That told me Sing knew "let's go" meant we were going for a walk. When she was older and just beginning to fly, she flapped her wings, lifting straight up into the air if I said, "Fly, Sing!" Until she mastered forward flight, she came straight back down, landing lightly in almost the same spot she had left. After she was actually flying, she took off and flew around above the field when I said, "Come on, Sing. Let's fly."

She responded to many things I said in a way that indicated she understood the meaning of the words. This is not surprising, as nearly all species of bird I have raised exhibited a similar ability to learn the meaning of English words. Crane parents continuously communicate with their young for as long as the chicks remain with them, usually about two years. Thus, the ability to learn communication skills is vital to a crane chick's survival.

Bob's father, Bus, with Sing, the Greater Sandhill Crane.

When Sing had become completely independent, we decided it would be best for her if we could find other Sandhill Cranes with whom to live. The rehabilitation center run by the Montana Department of Fish, Wildlife and Parks in Helena, Montana, had raised two Lesser Sandhill Cranes over the summer. They were going to release their youngsters in a wetland area near Helena and agreed to release Sing with them. Two days later, we put Sing in a large cardboard box and drove her to the Helena center. Leaving her there was hard for me, but I thought it would be best for Sing. As it turned out, that was probably not the case. The head of the center reported to me by phone that Sing and their two young cranes got along well. After a day or two for them to become better acquainted, they took the three youngsters to a wetlands area near Helena and left them. Their cranes had not grown up like Sing. They had been raised in a pen and were not at all independent, nor had they had the opportunity to learn to fly well.

The MDFWP rehabilitation center personnel determined their two were not going to survive in the wild, so they decided to take them back into captivity. Not wanting to leave Sing by herself, they recaptured her too. I didn't learn Sing was no longer free until much later. The head of the center said they had found a home for all three cranes at an aviary in Salt Lake City, Utah, and had sent them there to live out their lives in captivity.

Sing loved to fly, but there is no way a Sandhill Crane can really fly in an aviary. I would rather have released her near wild cranes, so she could have learned to migrate with them. She was neither technically imprinted on humans nor dependent on them; there was no reason not to give her the chance to live in the wild.

Unfortunately, we were not consulted regarding her future after she was recaptured, so she was doomed to spend her life in an aviary, essentially prison to a bird who was used to having total freedom. I have often wondered how long she lived. Cranes have been known to live over 20 years in captivity, so she could have had many years. While she would have a safe and easy life at the aviary, if given a choice, she would likely have willingly traded her life there for freedom and the joy of flight.

In 2014, I received two hatchling Sandhill Crane chicks. Someone picked them up, put them into a box, and set it by the gate of an obscure Forest Service campground. Fortunately, a kind person found them before they were eaten by a predator or died of starvation, dehydration, or hypothermia, and brought them to me. I raised them just like I had raised

Sing, except I wasn't able to let them out alone to forage for insects until their feathers were beginning to come in.

At that time, I put them in a room in our old homestead house where I keep recovering birds. When I opened the door of the room, they followed me to the field to practice finding their natural food. The two youngsters quickly learned to catch grasshoppers and other insects. Most interestingly, when I saw one, I could point toward it and the crane closest to where I pointed immediately looked in that direction. It then stalked the grasshopper, almost always catching it. They also spotted many by themselves, and caught most of them. Sandhill Cranes and their chicks are excellent grasshopper exterminators.

I have read studies stating most animals do not learn to look where a human points, but it didn't take the crane chicks long to understand what my gesture meant. When they were tired of catching insects, they followed me back to their room and walked in for water, game bird starter, and mealworms. Mealworms in a bowl are much easier to catch than grasshoppers and are a captive crane chick's favorite treat.

Like Sing, these youngsters liked to follow me when I drove my electric Club Car in our field. I could also leave it somewhere in the field and they would look for insects all around it without wandering too far. I was able to return to our house to feed other birds or work in the garden while the cranes foraged, feeling confident they would stay in the area. The field had only fairly short grass in it, not taller than the cranes like the alfalfa and grass were when we had Sing, so I could always see where they were. They were apparently more imprinted on the Club Car than on me. Once they were old enough to fly, they followed the little car at a run when I drove it through the field, then took off and flew high over our neighborhood, always returning to land in the field near the vehicle when I called to them.

One of the crane chicks was larger than the other and more masculine looking, so I assumed he was a male and the smaller one was a female. Both were fairly tall because the ones who nest here in western Montana are Greater Sandhill Cranes, about 5 inches taller than the Lesser Sandhill Cranes who migrate in huge numbers through the middle of Nebraska in spring and fall.

When the chicks were fully grown, I took them to the Montana Waterfowl Foundation near Ronan, Montana, where they keep unreleasable adult cranes and their chicks in large pens with nets over them. The head of the facility told me Sandhill Cranes raised by humans nearly always die if they are not at least two years old when released. When I heard that, I no longer felt bad about Sing being sent to the aviary.

The manager said all of the young cranes at his facility would be sent to a larger waterfowl facility when they were old enough. There they would be placed in a pen with wild adults and then released with them. In that way, the youngsters could learn naturally how to migrate and where to find food during the migration. It would take two or three years, but eventually the two young cranes and their new friends would fly free.

Courting sandhill cranes,
feather-light puppets, dance on
invisible strings.

CRANE SONG

When crane song echoes through crisp morning air
And long silver ribbons, undulating rhythmically,
Flow across the sky,
There are few earthbound humans, even those
Quite timid, who don't experience at least
A fleeting wish to fly.

CHAPTER 5
I LOVE YOU, GOOD BIRD

The doorbell was ringing *again*, it seemed for the thousandth time that week. It was July, the height of wild bird hatching and fledging season in western Montana. The year was 1991, a momentous one in my life because it was when Arnie, a pretty little songbird called a European Starling (*Sturnus vulgaris*), became my special friend. Our friendship, which lasted for 13 years, began that day with the ringing of the doorbell.

I put down a baby bird I was feeding and opened the door thinking, "Now what?!" On the porch stood a well-dressed woman and her small son Brian, who was four or five years old. He looked up at me with big brown eyes as sad as a scolded puppy's. Gently, he placed a small, cloth-covered box in my hands. I lifted the cloth and there in the center of a nest carefully made of soft tissue, was a homely, naked baby bird with gray downy tufts sticking straight up from its back and head. I recognized it immediately as a hatchling European Starling by its overly large, wide-at-the-base, brilliant yellow bill. Starling hatchlings always have a distinctive wide, yellow, clownish grin.

Starling parents make their nests in building eaves, old barn walls, and holes hollowed out by woodpeckers in tree trunks. All are dark places. The inner lining of hatchling starling bills adapted by becoming an almost iridescent yellow to help their parents see where to put the food they carry to their young. Starlings are an introduced species, brought from Europe and released in North America by people. It is not the starlings' fault they are here in North America. Though not native wild birds, they have successfully colonized all of this continent, similar to how people from other countries did.

The hatchling was undernourished and blue with cold. I carefully took the box from Brian's hands, thinking wickedly, "What a good snack for the injured Sharp-shinned Hawk." In my defense, injured and orphaned young birds had been arriving at my door that summer in numbers unprecedented in my then 22 years of rehabilitating wildlife. I was already caring for a clutch of five baby Mountain Bluebirds, two unrelated fledgling House Finches, several young American Robins of all ages, an even dozen baby Mallard Ducks, eight newly-hatched Ruffed Grouse, and several cat-bitten or otherwise injured adult birds.

All the hatchlings and fledglings, except the ducks and grouse (who can eat by themselves), had to be hand-fed every 20 minutes. I was also raising five orphaned white-tailed deer fawns who required bottles of warm goat milk every three hours. Once daily, the unreleasable birds (adult hawks, eagles, turkey vulture, and owls) I used in wildlife education presentations to clubs and school classes required food. And twice a day, I milked and fed the goats we kept to provide milk for the mammal babies. In my spare time, I made dinner for my husband and myself, washed dishes, and weeded and harvested the vegetable garden. I hadn't been getting much more than four or five hours of sleep each night. A baby starling made another mouth to feed every 20 minutes, all day, every day for several weeks, so was definitely *not* at the top of my wish list.

The boy's mother told me Brian had found the baby bird on the ground in their yard. She explained how she had looked but was unable find the nest from which it had fallen. Brian was in a preschool class where I had given a talk with the owls and hawks earlier that spring. He remembered my name and told his mother I was the one who took care of orphaned baby birds.

Brian's brown eyes filled with tears when he saw how still the little starling was. I assured him it would be fine when he asked if it would die. Baby starlings are tough little birds. Then, to show Brian the orphan was actually quite lively, I whistled. The small head popped up like a jack-in-the-box and eyes as brown as Brian's opened in expectation. Its broad yellow mouth gaped wide as it began begging for food. My syringe of special baby bird formula was only two steps away. The drop I squirted into his over-sized mouth quickly disappeared as the little bird swallowed. I carefully watched the glob of food, easily seen through transparent baby skin, slide down the esophagus into his stomach. Starlings don't have a crop, like chickens, pigeons, and doves do.

"Way to go, Arnie!" I said, spontaneously naming him after the hero of the three *Arnie The Darling Starling* books I had read the winter before. Brian's sweet, innocent eyes widened and his face lit up with a big smile. Arnie again opened his mouth, insistently asking for more food. I gave him another small squirt, followed by a few drops of warm water. The dry, cracked skin on his abdomen told me the week-old hatchling was dehydrated. With his insatiable baby starling appetite momentarily satisfied, Arnie promptly went back to sleep. I placed his box on a heating pad set on low to warm him. Then I helped Brian's mother fill out Arnie's admission sheet.

Baby birds digest their food very quickly, especially when they have been without any for several hours. Arnie was ready for more food by the time we had completed his sheet. His loud starling food call woke the baby finches, robins, and bluebirds. Brian watched as I fed all the demanding babies. After they were fed and asleep again, I took Brian and his mother to see the white-tailed deer fawns. They were both completely enchanted by the small, spotted babies with big brown eyes surrounded by movie-star eyelashes. The fawns, always expecting to be fed, poked their inquisitive wet noses everywhere, looking for a nipple to suck. It wasn't feeding time, so Brian had to be content with petting them, while they delighted him by sucking on his fingers.

After Brian and his mother left, I had to decide what to do with the baby starling. Ideally, I can put hatchlings with young of a similar size in one of the nests built by wild starlings in the walls of our barns and sheds. Usually in July, at least one pair of parents was tending hatchlings. Wild mother starlings will accept and raise an extra baby, saving me hours of work. I have successfully adopted out many baby starlings in this way. After the young birds fledge, the parents teach them how to find food and other important survival skills. Adopted starlings have a much better chance of growing up and surviving their first year in the wild than those I raise and release.

Fortunately for my continuing relationship with Arnie, all the surrogate mother starlings had just finished fledging their young ones or were incubating a new batch of eggs. There were no nests with young close to Arnie's age, so Arnie was stuck with me as his mother. I fixed a nest in a small cardboard box with soft tissue on top of old rags. Starling hatchlings eat a *lot* of food for their size. Their feces, also copious, are expelled in a soft sack the parents carry out of the nest in their bill. After they are well away from the nest area, they drop the feces sacks to the ground. Both parents do this, helping to keep the nest clean and dry. When I am a substitute parent bird, I try to pick up the sack as soon as a hatchling expels it. A recycled fruit can I keep nearby works well for disposing of the droppings. Occasionally, I am not quick enough and the sack disintegrates, soiling the tissue. Quite often, a little bird will back up to the edge of its tissue nest and expel its feces when I am not there to catch it. I use several boxes of tissue in a summer, even when I don't contract a summer cold.

I placed Arnie in his nest box, covering him with another tissue to keep off drafts. There was just enough room left for Arnie's box on the table, at the end of the line of boxes containing other orphaned hatchlings. Whenever he heard my footsteps, Arnie raised his head with gaping mouth giving his baby starling food call. After a couple squirts of baby bird food, I gave him a drink of water. Then I went down the row, feeding and watering all the other babies. By the time I was finished with the last one, Arnie was food begging again. After several more squirts of baby bird food, he was finally full. Then his head dropped down onto the soft tissue as his eyelids closed. He was instantly asleep. Baby birds definitely do *not* need sleeping pills!

This routine went on every 20 to 30 minutes all day. Fortunately, if they are well fed during the day, baby birds don't need to eat at night. I had to get up at 2:00 a.m. to feed the deer fawns their middle of the night bottles, so fed and watered the baby birds as well, since I was already up. I began the regular daily bird feedings at 5:30 or 6:00, just before taking bottles to the fawns. With all that nourishment, the birds grew fast, quickly graduating to bigger boxes where they could practice flying and feeding themselves.

Before they could be released, all the young ones had to learn to pick up their own food, whether it was seeds for the seedeaters or mealworms for the insect eaters. Starlings mature a bit slower than House Finches and bluebirds. Bluebirds learn to grab mealworms quite readily because their movement attracts the curious youngsters' attention. Seedeaters are often slower at picking up and shelling seeds, but House Finches, being ravenous little birds, quickly learn to peck at mushy baby bird food with shelled sunflower seeds mixed in. Young robins are thrushes like bluebirds and there is almost always a quick learner in the group. Once one youngster begins to pick up appropriate food, the others quickly learn by example. Or if I have an injured adult bluebird or robin in my care, I place the youngsters in its box where they easily learn to eat on their own by observing the adult.

Starlings eat both mealworms and grain but will food beg long after fledging, especially if they can get someone to feed them. Arnie was no different but learned to pick up, kill, and eat mealworms much faster as a fledgling than most young starlings I had raised. That may have been because I was so busy he often became quite hungry before I got back to feed him. However, I like to think Arnie learned new things more quickly than most young starlings because he was extremely intelligent.

By three and one-half weeks of age, Arnie's little pinfeathers had emerged as soft gray-brown feathers. He could walk or hop around on his long legs, flapping his wings to strengthen them while helping him maintain balance. As soon as he began actually trying to fly, I put him in a flight box. These are large cardboard boxes with a clear plastic window to let in light and allow the birds to see out. One side has a cardboard door that can be opened to feed the birds. Branches and/or hemp rope perches pushed through holes in the sides of the boxes are placed so birds can practice flying from perch to perch.

There were no other fledgling starlings Arnie's age, so he had his flight box to himself. He soon learned what "come here" meant, which may be why it was one of the first phrases he said when he began talking. When I fed Arnie, I opened his door while saying, "Come here, Arnie." He immediately ran over, hopping expectantly up onto the perch I had placed just inside the door. I could then easily put food into his gaping mouth. I fed him either mealworms or a mixture of Purina Game Bird Startina® and baby bird food, encouraging him to close his mouth on the bit of food I held in the tip of small forceps. They hold food in a way that is similar to how a parent bird's beak does. I pick up small amounts with the forceps from a little mound of food placed near the young bird. In that way, those without an adult bird as teacher learn by watching the forceps pick up their food.

After he had gulped down all the mealworms and baby bird food he could hold, along with several swallows of water, I said "Go home, Arnie." He obediently turned and hopped or flew to the perch in the center of the box. I left mealworms, small gravel, and a pile of food in small dishes on the floor of the box. Whenever he chose, he could practice pecking at the food and picking it up by himself. Birds with gizzards usually eat gravel, which goes into their gizzard to grind the food. Young starlings are very curious, regularly picking up and tasting new things to determine whether they are good to eat. Being extremely playful, starlings like to use feathers, colorful stones, beads, and other interesting objects as toys, all of which I supplied for Arnie's entertainment.

Whenever Arnie had eaten several mealworm beetles,* he soon regurgitated a pellet composed of pieces of indigestible beetle exoskeleton. Carnivorous and insectivorous songbirds, including starlings, are technically birds of prey, though are not classified as raptors. They catch live food, mostly in the form of insects, and after digesting it, regurgitate pellets just like the larger birds of prey. After ingesting insects and fruit with seeds, members of the thrush and lark families often cast up pellets made of both insect parts and indigestible seeds. This helps spread many kinds of seeds to new areas where they grow, creating new sources of fruit for birds and other animals.

*(Mealworms are the larval form of this species of insect. They hatch from eggs laid by the adult (reproductive form) which are beetles. Similar to butterflies, the full-grown larva forms a pupa from which the beetle later emerges. Arnie preferred the softer, light-colored beetles, those whose exoskeleton hadn't yet hardened after emerging from the pupa.

After reading the *Arnie the Darling Starling* books, having the opportunity to raise a baby starling and live with it as a friend intrigued me. Earlier in the year, I had met a starling named Lucky, raised by an acquaintance's daughter the summer before. When Lucky was seven months old, he began speaking English words. By the time I met him, he had developed a fairly large vocabulary including, "I'm a Lucky bird," "Eat your dinner," "Hi!" and many other words and phrases.

From childhood, I have been of the opinion that the intelligence of non-human animals, especially birds, has been shamefully underrated. The possibility of carrying on a meaningful conversation in English with a member of the bird world presented a whole new perspective on raising a baby starling. Of course, the bird would have to learn to speak English words, since I am unable to learn the language spoken by European Starlings. I never understood why people use the term "bird brain" as an insult. Judging by the birds I have been around, being called a "bird brain" is definitely a compliment. As Arnie's vocabulary grew and he could actually tell me in words how smart he was, I became even more humbled.

It is not surprising that starlings can say words of whatever language is spoken to them, since they belong to the Myna Bird family, known for their ability to talk. While reading the *Arnie the Darling Starling* books by Margarette Sigl Corbo and Diane Marie Barras, it became completely evident that Margarette's Arnie used words, phrases, and sentences meaningfully and in proper context. He, like Lucky, began talking at about seven months old. My Arnie began talking at just a week over three months of age. This was surprising as I was too busy to give Arnie the almost constant attention other talking starlings had received from their human friends when they were very young.

The first of Arnie's many linguistic surprises was the first sentence he said. Arnie had learned what "come here" meant as a fledgling, because that's what I said each time I fed him. If he was out in the room, he flew to me when I said it, landing on my arm. Arnie could fly well by the time he was a month old. Between his learning to fly and saying his first English words was a little over two months. I had thought if he did learn to say any words, they would be "Arnie is a good bird" or "Come here" or just "Good bird," phrases I most commonly used when he came to the door of his box or to me.

To my utter amazement, the first sentence Arnie said was something I had never said to him. One day in early autumn, I went into the bird room to feed a couple of injured birds. I said "Hi Arnie," as I always did. He replied in a voice that sounded something like mine and, in perfectly pronounced words, "Arnie is a pretty bird." Then he performed a wolf whistle. I definitely hadn't done any wolf whistles around him. I may have said, "Arnie is a pretty bird," but didn't recall ever doing so.

By that time, I had almost forgotten I had kept a friend's cockatoo, Berta, for two weeks in July, while she and her family moved to a new place in a different state. After they were settled, they returned for Berta, taking her to their new home. While she was with us, Berta lived in her cage in the corner of our living room at the east end of our home. Arnie lived in my studio, which had been turned into an intensive care room for birds, at the west end. Arnie was unable to see Berta, but he must have heard her. She repeated over and over in a clear voice, "Berta is a pretty bird," then made a loud wolf whistle. She also said some other things that were too indistinct for me to understand.

Arnie must have learned "is a pretty bird" by listening to Berta. However, according to most scientific reports on birds who learn to speak a human language, Arnie should have said, "Berta is a pretty bird." Many scientists still insist they only mimic words and sounds they hear, without truly understanding the meaning of the words. Arnie never in his entire life said the word Berta, even though he must have heard her say her name as often as he heard her say "is a pretty bird" and the wolf whistle. The only explanation is that he knew his name was Arnie. Somehow, he determined he should say "Arnie is a pretty bird" instead of just copying Berta's sentence. Even more interesting, Arnie was just learning to fly when Berta's family took her home. He was a preflight fledgling when he last heard her talk, more than two months before he first spoke to me.

Arnie also somehow knew what being a pretty bird means, because after he began talking, he asked me to bring him his bath by saying, "Arnie wants a bath. Arnie wants to be a pretty bird." Arnie constructed the sentence, "Arnie wants to be a pretty bird," by himself. He created many other new sentences using words and phrases he heard from me or other people. He knew his name was Arnie and that he was a bird. I could tell by what he said to other birds that he knew they were birds, too. He seemed especially interested in the young ones. He never tried to feed them but often talked to them while I fed them. He was never aggressive toward any bird who was in the room for rehabilitation.

By the time he was a year old, I knew for certain that Arnie knew the meaning of the words he said. He even appeared to understand the various uses for words with more than one meaning, such as the word good. He said, "You are a good bird," to me when I did something he asked me to do. When I fed him his favorite food, a soft mealworm beetle, he said, "Good bug." One day when I walked into the bird room and said "Hi, Arnie. How are you?" Arnie said, "Arnie is a good pretty bird," combining the two sentences "Arnie is a good bird" and "Arnie is a pretty bird" into one English sentence that answered my question. Another time he answered my question with, "Arnie is a pretty good bird." He never said the words in those sentences in any other way than the two grammatically correct English sentences. There are many other possible combinations of those six words, most of which don't make sense or form a sentence. He also said at various times in the proper context of our conversation, "Arnie is a bird" and "Arnie is a little bird."

When I named him, I didn't know Arnie was a male. It is impossible to tell the gender of a fledgling European Starling by the plumage, as both sexes look alike. However, the iris, the colored part of the eye around the pupil, is completely brown on male starlings. Females have a pale golden ring encircling their brown iris. Once a starling becomes a fledgling, gender is easily determined by looking for the golden ring. The irises in Arnie's eyes were completely brown. Male starlings appear able to learn to speak more readily than females. My original motive for keeping Arnie, rather than releasing him when he was old enough, was to observe how a starling learns to speak a human language. From a scientific perspective, it was good that Arnie was a male.

Over-wintering wild European Starlings living in our area appear to remain paired year around. In spring, the black bills turn bright yellow on both males and females. The changing of bill color is reported to be connected to exposure to sunlight. Since he lived inside a house all his life, Arnie's bill never turned yellow in the spring, even though his feathers molted into colorful, speckled, breeding plumage. In early fall, the bill color on a wild starling returns to black and remains so until the following spring.

Our resident wild starlings learned interesting food gathering behaviors during the difficult winter months. By watching magpies eat carrion, the starlings learned to peck pieces of meat from deer carcasses picked up by Bob as part of his job as a game warden. I had permission to butcher some of the accident-killed animals to feed meat-eating birds and mammals in my care. I put the remainder of the carcass out in the field where wild birds could eat from it. Starlings sat patiently while magpies filled their beaks and throat pouches. When they flew off to hide their caches, the starlings flew to the carcass to tear off as many bites as they could before the returning magpies forced them to leave and wait for another opportunity to feed. Starlings are small enough to fly freely in and out of the chain link kennel where at that time we often stored accident-killed carcasses for short periods when the weather was cool, protecting them from dogs and larger birds. In one afternoon, several starlings will eat quite a large hole in the meat of a deer leg. They could eat all they wanted in the kennel, uninterrupted by larger birds. After our wild starlings learned to eat carrion, they apparently taught other wild starlings in the area to do it.

A small flock of European Starlings began over-wintering at a local wildlife refuge, living mostly on deer meat. At the time, accident-killed deer carcasses were placed in a special area on the refuge for Golden and Bald Eagles, Ravens, Black-billed Magpies, coyotes, and other wild carnivores to eat in winter. When the refuge stopped putting out deer carcasses, starlings no longer spent that season there. Starlings will eat fruit, grain, or other seeds in winter when nothing else is available, but our wild starlings much preferred meat to grain or birdseed.

In early spring, before the swallows come back, wild starlings have another interesting food gathering behavior: flying around catching gnats, mosquitoes, and other similar prey species. They course back and forth through high-flying clouds of insects, looking very much like swallows as they snap them out of the air with their quick bills. By the time swallows, swifts, and other birds who live primarily on this food source return in spring, starlings have begun eating grasshoppers, caterpillars, leaf hoppers, and other ground insects abundant in the new spring foliage.

Many people dislike European Starlings, but for insect control, they are hard to beat.

After he began flying, I placed Arnie's cardboard flight box on top of an aquarium the same width as the box. I removed almost half of the bottom to make a large hole through which Arnie could jump down into the glass tank. Each day, I placed a plastic bath pan in the aquarium with about an inch and a half of water in it, just the right depth for a starling to bathe. Arnie loved to take baths, so it didn't take him long to learn to hop down through the hole to the edge of the pan and then into the water. Starlings splash more than a combination of a flock of ducks and a family of beavers, so the glass was necessary for splash containment. By the time Arnie finished his bath, most of the water was in the aquarium.

After feeding all the baby birds, I took Arnie's bath pan to the kitchen to put water in it. When I placed it in the aquarium, I said, "Here is your bath, Arnie." Arnie usually replied in a sincere tone of voice, "I love you. You are a good bird." Apparently, he understood such intangible concepts as love and good, because his use of the words was always correct, timely, and in the right context.

When I spoke to Arnie after he first began talking, I failed to consider that he would likely learn and repeat what I said to him. So, when I went into the bird room, I'd say, "Hi, Arnie. What are you doing," "How are you?" or simply "Hello, Arnie." I also said, "You are a good bird" or "I love you" at least once daily, while I worked in the bird room. He soon began saying, "Hi, Arnie" back to me. This went on for a couple weeks, until one day I said to him, "I'm Judy. You are Arnie. You are supposed to say, Hi, Judy." I was joking, of course, never expecting him to actually do it. But the next time I went in and said, "Hi, Arnie" he replied "Hi, Judy." He also began greeting me occasionally with "Hello, Judy," but he never called me Arnie again.

Arnie used different tones of voice when he talked to me or to other people, indicating irritation, impatience, contentment, happiness, and other moods. Right after I told him he should say, "Hi Judy," he started saying, "Hi, Judy. I love you." That wasn't surprising, because I said to him, "Hi, Arnie. I love you." Then a couple days later, when I was giving him his bath pan, he said, "I love you, Judy." Neither I nor anyone else had said that exact sentence in his presence. By the time he was six months old, it was evident that Arnie was able to make new sentences from words and phrases he had learned. The next day he said, "Judy, I love you," when I gave him his bath pan. From that day on, he told me he

48

loved me one of those two ways, until he was two years old. Then one day he said very tenderly, "I love you, Good Bird." That was definitely my favorite!

Some may believe Arnie was incapable of understanding an abstract word like love. By his actions, he showed his affection as well as verbalizing it. He often flew to my shoulder, gently nibbled on my ear with the tip of his bill, and told me in a sincere tone of voice that he loved me in one of the many ways he had of stating his feelings. He always used the word in the proper context. It was clear he loved me and I certainly loved him. How could I not love a beautiful little bird who told me he loved me several times every day in a tone of voice that would melt a stone?

For the first year after he began talking, Arnie often caught me by surprise by using phrases or sentences I didn't know he had learned. What he said was always completely in context with the conversation we were having at the time. I had often said, "Does Arnie want a bath?" or "Here is your bath, Arnie," when I put his pan of bath water in the aquarium. I started out by saying, "Arnie wants a bath" in hopes he would learn to tell me when he wanted a bath. As it turned out, it wasn't one of the phrases he said when he began talking. What I had not considered was how difficult it would be for a bird to make sounds like "baa" and "th."

One day in early spring, when Arnie was nearly a year old, I was dumping the water out of the other birds' water dishes into the soil of potted plants on the windowsill. When Arnie saw the water, he said, "Arnie baa. Arnie baa." It took me several minutes to determine what he was saying because he wasn't pronouncing the "th" on the end of bath. Also, I had always said, "Arnie wants a bath," not "Arnie bath." Usually, he spoke in whole sentences or even made them longer instead of shortening them. I was cleaning the other birds' boxes, when it suddenly occurred to me he had been trying to say "Arnie bath!"

When I filled his water pan and put it in the aquarium, he immediately hopped down into the water and began fluttering his wings to splash water up over his back. After that, he said "Arnie bath" or "Arnie wants a bath" every morning. At first, I couldn't hear the "th" but after a few days, Arnie pronounced "bath" perfectly. He didn't seem to have any trouble with the "baa" part of the word but had to practice a while before getting the difficult "th" sound correct. It was fascinating to me that he managed to learn to make that sound, which is made by the tongue against teeth when people pronounce it.

Starlings, like other songbirds, make vocal sounds with the syrinx, which is what their "voice box" is called. The syrinx is in the chest at the bifurcation of the trachea, where it divides to go to the lungs on each side of the chest. Arnie opened and closed his bill when he talked, but his sounds, whether a word or other sound like his wolf whistle, clicking noises, and clear, perfectly-pitched whistled songs, were made by air flowing through the syrinx in his upper chest.

About a month after he first said "Arnie bath," he surprised me one morning by following it with a short pause and then announcing, "Arnie is a dirty bird. Arnie wants a bath." I had said, "You're a dirty bird" only a few of the many times he left a dropping on my shirt. Apparently I said it often enough for him to learn the sentence, but I don't know how he figured out what it meant. He quite clearly understood that a bath would make him clean and pretty, which had nothing to do with getting my shirt dirty.

Some people have accused me of not being an objective observer. Arnie made many friends in his life and talked clearly in contextual sentences to the people he liked. Many were fairly objective witnesses to what he said and did. Mary, one of our best friends, offered to bird-sit Arnie when we went on vacation. Mary was also a wildlife rehabber, so she knew how to care for birds. She especially liked owls, but a visiting starling who could talk intrigued her.

The first time Arnie went to stay with her was in the spring shortly before his first birthday. I was away for two weeks. A neighbor who lived near us offered to feed the unreleasable birds I keep for educational presentations, but I thought Arnie should have full-time care. Mary agreed. We didn't want him to be alone in his room for all that time. While he was at Mary's house, Arnie had to remain in his large cardboard box; she didn't have a room where it was safe for him to fly free. He was quiet and subdued in his new surroundings. Mary talked to him often, listening closely for a reply. She didn't hear him say one word for the first week and a half we were gone. He didn't even ask for his bath. One afternoon, when Mary was standing near his box feeding a little bat she was also caring for at the time, she heard Arnie say in a sad, low voice, "I love my Judy." Mary said he sounded so sad it brought tears to her eyes. I am sure he thought I was not going to come back.

He was ecstatically happy to see me when I finally arrived to bring him home. He talked and sang continuously for the next several days, telling me he loved me at least a dozen times a day. It was quite clear he didn't

50

want me to go on vacation again any time soon. What I thought was most interesting was that Arnie had said to Mary, "I love my Judy." He had never used the phrase "my Judy" when talking to me. I thought it was very touching that he considered me his Judy.

Soon after things had returned to normal, Arnie amazed another friend, Adele, who also rehabilitated wildlife. When she came to visit me, I took her into the bird room to see the ones who were there. When we entered, Arnie was on his perch in his cardboard box. He said, "Hi." I replied, "Hi Arnie. This is Adele." Arnie looked straight at Adele and said, "Come here." Adele just stood there looking amazed. Again, Arnie said. "Come here." Curious as to what he wanted, I asked Adele to walk over close to the box and stand by the clear plastic window so he could see her better. Usually he didn't ask other people to come close to him and, in fact, was quite shy with strangers.

By coincidence, Arnie had just finished his bath and had damp, shiny feathers. He appeared to want Adele to see how pretty he was, strutting from one end of his perch to the other and then back to the middle, saying twice in a very proud voice, "Arnie is a pretty bird." When he stopped in the middle of the perch with his back to her, he whistled, loud and clear, the wolf whistle he had learned from Berta the cockatoo. Adele laughed, but before either she or I could say anything, Arnie turned around so he was facing her. Then he leaned forward toward her, looked her right in the eye, and said in a clear, emphatic tone of voice, "I *love* my Judy!" He placed special emphasis on the word love, left out the "you" he always put before Judy when talking to me, and said "my Judy" instead.

Adele looked at me with eyes as big as saucers and said, "That bird is amazing!" I thought so too. When speaking to Adele, he used the proper sentence structure for talking to someone other than me, as he had when he finally spoke to Mary. Even more interesting was the way he said it, as though he was telling her something important. From that time on, when he talked to others, he occasionally said to them in a confidential tone of voice, "I love Judy" or "I love my Judy." It is still a mystery to me how he knew to use the correct phrase, depending upon whether he was speaking directly to me or talking about me to other people.

While working in the bird room feeding young birds or cleaning up, I often whistled my favorite songs. If Arnie liked the tune, he included it in his spring songs. Each year in late winter, Arnie composed long, interesting courtship songs. When I wasn't in the bird room, he amused

51

himself by making up new versions of them. He was highly creative, musically speaking.

His songs usually began with "Arnie is a pretty bird" followed by his wolf whistle, then a perfect rendition of the first few bars of Yankee Doodle, then "I love you, kiss, kiss," emphasized by two smacking sounds like loud kisses, a few bars of his own whistled tunes, some weird TV sounds, and finally a string of hard-to-describe sounds starlings often make. Arnie's courting songs were similar to the long, varied ones created by wild male European Starlings in spring. Theirs consist of birdcalls, hawk screeches, whistles, and a variety of sounds made only by starlings, all strung into an amazing vocalization designed to impress their female partner. Judging by the number of young starlings produced each year, it works very well.

The whistled tunes Arnie made up sounded like a human whistling a song, but the notes were not a song I recognized. He repeated his long courtship song several times, and then created a different version by adding new parts or leaving out some of them. I could hear him singing from other rooms in the house. If I walked into the bird room, he stopped and talked to me in normal English sentences. When I stayed for long periods to work on an art project or with young birds, Arnie sang to me, usually while sitting on my shoulder. He made up new songs each spring for me, even though his bill never turned courtship yellow. Arnie did his best to impress me, having no other female audience. He was highly successful at it. What he said and did impressed me every day of his life.

Other people's reaction to Arnie's talking was always interesting, provided he decided to say something when they were present. He usually spoke when women came but often completely clammed up when men were there. Arnie immediately talked to Adele but usually would not say a word when my husband Bob or Adele's husband Don, were in his room. This resulted in some not-so-veiled implications concerning Adele's and my imaginations.

At two and a half years old, Arnie exhibited a new behavior when I was feeding him soft mealworm beetles, his favorite treat. He was on his perch, consisting of a hemp rope stretched from one side of his box to the other. Rope is much softer for a bird's feet than a hard, wooden perch, preventing foot sores from developing. As usual, I reached through the open side of the box to hand the beetles to him. He took each beetle, crunched it a couple times, and then swallowed it. He had eagerly taken two or three from my fingers without hesitation, but turned away when I offered another one. I started to put it back into the mealworm box, thinking he was full. Arnie came toward me on the hemp rope perch, saying in a very loud voice, "Come here, come here, come here!" Of course, I gave him the beetle. From that time on, whenever I asked if he wanted a beetle or even if I just picked one up, he said, "Come here." After he ate the beetle, he said "Good!" He even performed this feeding ritual in the presence of strangers. Most found it rather amazing that a starling could ask for food in English and then proclaim it to be good after he ate it.

Starlings can use their bills in ways most other birds do not. They pry things apart by placing the closed points of their bill between what is to be spread, then opening them. They push bark, grass, and weed stems apart in this manner to find insects and other choice invertebrates they like to eat that are hiding there. They also lift things from surfaces, putting the tip of the bill under an object before opening their bill to get at what interests them. Arnie used this skill to great advantage when he wanted to retrieve mealworms by himself from the pan where I kept the mealworm colony. I always place a layer of newspaper over the insects to help keep them from becoming too dry. Arnie lifted the newspapers, clasped the edge in his bill, and pulled them to the side, exposing the mealworms for his dining pleasure.

In early spring, when Arnie was three years old, he again stayed with Mary while we were on vacation. As before, we were gone nearly two weeks. This time Mary said Arnie talked, whistled, and chattered, seeming perfectly content in her home. He had learned I would eventually return and, of course, he remembered Mary. Arnie gave her a fright one day by flying out of his box when she opened the door to put in food and water. Arnie sailed around the room, and then did something he had never done in his room at home. He flew straight against a window. He must have bumped his head, because Mary was able to run over to the windowsill, pick him up, and put him back in his box while he was dazed. She was extremely concerned he might have seriously injured himself. Fortunately, he was fine after a short recovery period, but he never again tried to fly out of his box while at Mary's house. As before, he seemed extremely happy when I returned and took him back to his room, where he could fly free.

One day that summer, Arnie helped with a young man's education concerning birds. A woman called to ask if she could bring her son Bryce to see my education birds, those I used for presentations. She said Bryce loved birds, even wanting to begin a study program toward becoming an ornithologist when he went to college that fall. He was also an avid birder who was keeping a life list. (Bird watchers often maintain a record of all the different birds they see in their lifetime.)

When he and his mother arrived, I showed Bryce the unreleasable hawk, owls, and eagles I kept for nature talks. After that, we went out to look at wild birds living on our property. Several were eating sunflower seeds at the feeder, making them easy to observe. While watching the seed-eating birds, we were discussing Bryce's desire to become an ornithologist. I jokingly said I had a test he must pass before he could become a good one. I asked if he had learned the commonly taught misinformation that animals, including birds, did everything by instinct.

He answered, "Yes, that is what we learned in science class." I inquired as to whether he actually believed it.

"That's what it says in the science books. Isn't it true?"

My response was, "I will take you to meet Arnie. You can draw your own scientific conclusions."

Arnie was delighted to have company and, with everyone's attention on him, he was even more talkative than usual. He took an immediate liking to Bryce, probably because he could sense the young man loved birds. Without hesitation, Arnie flew straight over to him, landing unafraid on his shoulder. He often flew to bird lovers, perching on their shoulder or arm to talk to them, while totally refusing to go near other people. He especially would not approach most men. Apparently, Arnie considered Bryce an exception.

Arnie was linguistically impressive that day, maybe because he decided the young man was special. As soon as he landed on Bryce's shoulder, he said "Hi." Then he proclaimed, "Arnie is a good bird, Arnie is a pretty bird," followed by his wolf whistle. Meanwhile, I was finding some of his favorite mealworm beetles. I held one up and Arnie flew back to my shoulder saying, "Come here" in a demanding tone. I gave him one of the beetles, which he quickly ate, following with "Good bug." He repeated, "Come here" for each of the rest of the mealworms I held up, and said "Good" after eating each one. He followed that impressive performance with, "I love you, Judy." He promptly proved to be a fickle little bird by flying from my shoulder back to Bryce's arm. As soon as he landed, Arnie said "Hello," followed by a short pause, and then emphatically stated, "I love my Judy Bird."

All that had happened almost too quickly for Bryce to grasp. He looked at me like I had shown him an alien from another planet rather than a pretty but ordinary-looking European Starling. I asked him if he still believed what the books said about birds doing everything by instinct.

He was obviously a quick learner, as he stated very positively, "Your bird makes me think the science books must be wrong." I told Bryce he was now destined to become a good ornithologist and Arnie proclaimed Bryce to be a "Good Bird!" making both Bryce and his mother laugh.

One summer day when Arnie was four, Laura, the daughter of an acquaintance, brought me an abandoned baby domestic rabbit for whom to care. After I made the little bunny comfortable, Laura asked if she could see some of the birds. The first one we visited was Arnie. He immediately said "Hi" when we entered the room. I asked if he wanted a beetle. As usual, he said, "Come here." After eating two or three, he said "Good bug." Once he had warmed to having company, Arnie said several other sentences, including, "I love Judy," and "Arnie is a pretty bird" with his usual wolf whistle. Then he said, "Judy is a good pretty bird" and "I love my Judy bird," concluding by saying "Arnie wants a bath." I put some water into his pan, which he immediately entered to enjoy a very splashy bath. Laura was duly impressed by Arnie's ability to verbalize what he wanted in English. When she arrived back home, she told her father about the talking starling she had seen and heard. He said he didn't believe her.

A little over a week later, Laura called to ask if she could bring her friend Sandy along when she came to see the baby rabbit. They also wanted to visit Arnie, of course. Laura explained that her father didn't believe what she had told him about Arnie, especially that a starling could talk in complete English sentences. She wanted Sandy to hear Arnie to corroborate her story. As usual, Arnie greeted them with a "Hi" when they went in to his room, continuing with "Arnie is a pretty bird," followed by the wolf whistle. I held up some mealworm beetles for him to see. He said "Come here" to indicate he wanted them, then as always, said "Good" or "Good bug" after he ate each beetle. He embellished this by proclaiming, "Arnie is a good pretty bird." He then emphatically stated, "I love my Judy bird." After that statement, both young ladies were bent over with laughter.

Although what he said was standard Arnie vocabulary, hearing clearly-stated English sentences come out of his mouth (actually from his syrinx) was obviously as astounding to Laura and Sandy as to all who had previously met Arnie. Like most people, they were conditioned to believe birds are not very intelligent. Laura's father was completely convinced they do everything by instinct. I am not sure he believed a bird could speak English, even with Sandy as a second witness. He never came to see Arnie, although Laura had to come back to get her bunny when it was old enough to wean. It appeared her father didn't want his beliefs to be proven false.

One summer day, a fledgling swallow was rescued and brought to me. A highly inconsiderate* boy had thrown a rock at its nest built on a bridge beam, knocking it and four siblings into the river. A quick-thinking little girl rescued one of the babies before it was carried away to drown with the others in the fast-flowing water. Many swallows are lost each year in this way. The parents attach their mud nests to the bottoms of numerous cement bridges that span the Bitterroot River. During summer, when swallows are nesting, people go to swim in the river near the bridges. For some unfathomable reason, many people, usually younger males, think it's fun to knock down nests and watch the babies drown. Swallows eat many flying insects each day, especially mosquitoes and a small biting insect locally called a no-see-um. Their ability to deplete mosquito populations is particularly beneficial to humans. While sucking the blood of birds and mammals, they can spread diseases. With people being so fearful of mosquito bites giving them or their livestock mosquito-borne diseases, including West Nile Virus, they should afford all swallow species and other mosquito eating animals the greatest protection possible.

*(The words I would like to use for such behavior are not suitable for print.)

One morning a few days after the swallow arrived, I went into the bird room to feed it for the fourth or fifth time. The fledgling, now fully grown, was in a big flight box on the opposite side of the room from Arnie's, where he was perched at the time. I had been busy with the other birds and several deer fawns, so had been neglecting Arnie. I gave him his food and bath, but hadn't spent as much time with him as in the winter when I worked on various projects in the bird room. Then it was an art studio, where I created wildlife paintings for hours at a time. Arnie would sit on my shoulder, practicing and perfecting his long spring songs, whistling tunes I had taught him, or asking me questions, which I answered. Thus, during winter, he had become accustomed to almost constant attention, which suddenly stopped when I became busy with all the summer chores like gardening and caring for the many critters who arrived in spring and summer.

I had fed the swallow one mealworm, when I heard Arnie say, "Hi, Judy."

I replied, "Hi, Arnie," without really thinking about it, since we often exchanged greetings when I went into the bird room.

Then he asked, "What are you doing?"

"I'm feeding a little bird."

I didn't expect a reply but, after a long pause, Arnie said in a clearly jealous tone of voice, "Arnie is a little bird."

I was so surprised, I almost dropped the baby bird food. That was the first time I had heard him use the word little, but more importantly, his cryptic declaration was completely appropriate, sounding exactly like a small child who feels neglected.

Arnie usually asked for his bath every morning, especially if I didn't bring it as soon as he wanted. Sometimes, he said, "Hi Judy! Arnie wants a bath," as soon as I walked into the room. If I had baby birds, I fed them before doing anything else. This delay was quite upsetting to Arnie. He repeated, "Arnie wants a bath" and added, "Arnie is a dirty bird." I replied, "I will get your bath in a minute. I'm feeding the little birds." After the incident with the swallow, Arnie often reminded me in a perturbed tone of voice, "Arnie is a little bird." Other times, he would try to get me to pay more attention to him by saying, "Come here, Good Bird," using his pet name for me before repeating that he wanted his bath. His jealousy was so obvious it often made me laugh. Unlike some animals, Arnie never seemed to have hurt feelings when I laughed at him.

The next winter, when I went into the bird room to feed and check on a Cedar Waxwing and a Pygmy Owl, Arnie said his usual perky "Hi, Judy." The two birds had been brought to me the day before because each had been injured by flying into a window. After a pause, he said, "I love you," which often preceded a request from him. He had learned I was a pushover for sweet talk, knowing I would bring him what he wanted faster if he told me "I love you" in his most persuasive tone of voice. Predictably, he asked for his bath as he did nearly every morning, saying, "Arnie wants a bath. Arnie is a dirty bird. Arnie wants a bath." As I was busy getting mealworms for the Cedar Waxwing, I told him, "I will get your bath in a minute." After a short pause, Arnie repeated, "Arnie wants a bath." Then he stated emphatically, "Arnie wants to be a pretty bird."

I hadn't heard him say that before. I thought maybe I had not heard him correctly, because I had never said that to him. A couple days later, he told me as usual, "Arnie wants a bath" followed by declaring, "Arnie is a dirty bird." I never figured out how he knew that taking a bath would fix being a dirty bird either. I may have called him a dirty bird a few times when he was young, but how could he know that a dirty bird needs a bath? After a short pause, he again stated emphatically, "Arnie wants to be a pretty bird." I laughed all the way to the kitchen to get the water. He never said, "Arnie is a funny bird," but he could have, because he certainly was.

For some reason, I began saying "Hi, Arnie-Arnie" in a cheerful voice when I went in to see him or to feed other birds. I thought it sounded rather musical. A week or so went by with me repeating the new phrase each time I saw him. One afternoon, when I said it in a happy, upbeat tone as I walked into the room, he quickly replied in the same tone, "Hello, Judy-Judy," a completely different phrase that he made up entirely on his own. After a few days, he began saying the greeting in two ways: "Hi, Judy-Judy" and "Hello, Judy-Judy."

Each morning, especially during spring and summer, I had to clean all the recovering adult birds' boxes, as well as those of the fledglings, and resupply them with food and water. While I worked, Arnie and I kept up a running conversation. He always requested his bath, sometimes he asked me to come to him, and occasionally he said to me questioningly, "Go to bed?" When I said, "Go to bed," I meant for him to go into his box for the night so I could turn off the light, but I wasn't sure what he wanted from me. I was certainly much too big to share his box. He sometimes suggested seductively, "I love you Judy, my good pretty bird. Go to bed?" I never knew if he really meant what that implied, but I assume he wanted me to come into his box with him. Jasper, the male American Kestrel had sexually imprinted on me and even deposited semen on my head. It was possible and even likely that Arnie considered me his mate, since he had no available female starling.

After raising Arnie, I looked up research on birds who could talk. I read about Irene Pepperberg, an animal research scientist who taught Alex, her African Grey Parrot, to recognize and name various shapes, identify different materials, count objects, and learn the sounds of letters. Alex talked to Irene and other researchers like Arnie talked to me, making up new words, creating his own names for unfamiliar objects, and asking for things he wanted. Alex also told researchers where he wanted to be taken, as his wings were clipped so he couldn't fly. Thanks to Irene and

Alex, many people now understand that birds are extremely intelligent and can communicate with other species, including humans.

In 1997, Dorothy Hinshaw Patent decided to write a children's book about Irene and Alex, called *Alex and Friends: Animal Talk, Animal Thinking*. Dorothy called me that summer to ask if she could include information about Arnie and me. I told her we would be honored to be in her book, and suggested she might also include my friend Adele and her Chattering Lory, Nicki. Dorothy's photographer friend, William Munoz, took the photos for her book. William had previously been to our place to photograph my unreleasable education owls and hawks. A great one he took of Arnie sitting on my shoulder, mouth open so it looks like he was talking, which he likely was, is in the book. William also took delightful photos of Nicki playing a game and sitting on Adele's shoulder.

In the book, Dorothy described some of the things Arnie and Nicki could do and say. She discussed intelligence and ability to communicate in other birds and animals such as chimpanzees, sea lions, and dolphins. Of course, the book was mostly about Alex, Irene, and their research together. When Dorothy went to Arizona to interview them, she told Irene about Arnie and Nicki. William took many interesting photos of the various birds and animals, which helped make Dorothy's book a big hit with both children and adults. Unfortunately for Irene and her research, Alex died suddenly during the night on September 6, 2007, when he was only 31 years old. African Grey Parrots usually live to be over 50. Even though I never actually met Alex, I felt and still feel like I lost a dear friend. He will be missed by all who were grateful for his intelligence and cooperation, enabling Irene Pepperberg to prove that birds have the ability to think in a cognitive manner, do communicate with other species, and are intelligent, compassionate individuals deserving of consideration and respect.

When Arnie was eight years old, he added another new sentence to his repertoire. I was working in the bird room late that spring, feeding a brood of baby Mountain Bluebirds. The little guys were food begging loudly, making funny gulping noises when they swallowed what I placed into their gaping mouths. Arnie was watching them from his perch on my shoulder when he suddenly asked, "Is that good?" He seemed disappointed when none of them answered him.

I was nearly finished feeding the bluebirds when the portable phone I carried with me rang. Arnie was still on my left shoulder, so his face was fairly close to the receiver of the phone as I talked. The caller was a man

I didn't know, who wanted to speak to my husband about his recently-constructed fish pond. At that time, part of Bob's job as a game warden was to inspect ponds for the Montana Department of Fish, Wildlife and Parks to make certain stocked fish (those introduced into ponds by landowners) could not escape into rivers and streams to mix with wild fish.

I asked the man for his name and phone number, saying I would give Bob the message when he returned home in a couple hours. While I was writing the information, there was a pause in our conversation. Arnie, unfortunately, picked that moment to say very clearly and quite loudly, "I love you." Because Arnie had learned to talk by listening to me, his voice sounded quite similar to mine.

The man on the phone replied, "What did you say?" in a shocked and angry tone of voice.

I quickly told him, "Don't pay any attention to that. My pet starling was talking to me."

The man repeated, "What did you say???" His tone clearly indicated he could not comprehend starlings that talk or say "I love you" into a phone.

Before I could explain further, he said in a clearly irritated tone, "Just have your husband call me!"

Then he hung up, leaving me laughing so hard Arnie had to fly off my shoulder to avoid falling. When Bob returned the call later in the day, the man didn't mention his conversation with Arnie, so I guess he thought it best to forget the whole thing. I had told Bob the story as soon as he arrived home. He thought it was funny, too, giving us both a good laugh.

People often ask me questions in complete sincerity that seem on par with "Do you believe the earth is round?"

An example was the question, "Do you believe birds can act consciously?"

I responded, "Once in a while they behave instinctively, just as we do, but most of their actions are completely conscious."

We were interrupted just then, so I was unable to ask the person how she thought a bird or any other animal could survive if they didn't act consciously. Only a few behaviors are instinctive, so it would be extremely difficult for them to function if they were not conscious of what they were doing.

Considering what Arnie did and said each day, there can be no doubt that nearly everything he did was a conscious act. I would like to believe he didn't actually think about unloading his droppings down the back of my neck when he was sitting on my shoulder saying "I love you" in my ear, but I wouldn't have put it past him. He did consciously decide to fly to my shoulder. He consciously proclaimed, "I love you, Judy." Those are neither instinctive nor involuntary behaviors. I have to admit unloading droppings whenever and wherever the need arises is probably an involuntary behavior for a bird. It is difficult to paper-train them, but I have heard it is possible.

Arnie had always decided which individuals with whom he came into contact, human and avian, were worthy of being his friend. While Arnie lived with me, he had interacted with many of the birds I cared for in the bird room. In fall 2000, one became his special friend. A fledgling Barn Swallow from a late hatch was found on the ground after the other young had flown. Swallows must be fully-grown and able to fly before leaving the nest. This one was unable to fly with the others, so was left behind. The couple who owned the barn where its nest was located found the little bird flopping around on the ground and brought it to me. I named the swallow Barney, not knowing its gender.

Initial examination showed it was thin and dehydrated, and its face and top bill were malformed. Underdevelopment of the upper facial bones is caused when the skull and the bone of the bill grow too slowly or prematurely stop growing during development in the egg or as a hatchling, resulting in the upper bill being shorter than the normal lower bill. This malformation has become quite common, sometimes forcing birds to cross the bills in order to close the mouth. Barney's had already begun to cross. If I receive an affected bird before it is fully grown, it takes two days for the face to grow to normal if I give it a tablet of a homeopathic cell salt (Hyland's Calc. Phos. 6X or 30X®) four times a day. This is a type of electrolyte that helps calcium go into cells that need it. When the cells are stimulated to take in sufficient calcium, growth of the upper face and bill resumes, continuing until the bones are normal in size. It works the same on newborn mammals with underbite, but their underdeveloped facial bones usually take up to 13 days to grow to normal or longer for a severe underbite.

I had decided to consider Barney a female because, at the time, that particular malformation occurred more often in female young of vertebrate animals than in males. By 2007, underbite was nearly as frequent in males as in females of mammal species and the prevalence was extremely high in grazing animals. Both underbite and overbite are reported to be quite common in children of both genders.

A homeopathic pill consisting of 12 cell salts (Hyland's Bioplasma®) causes seriously dehydrated and starving animals to become hydrated much faster when added to liquid electrolytes than just giving the electrolytes alone. I quickly dissolved a tablet of calc. phos. 30X and one of bioplasma in the electrolyte solution, filling a small syringe with the mixture. Placing a tube attached to the tip of the syringe into Barney's mouth and gently pushing it down into her crop, allowed me to give her a half cc of fluid. Then I settled her in a box with a soft cloth as a nest and a heating pad underneath. Lying on the ground for a long period without food had caused Barney to become hypothermic, even though the outside temperature was in the 70s that day.

She soon warmed, quickly absorbing the small amount of fluid while I had the couple who brought her fill out Barney's entrance form. As soon as they left, I gave her another dose of the electrolyte combination. The little bird indicated she was feeling much better by food begging. I had mixed a small batch of baby bird food to give her initially because it is more easily digested than insects. An hour later, after two or three crops-full of baby bird food, I fed her the soft internal material from several large mealworms. She was soon standing, flapping her wings, and trying to fly. I fixed a flight box for her, with a perch where she could see out through a clear plastic window.

Before putting Barney in the flight box, I trimmed her lower bill as much as possible without harming her, hoping to get the upper and lower parts to grow into a more normal position. After several days, they were nearly perfect, with just the slightest offset to the upper bill. Her skull and upper face had already grown almost to adult size and conformation, which was surprising. I had thought because Barney was fully-grown her bones wouldn't begin growing again but knew it couldn't hurt to try the homeopathic cell salts. Birds and other critters have often proven my assumptions wrong with their propensity for survival and healing.

Barney soon learned to fly down to a dish full of mealworms, pick one up, and eat it by herself. This in itself was an accomplishment, since swallows usually feed on insects snatched out of the air while flying. They seldom eat off the ground, except for occasionally landing to eat gravel or pick up mud and grass to make nests. They even drink by flying low over a pond or slow-moving area of a stream or river, scooping up a small amount of water with their lower bill.

As soon as Barney began flying, I released her in the room, watching closely for Arnie's reaction. He seemed interested in the smaller bird but not at all disturbed by her presence. I had taped branches to the tops of boxes to make perches where Arnie could land. I put up even more, creating plenty of landing options for both birds. Arnie could run and hop on his long legs, but Barney, with her short, swallow legs, had to land where she could take off again. To my surprise, she was soon sharing Arnie's hemp rope inside his box, sitting close beside him. She flew in and out of the open side of the box just as she had seen Arnie do.

When Barney landed beside Arnie, she made twittering Barn Swallow sounds. Soon, Arnie was twittering back to her in what sounded like the same language with a bit of a starling accent. They often chirped back and forth for long periods. Arnie occasionally threw in a bit of English, likely for my benefit. He may have realized I was a seriously linguistically-challenged human and didn't want to leave me completely out of the conversation. Barney was highly intelligent, learning new things quickly, but she never learned to speak English, perhaps because her swallow syrinx couldn't make those sounds. I was at a loss to know what their many conversations were about.

I had placed a dish of mealworms on top of one of the boxes where Barney could easily eat them. Arnie had a bowl of them in his box. She may have eaten out of his dish, but I never saw him eat out of hers. Arnie seemed to like her very much, which turned out to be a good thing. Barney appeared to have lung damage as well as disrupted bone growth. If she flew around the room more than two or three times, she panted so hard I was afraid she would have heart failure.

I began putting a small amount of MSM (methylsulfonylmethane) in her water. That compound had helped my lungs and those of many birds and animals who had been in my care. I always put one tablet each of the two cell salts in both Arnie's and Barney's water to help keep their cells working properly and to boost their immune systems. Arnie was in the room for years with all kinds of birds who had many different health problems, but he had never been sick.

Unfortunately, after several weeks it became apparent that Barney's lung damage was probably permanent. Fall came and then winter; still she would fly a short distance, land, and pant. I could relate, as I had developed shortness of breath in summer 1994. Three doctors, after viewing the CT scan of my lungs in fall 1996, proclaimed that I was going to die in six months to a year if they were not able to reduce the amount of fluid in my lungs. I began taking MSM then, helping to heal my lungs. Fortunately for me, the doctors were wrong about my imminent death.

I still had hopes that when spring came, Barney would be releasable, but she seemed to have even more shortness of breath in March. It was 2001, the period of time I called the Death Spring here in Ravalli County. More than 50 foals were euthanized because of birth defects and many more were born dead during that time. Calves and lambs died by the hundreds. Many piglets had both male and female reproductive organs. Horse, cow, sheep, goat, white-tailed deer, mule deer, and elk young were born with an underdeveloped skull and upper face, and consequently had underbite, sometimes severe. Others had crooked legs and soft-tissue malformations. Some individuals I necropsied had all of those issues plus others. The dead malformed animals born on ranches were not tested. They were burned or buried and nothing was said. Ranchers were told by their veterinarians the cause was inbreeding or improper feeding, so no testing was done of feed, forage, water, or air. Not wanting anyone to know about the malformations, ranchers did what is often done here in Montana. They used the three S policy: shoot, shovel, and shut up.

Watching so many young animals die or be born with malformations made it a sad spring for me and, as it turned out, for Arnie. By April, it was becoming painfully clear that Barney's lung problem was growing worse. I considered euthanizing her, but Arnie was so attached to her, I decided to let her remain with him for as long as she retained the ability to fly and eat by herself. On the second day of May at 9:15 in the morning, I found Arnie's swallow friend lying dead on top of the box near her food bowl. Barney had looked the same as usual to me when I filled her and Arnie's bowls earlier that morning. She was still able to fly short distances from perch to perch, so could reach her food and water. There had been no warning her death was imminent. She appeared to have just fallen over, with no struggle. Necropsy revealed a severe case of lung tumors which appeared to be cancer, though I didn't have them tested. Even though it was spring, the season he usually spent hours singing his courtship songs, Arnie was unusually quiet and subdued for many days after his little friend died.

The previous December (2000), when Arnie was nine and a half years old, I decided to see if he would learn and say a specific new phrase if I repeated it. At that time scientists who studied birds said males, including European Starlings, can't learn new songs after they are more than one year old. Not many live to be nine years old in the wild, but some do. The oldest European Starling on record was a captive bird who lived to be 17.

As a test, each morning I said the new sentences: "Arnie is a smart bird. Arnie can talk." At the time, he didn't act like he was paying much attention. He still had his Barn Swallow friend for a companion, perhaps a distraction keeping him from listening to me. After a couple weeks, I forgot all about the test. I had begun to whistle "Music of the Night," a melody from "Phantom of the Opera," to see if Arnie could learn it. In a few days, he whistled it much better than I did.

In February 2001, two and a half months after my test to determine whether he could learn new sentences, Arnie completely surprised me by announcing, "Arnie is a smart pretty bird." Several days later while I was working in the bird room, he said, "Arnie is smart" and then "Arnie is a good smart bird" and a while later, "Arnie can talk." By the time spring came, he was saying to me quite often, "Judy is a good, smart bird" or simply, "Judy is smart." Sometimes he gave me those compliments and followed them with "Judy is pretty" and his wolf whistle. It was important for me to not take all his compliments too seriously. I didn't want to have to buy a larger hat for my swelled head.

His first sentence, "Arnie is a pretty bird," followed by his wolf whistle, was still his favorite. He said it more often than any other sentence. After he first said, "Arnie is a smart bird," he began combining the sentences into a longer one, saying either, "Arnie is a pretty, smart bird." or "Arnie is a smart, pretty bird." The longest sentence he made from those two was, "Arnie is a smart bird and a pretty bird." I originally said to him as my test, "Arnie is a smart bird. Arnie can talk." While he did learn those sentences from me, he made up the others by himself, and he didn't stop with those.

Arnie changed the sentence again on June 9, 2001, when he said, "Arnie is a good, smart, and a pretty bird." After saying those sentences in the many variations he constructed, he created a completely new sentence in December 2001. After our usual greetings one morning, he said, "Arnie is a smart, pretty bird." Then after a pause, he said proudly, "Arnie is a smarty." I had never said the word "smarty" in his presence, nor had I heard him say it before that day, but he said it quite often from then on. Of course, my favorite variation was "Judy is a smarty." He proved to me quite definitively that an older European Starling is able to learn new words and whistle new songs. Arnie was also able to construct new words and sentences, something I was told birds can't do at any age.

Arnie learned or made up new sentences and new variations of his spring songs until a few weeks before he died at nearly 13 years old. He didn't say anything new the last three or four weeks of his life, but he carried on his usual conversations with me right up to his last day.

It appeared throughout his life, as Arnie learned words or sentences, that he was able to somehow understand what they meant. For example, he knew the words good, pretty, and smart are complimentary, using them as adjectives in the correct place in sentences. I went to high school with teen-age humans who couldn't make correct English sentences as well as Arnie did. Many of them had to repeat English class. To me, the big mystery was how Arnie knew where to put new words to make new sentences he had never heard spoken. Or how he could put two sentences together into one perfectly understandable and grammatically correct English sentence. That is something a candidate for Vice President a few years ago was often unable to do.

Even more amazing to me was how Arnie used sentences he constructed himself. He could apply them in the proper context, apparently knowing exactly what they meant. If I was kept in a room in China where someone said a few things to me in Chinese, with no real way to know what they were saying, I wouldn't have been able to learn the Chinese language or make new sentences in Chinese. Compared to Arnie, I am severely linguistically challenged.

Another mystery I was never able to solve was how Arnie knew which pronoun to use, or how he knew he should change the word Judy in "I love Judy," when he spoke to others to the pronoun "you" in "I love you," when he was talking to me. He also made up different ways to say he loved me. Each year of his life, he added many new words, phrases, and sentences to his vocabulary.

One day in December 2003, Arnie was unusually quiet when I went in the bird room to clean boxes and feed occupants. He didn't fly around or come to land on my shoulder. He simply stood quietly on top of one of the bird boxes. Even when I went over to him, he just stood there. I asked him if he was all right. His legs suddenly folded and he sat down, like he was sitting on a nest. I picked him up without his usual objection to being held in my hand; he just sat there looking up at me. Then his head drooped down and he was gone. It was like his heart just suddenly stopped.

Arnie was extremely affectionate. His favorite place to be was sitting on my shoulder, where he could nibble on my hair and say nice things to me. It was a delight and an honor to have him for a friend. He taught me something new every day about how birds think, learn, piece together their songs, and communicate with other birds and other species. Arnie showed me how perceptive, compassionate, and empathic a bird can be. Every day he told me he loved me and he made me laugh. I am extremely grateful to have had such an amazing little friend in my life.

**Animals can tell
us how to live wisely; we
must learn to listen.**

An adult Tree Swallow (*Tachycineta bicolor*) with a short upper bill photographed in the wild by Eugene Beckes. Swallows seem to be especially affected by what causes the upper facial bones to have disrupted growth.

A European Starling in breeding plumage with a bright yellow bill. The bills turn yellow in late winter and then turn dark brown after nesting season. Starlings molt in fall and their new dark feathers have bright white tips. The white tip wears away by spring, leaving the feathers shiny black with iridescent colors, a change called "wear molt." Starlings are extremely beneficial to agriculture, eating pests such as clover-leaf weevil, Japanese beetle, May beetles, cutworms, and grasshoppers. Photo by Eugene Beckes.

CHAPTER 6
NICKI

Because of her interest and amazement concerning Arnie's linguistic abilities, my friend Adele decided to purchase a small parrot from my sister and brother-in-law, Nancy and Gary Miller, who owned a small parrot breeding operation. Adele wanted a bird with whom she could communicate and have a close relationship, while directly observing the bird's learning processes. She chose a two-month-old, hand-raised male Chattering Lory (*Lorius garrulous*) and named him Nicki.

Chattering Lories are not native to North America. They are a forest-dwelling parrot endemic to North Maluku, Indonesia, in Southeast Asia, where they dine on pollen, fruit juices, and nectar from large flowers, supplemented with insects for protein. Lories and lorikeets are often called brush-tongued parrots due to their papillae-covered tongues, designed to better collect liquid and pull it into their mouths. Because of their mostly liquid diet, some time in their distant past lories and lorikeets developed a digestive system with weak-muscled organs composed of thin, elastic tissue, including the crop, proventriculus, and ventriculus or gizzard. The proventriculus is the first part of a bird's stomach between the crop and the gizzard. These organs have thick powerful muscles in most bird species, especially the gizzard. After the bird gathers and swallows small stones, the gizzard acts as a grinder to pulverize seeds and other foods it eats. Digestive organs composed of strong, thick muscles are of no use to parrots who eat nectar, insects, fruit, and greens.

Chattering Lories are captive-bred in many countries and advertised by breeders as having great character and energy. Capturing wild lories for the pet trade and habitat destruction is reported to be endangering native Indonesian populations. Parrots and other birds sold as pets should only be purchased from reputable breeders who deal solely with captive-born birds and never buy or sell wild-caught birds. Anyone purchasing a parrot should also consider the long-term commitment they are making. Most parrots live 30 to 70 or more years. People who can only have a pet for a short time because of age or other circumstances should never purchase a parrot because it will have to be moved to a new home with strangers, perhaps many times in its life. Those who do buy a parrot should strongly consider building a much larger containment area for it to live in than the small cages sold in most pet stores.

Other characteristics also need to be considered before purchasing one of these undomesticated, highly social, intelligent, sensitive beings. They are active, often aggressive, messy, destructive, and noisy. Screaming is normal for them, as is chewing up anything they can reach with their beaks, such as wood molding, curtains, walls, books, plants, and furniture. Parrots may bite unexpectedly, even years after they have become familiar with their people. Because of their high metabolic rate, birds eat and therefore eliminate a lot, without regard for furniture or carpets. Feathers are shed (molted) regularly, and flapping wings spread feathers as well as seeds or shells outside the area of their cage.

Parrots are highly intelligent so require a great deal of mental stimulation to keep them occupied; boredom and/or stress can seriously damage them emotionally. These birds normally live in large flocks and need others of their own kind for companionship. Observing and protecting them in their natural wild state is by far the most compassionate way to treat them. Adele loved Nicki dearly but for many years was saddened that he lived his life in captivity, even though she provided him with a large cage, extensive human companionship, and many toys.

Nicki and I quickly became friends and he was always excited to see me when I went to Adele's home. We carried on many interesting conversations, including on the phone when Adele and I called each other. He loved to dance, often demonstrating his moves during my visits with him. Nicki was another of my amazing bird friends.

Just as Arnie had, Nicki carried on conversations with people. Both learned to talk much as young children do. They jabbered a lot to themselves while playing, carefully observed what was going on around them, and continuously practiced saying words, phrases, and sentences. Both asked and answered questions and made statements consistent with the topic of conversation. Adele kept me informed on Nicki's linguistic progress and other antics, about which I kept a journal.

He had a keen sense of humor, as did his father, Elliott. Nicki's parents belonged to my youngest sister Nancy and her husband Gary. Nicki was hatched on September 4, 1994, after being incubated by his mother. As is common among parrot breeders, he was taken from her at about two weeks of age, to be hand-raised with the intention of making him a better pet. Some studies have shown this practice to be unnecessary and often damaging to the birds, not to mention unkind to both babies and parents.

About a year before Elliott's mate laid the egg that produced Nicki, I visited Nancy at her home, the only time I interacted with Elliott. I talked to him for about 10 minutes, trying to get him to reply, saying, "Hello Elliott, good bird, how are you, Elliott wants a cracker," and every phrase I thought a parrot might know. Elliott stared intently at me in a way that indicated he considered me slightly daft but steadfastly refused to say a word. Finally, I held up my index finger and asked, "Do you like fingers, Elliott?" Clearly and enthusiastically, Elliott replied, "Yum, Yum!" It took me quite a while to stop laughing. I have to admit he did answer my question.

Although my sister claimed Elliott knew more swear words than a present-day comedian, I consider his greatest achievement to be his son, Nicki. I admit to being prejudiced. Adele bought Nicki on November 1, three days before his two-month birthday. His feathers were still growing so he was unable to fly, and he was still being hand-fed with a syringe. From that time on, Adele and I compared notes on our talking bird friends. Arnie was three years old then and extremely linguistically talented, but it didn't take long for Nicki to catch up. He was an incredibly fast learner, both at developing language and at manipulating Adele to do his bidding. Patience wasn't one of his many virtues. If she took too long, he became quite upset with her and stated, "Dammit, Me!" in an obviously annoyed tone of voice and then repeated what he desired, "Nicki want a carrot, a cricket, a shower," or whatever it was he was demanding.

Nicki at first referred to Adele as Nicki, just as Arnie often called me Arnie when he began talking. He knew he was Nicki but apparently thought Adele was also Nicki. Just as it takes small children time to sort out which name belongs to whom, it seemed to be the same with both birds. After several months, Nicki also used the words she, Me, or Adele, while continuing to say "Nicki!" to get her attention at times. Perhaps mated pairs use the same or a similar sound to refer to each other as opposed to different members of their flock.

Adele believes Nicki thought of her as Me because that's what she called herself when talking with him (as in "Do you hear me?" or "Don't bite me."). He knew Don's and Adele's names, using them correctly when talking to someone else about them. For example, if Don was away somewhere, Nicki said to Adele, "I wish Don was here." When Adele was gone, Nicki said to Don, "I wish Adele was here," usually in a sad tone of voice.

One terrifying day in December, when Nicki was only four months old, Adele spent many hours thinking, frantically, "I wish Nicki was here!" She had gone into town that morning to help her sister-in-law do some painting. Nicki had learned to fly perfectly by then, navigating around the house, creating havoc wherever he went. When Don opened the door to let their dog Ginger go outside shortly after Adele left, Nicki zipped right out over Don's head, apparently looking for Adele. He flew high above the house, circling to get his bearings, then took off in the direction Adele had driven when she left for town. After Don called Adele to report what had happened, she drove home as fast as she could, hoping to quickly find Nicki.

Don called the police, animal shelter, neighbors, and radio station in case anyone saw a bright red parrot with green trim flying around like an unusual airborne Christmas decoration. That was definitely *not* a normal occurrence in western Montana, especially in December. There was snow on the ground that day, with occasional freezing rain, certainly not safe weather for a small tropical bird. Don and Adele searched everywhere around the rural area, calling for him until nearly dusk. Adele finally gave up in despair, thinking a hawk may have eaten Nicki or, at the least, imagining him huddled terrified, wet, and hypothermic under a tree, waiting for her to rescue him. Feeling sure he couldn't have survived the whole day in that weather, she curled up on her bed to grieve, determined to never live with another animal because this was entirely too painful.

Suddenly she heard a familiar whistle outside the bedroom window. She called out, "Nicki!" who replied in his most demanding tone, "Nicki, come here!" Adele dashed outside, tripping over untied bootlaces, clumsily climbing the fence into a neighbor's pasture, desperately calling him. Because it was becoming dark, Nicki was anxious to go inside to his sleeping cage. He flew down to Adele's shoulder from the pine tree where he was perched, showing how happy he was to see her by nibbling on her hair. She picked him up, snuggling him under her chin for warmth, unwilling to risk his flying again. Nicki was shivering and smelled strongly of pine trees but seemed unharmed. Being a nectar eater, he must have tried eating sap when he became hungry, or perhaps he chewed on pine needles. Nicki remained calm in Adele's hand while she walked into the house, where he could eat his own sweet, powdered food especially made for lories and drink his papaya nectar. Adele was extremely relieved and happy to have her little bird friend back.

Over time, Nicki acquired a large vocabulary. He put the words he learned together into new sentences, which were sensible, grammatically correct, English sentences, exactly like Arnie did. Nicki had an even bigger vocabulary than Arnie, perhaps because he lived in a large wire enclosure (4' x 8' wide x 6' tall) in a room where he could see and talk to Don and Adele most of the time. Nicki knew he was a bird and that other birds were also birds, but, interestingly, he created categories for other creatures he met: insects, including his favorite mealworms, were crickets, the first insects he found to eat; goats, sheep, and fawns were goats; dogs were Ginger, after the first dog he knew.

Nicki made an amazing variety of sounds copied from his environment: wolf whistles (taught to him by a friend); excellent raucous Black-billed Magpie and Clark's Nutcracker imitations (the soft, soothing sounds of mourning doves or chickadees apparently weren't nearly as fun to him); ketchup and air squirting from a squeeze bottle; repeating sound from a pump bottle of window cleaner; click of a cigarette lighter; squeaky opening of the wood stove door; laundry machines controls; pills rattling in a bottle. He barked, laughed, coughed, and perfectly made the sound of running water. All were appropriate to what was going on around him. For example, if he saw the window cleaner bottle, he made that sound before it was actually used. When someone went to the stove to add wood or reached to open a window, he perfectly copied the sounds before the action occurred.

Like Arnie, Nicki was curious and astoundingly aware of his environment. He asked questions, did what he was asked to do (when it suited him), and appeared to understand what people said to him. Also as Arnie did, Nicki used words and phrases in several contexts appropriate for the situation. For example, Nicki answered the same question, "What are you doing, Nicki?" with different answers, depending on what he was actually doing at the time. When he was taking a bath, which he called a shower, he answered, "Taking a shower."

One day, he was dashing around the room throwing things. Hearing all the commotion, Adele asked, "What are you doing, Nicki?" He answered, "Being a shit," saying a bad word he learned from Adele, which to him meant the opposite of being good. When Nicki shoved a full glass of water off the kitchen counter, showing great pride and interest as it shattered on the floor, Adele said in a disgusted tone of voice, "Ahh, shit!" Nicki obviously connected the word shit with him doing something Adele didn't like. When he was playing quietly, and Adele asked, "What are you doing," he sweetly answered, "Being a good bird" or sometimes, "Being a bird." Like most young children, he knew the difference between right and wrong or good and bad, not that he always made Adele's preferred choice!

Nicki not only thought he was a shit when he was bad, he considered Adele a shit when she did something he didn't like. For example, he couldn't tolerate anything white in Adele's hand, especially if it was floppy like a hand towel or tissue. If she had an unacceptable item in her hand when he was nearby, Nicki flew at and attacked her hand. For some reason known only to him, he didn't attack the actual object. Instead he tried to bite her.

One day when he was sitting on her left hand, she unthinkingly picked up a white towel with her right. He instantly flew to the offending hand, landed on the towel, and bit her hard. It hurt and startled her, causing her to drop the towel with Nicki on it. He landed safely on the floor, glaring up at her. Then he stood up as tall as he could and demanded in an extremely irritated tone of voice, "What is the matter? You're being a *shit*!" He apparently didn't understand he had played a considerable part in causing her to drop him or that he himself had acted badly. Nicki was totally self-assured with no concept of low self-esteem.

Like many small children, Nicki was adamantly possessive. When I was there and Nicki was given a mealworm to eat, he often said to us, "Go eat yours." Apparently, he didn't want us to eat his mealworms. We told him we didn't want to eat his cricket, his word for all insects. (Some people do eat mealworms, but I find a mouse more appetizing.) Even when he picked up Adele's food from her plate, he told her to "Go eat yours." Adele reminded him the food on the plate was hers, so he should go eat his juice.

Nicki invented a dance where he jumped up and down in one place, tapping his feet independently in an amazingly fast rhythm, sometimes turning in a circle. As he danced, he often asked "Do you want to dance?" He especially liked dancing on a small cardboard box, plastic tub, or on top of a leather-covered easy chair, because his feet made interesting drumming sounds on those surfaces. He seemed to thoroughly enjoy his dancing, often putting on quite a show. One day, when Nicki was in the car with Adele, he was perched on the back of the front seat. Suddenly, he began to dance. Ginger, his dog friend, was sound asleep in the back seat.

Nicki, likely contemplating some mischief.

Nicki apparently wanted a dance partner, so he said loudly, "Ginger, dance!" Ginger opened one eye and looked at Nicki but politely refused his invitation.

One summer, when Nicki was in the forest with Adele and Don on a camping trip, he was perched on a stump while Adele was helping Don. Adele had trimmed Nicki's wing feathers so he could fly enough to be safe from falling but was unable to fly away when he was outside. Suddenly a small brown bird landed on the stump beside Nicki, most likely to get a closer look at such a large, dazzlingly red, male bird. Nicki graciously greeted the little brown female by saying in a soft, sweet voice, "Hi, Bird. How are you?" If the little bird answered, it was not in English, so we don't know what she said, but it was likely, "Hi, Handsome."

Nicki had a delightful sense of humor, especially when he was playing a trick on a human or another animal. However, if he was the one being laughed at, unlike Arnie, who didn't seem to mind when I laughed at funny things he said, Nicki didn't take it at all well. One sunny day, he was keeping Adele company while she worked in the forest. In an attempt to get to a higher perch, he clambered up the flower stalk of one of the many beautiful beargrass plants that were blooming that year. When he got near the top, his weight began slowly bending the stalk toward the ground. Within a short time, Nicki was lying on his back with the large beargrass blossom covering his face. He was unharmed but looked so shocked that Adele spontaneously laughed out loud. When Nicki let go and regained his feet, he stood as tall as he could stretch, demanding indignantly, "Quit it! *Quit it!*" He clearly knew the difference between laughing with him, which was fun, and laughing at him, which was not acceptable.

While camping in the woods with Don and Adele, Nicki slept with Adele in her sleeping bag to keep warm. The bags were on cots placed against the side of the tent. There was a big cushion behind the sleeping bag for Adele to lean against while she read books at night. While Adele was reading, Nicki played on top of the cushion right above Adele's head. Twice, he unintentionally hit Adele on the head with a big, wet dropping. Nicki's diet was mostly liquid so his feces were as well; having them running down the side of her head while living away from hot, running water for washing her long hair was not pleasant for Adele, to say the least.

That prompted Adele to try to teach Nicki to point his tail over the newspapers she placed on the floor below the end of the cushion. When it was obvious Nicki needed to do his job, she pushed him to where the newspapers were directly below his tail. Nicki dodged away and tried to get to the tent side. After being interrupted several times when he was all set to go, he ducked under Adele's hand one last time, running quickly over to the other side. Before Adele could stop him, he squirted a big, wet stream onto the side of the tent, simultaneously proclaiming, "Oh, *God!*" in a deep, loud, disgusted tone of voice, probably exactly as Adele had when he pooped on her head. Adele laughed so hard she nearly fell off the bed. Nicki's expression was partly what was so funny. He looked completely confused, having no idea what had caused Adele's hysteria. He even tried to laugh with her, but it sounded forced, unlike his usual spontaneous, delighted laughter. Fortunately, Nicki couldn't hear me laugh when Adele told me about that escapade over the phone. I wouldn't want him to be angry with me.

Because the first animal Nicki met other than the dog Ginger was a goat, Nicki categorized all animals who resembled or even sounded like them as goats. Adele's goats had lived in the house for a while when they were small, bottle-fed babies. Nicki saw and heard them then and through a window near his cage when they were outside. Once when Nicki and Adele were in the tent, a small herd of cattle walked by, making stomping and mooing noises in the woods. Nicki listened intently, then asked Adele, "What is that? Goats?" At home, Adele's pet goats often made clattering noises with their hooves when in the house, and their voices are somewhat similar to those of calves. Nicki apparently thought the sounds meant there were goats in the forest.

One day at home when Adele, with Nicki perched on her shoulder, was standing on the front porch, one of her pet goats was dashing around the yard, jumping and playing. Then it ran to the porch, leaping up to land beside Adele for some neck scratching. Nicki looked inquisitively at the goat and said "Hi, Goat. What is the matter?" Nicki not only expected Adele to answer his questions, he thought other animals should as well. Unfortunately, most other animals cannot speak human languages, or we could all have some fascinating conversations.

When Adele took in a baby domestic sheep to raise, Nicki was curious about the tiny lamb. After a thorough inspection of the small animal, Nicki said in his polite way, "Hi, Goat. How are you?" and that is how a little lamb came to be named Goat. Nicki talked to the lamb quite often while he was in the house, always calling him Goat. One day when the lamb was wandering around bleating for his bottle, he went over to Nicki's cage crying loudly. In a concerned voice, Nicki asked the lamb, "What's the matter, Goat? You want some juice?" Adele soon provided a bottle of warm milk for the lamb, so Goat got some of his own "juice" to drink.

Often when Ginger went outside, Nicki asked, "Where is Ginger?" "Is Ginger with Don?" or "Is Ginger outside?" If Adele said Ginger was outside, Nicki often asked, "Do you want to go outside?" or he'd say "Go see Ginger," which meant he wanted to go outside too. Ginger was tolerant of Nicki, even when he nipped her toes, but she preferred to avoid him. Unfortunately, she was old when Nicki became part of the family. Don and Adele adopted another dog before Ginger died, and a second one after. Nicki called all dogs Ginger, so whenever the new dogs were outside he still asked, "Where is Ginger?"

When Don went somewhere, Nicki asked, "Where is Don?" then "Is Don gone?" To which Adele answered, "Yes, Don has gone to town." Then Nicki, seemingly satisfied, resumed playing with his toys. Interestingly, he often said, "Don is here" several minutes before Don arrived in the yard and prior to his pickup even being visible on the highway. Sometimes, just to tease the dogs, Nicki said, "Don is here! See! Here's Don!" when Don really wasn't there. The dogs, who always became excited and rushed to the door when Don returned home, were quite disappointed when it was one of Nicki's jokes. Nicki thought it was extremely funny.

Adele sometimes kept crickets to feed various animals who lived in her household, including pet tarantulas, tropical frogs, and wild insect-eating birds. One day Nicki spotted a cricket escapee running across the kitchen floor. Trying his best to catch it, he ran after it, but it eluded him by dashing under the electric stove. Nicki leaned way over, trying to look under the stove with one eye. At the same time, he repeated several times, "Where are you?" in a perplexed tone of voice. He also tried coaxing it out by saying sweetly, "Come here." When he gave up, Nicki announced emphatically, "Lost ya!"

He said similar things to a pair of three-week-old Yellow-bellied Marmots Adele received one spring for rehabilitation. The two little rodents were in a five-foot long terrarium with a wooden box at one end where they could sleep or hide. Nicki was fascinated with the small mammals, watching them with great interest when they were out running around in the cage. One day while he was watching them, they disappeared into their box. Nicki called, "Come here, come here." When the marmots didn't reappear, he shrugged and said, "Lost ya."

Even though Nicki didn't appreciate being laughed at, his interactions with other animals were frequently comical. When Nicki saw an ant crawling across his cage floor, he cocked his head to watch it with one eye. After observing the ant for a while, he said inquisitively, "What's your name?" Nicki didn't know what an ant was called and obviously assumed the ant would tell him.

People's reactions to Nicki were often even more comical than Nicki's antics. When Don, Adele, and Nicki were on vacation in Yellowstone National Park, they went to Old Faithful. While waiting for the geyser to erupt, Nicki was perched on Adele's head, gaining a good view of the area. Adele kept his wing feathers trimmed after the time he escaped out the door, so he always remained on her head or shoulder when away from home. In fact, he tried to make certain she didn't get far from him, no matter where they were. Adele called it wearing her parrot. Upon seeing Nicki, a man walked up to Adele and said, "Do you know you have a bird on your head?" I hope he intended to be funny, because he certainly succeeded.

Unfortunately, many people still believe everything birds do is strictly instinctive. In December 1994, I argued with a group of bird watchers over whether birds can think and reason, with over half of them believing a bird's behavior is strictly due to instinct. Many studies have shown birds have feelings, reason intelligently, learn new things, and only do some specific behaviors by instinct, similar to humans and other animals. After considering the stigma I was confronting, I decided Nicki would be an excellent advocate for bird intelligence. I made arrangements for Adele to bring him to the monthly Bitterroot Audubon Society meeting in January 1995.

Before his part of the program even started, Nicki began educating his audience, especially the group who believed birds can't think and reason. Adele had arrived early, before the meeting was scheduled to begin. She wanted Nicki to become accustomed to the new surroundings and get used to having strange people around him. He sat on Adele's shoulder while she walked around the room, hoping he would be at ease when it was time for his part of the program. Several people approached Adele to observe Nicki up close. His brilliant red and green feathers always attracted attention, especially that of bird lovers.

Adele was standing in the center of the group, when Nicki said very plainly, "You want some water?" He often asked Adele if she wanted something when it was actually what he wanted. When Adele said, "No, I don't want a drink of water," Nicki promptly stated, "Nicki want some water!" Adele took out Nicki's water bottle and gave Nicki a drink. He actually took several drinks, because he was obviously quite thirsty. It was always clear by his inflection whether he was asking a question or making a statement. After watching Nicki ask for water, then drink several times, a woman asked Adele, "Did he really want a drink of water?" The thought occurred to Adele it was not bird intelligence that should be in question.

Nicki then said, "Hello. How are you?" Before any of the people had time to comment or answer, the chairman said it was time to begin the meeting. After the usual announcements, he introduced Adele and Nicki.

Nicki wowed the audience by playing "Pick it up" with Adele, dancing when she said "Dance, Nicki!" and clearly asking several questions of Adele in English. When he became hungry, he asked for his juice by saying "You want some juice?" When Adele declined, he said, "Nicki want some juice!" Of course, she gave him his juice. Adele also had taken a few mealworms, one of his favorite treats. As soon as he saw one, he announced, "Nicki want some cricket!" After he ate it he said, "Good cricket."

The Audubon members attending the meeting that night were quite impressed with Nicki's intelligence and abilities. That he asked for things by name, in English, when he wanted them, should have proven to everyone he had to be thinking and was exhibiting cause and effect reasoning. It is actually impossible to ask for something without thinking and it certainly is not instinctual for a bird to ask for things it wants in a human language.

Nicki created the game of "Pick it up" all by himself when he was quite young, prior to having his wings trimmed. He found a margarine lid on the kitchen counter, picked it up in his bill, and threw it, like a Frisbee. He then flew down to the lid, picked it up, and threw it again. He repeated this until the lid was close to Adele, who was sitting in a chair watching him. When he saw the lid was close enough for her to reach it, he said "Pick it up!" So, she did and threw it across the room. He partly ran and partly flew to the lid, repeating the whole procedure until he tired of the game. One day while playing "Pick it up," Nicki accidentally threw the lid a few feet straight up into the air. It then dropped straight down, nearly hitting him. As he dodged out of the way, he said, in a startled tone of voice, "Oh, shit!" Apparently, he had figured out that word was for incidents other than when he deliberately shattered water glasses or bit Adele.

Nicki and I often talked on the telephone. Adele held it close enough for him to hear me. When I said, "Hi, Nicki," he immediately replied, "Hi Judy, Judy. How are you?" I don't know why Nicki repeated my name twice when we talked on the phone, but he almost always did. When I was talking to Adele, he asked, "Is that Judy?" Adele replied," Yes, Nicki, it's your friend, Judy." Sometimes, after he said, "Hi Judy, Judy. How are you?" he rushed to the towel on the floor of the small, hanging cage where he slept at night, crawled under it, and demanded, "Where are you?" Then he peeked out at Adele with one eye, and said with great joy, "There you are!" I presume because he couldn't see me but could hear me, he thought

I was hiding, so he played his peek-a-boo game. His whole life, he loved playing this game with Adele when she wasn't talking on the phone. He considered himself hidden if his head was covered so he couldn't see, even though his beautiful tail was exposed.

In January 2000, Nicki stayed home with Don while Adele went on a two-week trip to Oregon to visit and help a friend with her new baby. I called Don one day to ask about Adele, the baby, and the new mother. After Don told me all were fine, I asked to speak with Nicki, missing him after not having contact for a while. Don hadn't facilitated that before so I explained he should hold the phone close to Nicki so I could say "Hi." Nicki became excited, jumping up and down and bowing, while saying, "Hi Judy, Judy." Don was quite surprised at his reaction. He had apparently never been around when Adele took the phone to Nicki so we could chat.

Nicki was never happy about Adele leaving him, even for short trips. One day she drove to Idaho to pick up a baby wallaby she was adopting. That morning, Adele began packing all the things she needed for the trip, putting them into her vehicle as they were ready. Nicki could tell she was preparing to go somewhere other than a short trip to the grocery store, so he tried his best to distract her.

First, he asked, "You want some juice?"

To which she answered, "Not right now, Nicki. Thank you."

"You wanna take a shower?"

"No, I already took a shower."

So he tried a different tactic, asking, "You wanna take a nap?"

"No, Nicki, I don't want to take a nap. I have to go get a little wallaby. I'll be home later."

When she was ready to leave, Adele picked up her keys, walked over to Nicki, rubbed his head, and said, "Goodbye, Nicki. See you later."

Nicki said in a soft, dejected tone of voice, "I wish she's tired."

Because Adele gets up quite early in the morning, she occasionally takes a nap in the afternoon. Before she went to lie down, she always told Nicki she was going to take a nap. He usually considerately avoided screaming for a while then. Nicki had often said, "She's tired," but Adele had never heard him say, "I wish she's tired" until the day she left for Idaho. He apparently thought if Adele was tired, she would stay home and take a nap instead of going away and leaving him.

Nicki enjoyed making loud noises but sometimes used them as a threat and punishment when Adele wasn't behaving appropriately, by his standards. Before he began screaming he demanded, "You want some screaming?"

Adele said, "No, I don't want screaming."

Nicki emphatically declared, "You need some screaming! I'll get you some screaming!" Upon saying that, Nicki made the obnoxious screaming noises a few times, looking pleased with himself afterwards.

This continued for a while, depending on how angry he was or how slow Adele was to give in to his demands. He'd say, "You hear me screaming? Screaming and screaming!" And then he'd scream even louder, insistent, demanding screams that seriously grated on the nerves. Don and Adele lived out of town some distance from the road, but the neighbor on the other side of the road could hear those screams with all windows closed. They were a highly effective part of Nicki's training tools.

A not-so-funny practical joke Nicki sometimes pulled on Adele began with an actual traumatic event soon after Nicki first learned to fly. One day when he was playing by a window, he somehow wrapped a curtain string around his neck and was unable to free himself. Nicki screamed a loud, distinctive panic scream, bringing Adele on the run. She untangled him, removed all curtains with pull strings from the house so that couldn't happen again, and all was well. But it taught Nicki how to get immediate attention when he wanted it. He occasionally gave his "Help! I'm caught!" scream whether he was caught or not, because Adele and/or Don always ran to rescue him. He'd laugh when they realized he was just playing. Adele should have told Nicki the story of what happened to the boy who cried wolf.

Nicki's special juice and a powdered lory diet were in containers in the small sleeping cage that hung from the top of his tall, almost room-sized flight cage. At night, Adele cleaned, refilled, and replaced his food dishes because he liked to fill up before going to sleep, and lastly, she straightened the towel on the floor of the little cage. For some reason, Nicki preferred to sleep under the towel, so the small cage didn't have perches.

Each night, they had a bedtime routine before Adele closed the little door and draped a large towel over the cage. He then slept quietly all night. In the morning, Nicki really needed to get out of his little cage because he didn't eliminate where he slept. If Adele didn't get up soon enough to suit Nicki, he would swing upside down from the hanging powder dish, as though his toenails were caught, and scream his "Help!

82

I'm caught!!!"call. He understandably considered his full cloaca an emergency that required her immediate attention. His behavior was certainly effective but not a pleasant way for Adele to wake up and start her day. Fortunately, it didn't happen often after she learned to get up before Nicki woke up, a reason she needed a nap in the afternoon.

People loved watching Nicki take his shower because he was so enthusiastic about it. He was always ready to be the entertainment, so he enjoyed it even more with an audience. He jumped into the bathroom sink, stood under the small stream of water, and flapped his wings, splashing everyone in the room and vocalizing loudly. He didn't usually say words, just made happy, energetic sounds including laughter. He'd hop out of the sink, dance across the counter, and then dive back into the sink, rolling on his back under the water to get his chest and belly wet. This continued for at least 10 minutes and always brightened Adele's day. It was worth the chore of drying off the bathroom after he finished.

One time when Adele wasn't around for some reason, Nicki began his request for a shower by saying, "Don." There was a pause before he called "Don!" in a louder, more demanding voice.

Don answered, "Yes, Nick."

Nicki asked, "You gonna take a shower? Nicki wanna take a shower!"

So Don took him into the bathroom, turned on water in a small stream, and let Nicki hop down from his hand to the counter. He jumped into the water in the sink, then quickly leaped right back out, saying in a startled tone of voice, "It's hot!" Not believing Nicki, Don put his hand in the water, which was indeed too hot.

One of Nicki's favorite tricks to play on Adele was to talk her into taking him into the bathroom for a shower when he didn't really want one. After she had cleared the counter of objects he could throw on the floor and started water running into the sink, he would refuse to hop from her hand to the counter. Instead he would firmly clasp a finger with his feet, looking up at her while laughing gleefully. His laugh was so infectious, even when at her expense, that Adele couldn't help laughing with him. Though he'd become angry sometimes, Nicki never seemed to hold a grudge. He was usually a bubbly, cheerful little guy who was always ready to have fun. Nobody could enjoy himself like that adorable little bird!

When Nicki was seven years old, Don and Adele adopted two African Grey Parrots, Tisha and Simon. Both had had difficult lives before they came to their new home. Nicki could see the parrots from his cage in the

83

adjoining room through a large archway in the wall. A nest box was next to Tisha's cage. One afternoon, Adele went to help her brother at his store in the nearby town. When she returned, she noticed Tisha was in her nest box, an unusual place for her during the day. Adele immediately went over to make sure nothing was wrong. Nicki, quietly observing, asked Adele in a concerned tone of voice, "What's the matter with Tisha?" After a short pause, he answered his own question, saying emphatically, "She's tired."

Nicki understood that animals sleep when they are tired, and that when people are tired, they go to bed. One day when Nicki was sitting on Don's shoulder while the two of them were watching television, Don fell asleep. Nicki climbed down to the floor, running (Nicki never did anything slowly) straight to the kitchen where Adele was reading a book. He climbed up onto her shoulder, leaned around in her face to get her attention, and announced, "Don go to bed!" Another time in the evening, as Adele was preparing Nicki for the night, he sleepily proclaimed, "It's tired here."

Nicki was far from tidy when he ate, so Adele had to clean his dishes at least twice a day. One evening when she was cleaning his sleeping cage, she pulled out the tray at the bottom and said, "This is a mess!"

He replied in an unconcerned tone, "Go wash it." Obviously, he considered Adele his chief dishwasher.

Even though he considered her his caregiver, Nicki was always sympathetic and in tune with Adele's feelings. One day, when she was somewhat depressed, she settled in a chair to think about what was bothering her. Nicki stopped playing, walked over to her, and climbed up onto her shoulder. He peered directly into her face and asked in a soft, concerned tone of voice, "What's the matter? Are you all right?" Then after a short pause he said gently, "Do you want some carrot? Go eat your carrot." Carrots were one of Nicki's favorite foods, so he must have thought eating one would make Adele feel better.

Occasionally I went to Adele's home to deliver mice and mealworms for birds she was rehabilitating or to pick up a bird for which she had provided initial care. I put her recovered rehab birds in our flight rooms to build up their muscles, as Adele didn't have a suitable place for small birds to fly. She was sometimes in her office where she couldn't see me when I knocked on their door, but Nicki could see anyone who was there from his large cage at the front of the house. He always said to me, "Hi, Judy. Come in." He didn't say that to anyone else who came to their door.

After I went in, Nicki, Adele, and I visited for a few minutes about whatever was going on that day. Once, when we were admiring a bright red feather that had fallen from Nicki's wing during his molt, I asked if I could have it to dress up my Stetson hat. As I tucked the brilliant red feather into my hatband, Nicki proudly announced, "Nicki is a pretty red bird!"

Another time, when he was sitting on Adele's leg while she stroked his head and back, Nicki looked up at her and asked in a quiet tone of voice, "Are you being a bird?" Adele had never said that to him, but he apparently thought her finger sort of preening him was equivalent to her acting like a bird.

Chattering Lories can live 25 to 30 years. Unfortunately, a tumor developed on the left side of Nicki's abdomen, causing his leg on that side to have nerve damage. Even with veterinary care, his health continued to deteriorate until, when he was no longer having fun, we had to euthanize him in spring 2015 when he was almost 21 years old. All those years, each time I had gone to visit Adele and Nicki, when I went to the door to leave, Nicki said, "Bye, Judy. See you later."

"See you later, Nicki."

**Friendship is precious.
Like a rare flower, it should
be deeply cherished.**

Cedar Waxwings (*Bombycilla cedorum*) are extremely friendly and cooperative with each other. A courting pair often touch bills during courtship as shown in this photo by Eugene Beckes. Cedar Waxwings' year around diet is mainly fruits, such as juniper and mountain ash berries, honeysuckle, crabapple, hawthorn and cedar berries, from which they get their name. They also eat insects in the warmer months, including mayflies, dragonflies and stoneflies caught on the wing, and spruce budworm and leaf beetles picked directly from foliage.

CHAPTER 7
DUCK TALK

We moved into our home at the bottom of what is known as Brickyard Hill a short way east of East Missoula, Montana, in spring 1970. Two springs later, I received a single hatchling Mallard (*Anas platyrhynchos*) for care. When I lived on a ranch as a youngster, I had cared for ducks, geese, and chicks, but this little female hatchling was the first wild duck I was privileged to raise. At the time, I didn't know it isn't advisable to raise a wild duck the same way as domestic birds. Wild animals and birds need to learn to be afraid of and avoid humans. They should not come running when they hear a human voice and definitely should not learn to follow humans around.

Single baby ducks are harder to care for than two or more ducklings. One gets lonely, tries its best to escape from its box to look for others, and frantically calls its baby duck cheep almost constantly, except when asleep. I have learned to wrap a loudly ticking alarm clock in a towel to keep single ducklings company. By placing it in their box under the heat lamp where they like to sleep, they can nestle close beside it or sit on top of it. The ticking seems to comfort them, possibly sounding somewhat like the beating heart of their mother as she sat on the developing eggs.

Wild precocious hatchlings can run around, follow the mother, and catch their own food within a day or two after hatching, instinctively attracted by movements of live insects. When raising wild ducks, I catch small insects such as leafhoppers with a butterfly net, sprinkling them in a shallow pan of water (usually a pie pan for several ducklings or a low bowl for one). If I also sprinkle 30% protein Purina Game Bird Startina® with the insects, the little ducks go after the moving insects, eating both insects and starter. In this way, they learn the starter is also good food, even though it doesn't move. Soon, they are eating dry starter alone from a dish, saving me from having to catch so many insects.

Ducklee, as I named this new orphan, was soon gobbling down as much game bird starter, insects, and cut-up earthworms as she could hold. The little duck quickly stopped trying to jump out of her box and spent her time eating and sleeping, or swimming in her baking-pan pool. She was quite well behaved for a single duckling. Several times each day, I

87

carried her to the garden or out to the grass where she could catch insects. While she was small, I stayed nearby to protect her. She soon learned to follow me or come when I called her. When she had doubled in size, she was big enough and sufficiently well-trained to run around in the garden while I weeded the newly sprouted vegetables. Having her follow me and come when I called her seemed like a good idea at the time, but it is definitely not the best way to raise a wild duck who is to be released.

Ducklee at two weeks old.

It wasn't long before Ducklee could understand some words and phrases. Several times a day, I carried her out the back door and put her down on the ground, walking around the yard with her while she found things she liked to eat. If she wasn't finding adequate numbers of insects, I would say, "Ducklee, let's go to the garden and get worms." She would immediately run toward the garden, even though I hadn't moved at all. She had learned that, by going there, she would get worms and insects to eat. Eventually all I had to say was, "Let's go get some worms!" and she would dash for the garden as fast as her short duck legs and big webbed feet could take her.

If I wanted her to sit down and remain in a certain place while I went somewhere else, I simply said, "Stay here." When I returned, I said, "Let's go, Ducklee," to let her know she should follow me again. While she was little, she always remained close to me when we were outside, as she would with her natural mother, unless I told her to stay. After reaching adult size, with fully-grown feathers, she became more independent, often leaving me to explore on her own.

One day when Bob had company, he and the two men who had come to visit sat in the kitchen around the table. I was working outside weeding a flower garden with Ducklee foraging nearby, or so I thought. I eventually realized she wasn't anywhere in view and that I hadn't seen her for a while. I called her name with no response. After walking around the house, searching the garden, and looking in the garage without finding her, I finally went into the house to ask Bob if he had seen her. He said he hadn't, but from where I was standing by the door, I could see under the table. There in the middle of six human feet sat one little duck. She must have snuck in unseen when Bob and his friends went through the door and into the kitchen. None of them saw her walk across the room or go under the table, nor were they aware a duck was sitting contentedly under the table listening to their conversation, happy to find a flock of humans for company.

As Ducklee became more mature, Bob said, "That bird needs to learn to be a duck." I agreed. After another week, at which time the flight feathers in her wings had completed their growth, we began looking for a good release site where Ducklee could be with others of her kind. I often said to her, "You've got to learn to be a duck, to fly and be free." The sentence expanded into a whole song I sang to her while I worked in the garden or dug worms for her. She didn't seem to mind my singing voice, which usually scares other animals and annoys humans. Eventually, after Ducklee was released in a friend's large pond where there were other young wild ducks, I wrote down the song, adding more verses. Being an elementary school teacher, I constructed the main verse so children could make up their own phrases about any wild animal by changing a few words. A music teacher at the school kindly wrote music to go with the words, when I sang it to her. Fortunately, like Ducklee, she didn't seem too annoyed by my singing. I had the song, called *Critter Song,* copyrighted so we could use it in the school where I taught.

Although originally written about a duck, the words in italics could be changed to different animals to make new verses about what they do and where they live. When I used it in my classes, I asked the children to think of another animal's name to substitute wherever the word duck appears in the song. Some of the animals for which they made verses included bear, deer, fish, hawk, lion, elk, skunk, bat, bee, and ant. The children also had to consider what their animal would be doing. Actions they suggested were run, swim, soar, fly, dash, walk, buzz, and crawl. They decided where it would be most at home; for example, in the sky, in the forest, on the prairie, hiding in grass, living in the soil, under rocks, or in other places. The students even made up movements to imitate their animal while singing the song, such as running in place or flapping their arms to simulate flying. The critter song was a fun activity in the gymnasium on a rainy day.

Several years later in 1994, my friend Clara Pincus, who produced and filmed news and children's videos at Dancing Backwards Productions in Corvallis, Montana, decided to create a children's movie with background songs illustrated by a video of live wildlife and wildlife artwork done by children. She asked if she could use my song on it. I told her I would be thrilled and honored to have it on a video for children. She asked Chip Jasman, a local singer who often works with school children, to sing the songs with a talented group of young people accompanying him.

The other song on the video was *All God's Critters Got a Place in the Choir* written by Bill Staines, a New Hampshire songwriter. While Chip and the children sang *Critter Song*, Clara illustrated the words with video clips of live wild birds and animals. I helped her film young deer and elk playing, a mother pigeon with babies, a pair of blue birds, and other wild critters doing what they do. *All God's Critters Got a Place in the Choir* was illustrated by artwork created by school children for an art fair. Clara called the video *Critter Songs* and marketed it with an interesting and informative teachers' guide. *Critter Songs* won an award for Clara. Children and their parents enjoyed watching the animals and singing along with Chip and the young singers. The following is the verse I wrote for Ducklee:

CRITTER SONG

You have to learn to be a *duck,* to *fly* alone and free.
You have to learn to be a *duck.* You can't just follow me.
For there's a big, big world out there that's waiting just for you.
You have to learn to be a *duck* and do what *ducks* can do.
But when I see you *flying* through the *sky* so wild and free,
I think that's what I'd like to do. A *duck* is what I'd like to be.
But I have to learn to be myself and do what I can do.
I have to learn to be myself; I can't just follow you.
For there's a big, big world out there, just waiting for you and me.
We have to learn to be ourselves, if we want to be free.

The friend on whose pond Ducklee was released soon reported the good news that she had joined the group of young mallards living there. She had quickly learned to find food, such as land and water insects, worms, and pondweed along the shore of the pond, and to dive underwater to safety whenever there was a threat. I was happy Ducklee had finally learned to be a duck, flying free with the other mallards. She left with them when they migrated in the fall.

I raised a little family of five ducklings the next year, taking them out for walks and talking to them, just as I had Ducklee. They all sat down at the same time and remained motionless when I told them to stay. They came when they were called and all ran to the garden when I said, "Let's go get some worms!" just as she had. Even though she was quite amazing, Ducklee wasn't an unusual duckling. They can all learn to understand and respond to human words, just as they do their mother's quacked commands. Even though they can't speak in human language like Arnie and Nicki did, ducks and other birds can learn to communicate with humans quite well.

**Multicolored sky
wrapped in white goose ribbons, a
gift from prairie lakes.**

A YELLOW DUCK TALE
(A Read-Aloud Poem for Children)

A little yellow duckling with big orange feet
Waddled to the meadow to find some worms to eat.
She ate a big green worm with red spots on its head,
Making Yellow Duck so sick, she had to go to bed.
Her eyes turned pink and her bill turned black.
And large purple spots broke out on her back.
Her mother tucked her into her little brown bed,
And put cool white feathers on her hot yellow head.
As she lay there peeking out at the big blue sky,
She began to wonder how it would feel to fly.
A good little duck, so her mother explains,
Gets long silver wings like those on airplanes.
Yellow Duck was so happy she got well right away.
She has been well behaved ever since that day.
She politely says please and thank you
And does chores she's asked to do.
That should tell you what her future brings.
When she grows up she will get her wings.

CHAPTER 8
FOXY FINDS HELP

In early spring 2005, long after we moved to our place in the Bitterroot Valley, a pair of Red Foxes (*Vulpes vulpes*) made a den on top of a bench northeast of our land, where they raised their litter of pups. Unfortunately, the den opened in the side of the ditch beside a much-traveled road. When the young foxes were old enough, they began coming out to play, sometimes straying onto the road. Predictably, a passing vehicle hit one of the playful fox pups, a little female, breaking her humerus, the bone between her shoulder and elbow.

The pup, whom I named Foxy when I received her for care, could not compete with her siblings for food with a broken leg, so she became hungrier and hungrier. For some reason, she hobbled to a man's house about three quarters of a mile west of the den. It wasn't the closest human residence; several houses are between the den and the house where she chose to find help. Something about his home, or about him, must have seemed safer and less threatening than other nearby houses. She climbed up onto the porch and sat down near the door, where the man found her when he went out to do his afternoon chores. Quite uncharacteristically for a fox pup who was about five weeks old, she allowed him to pick her up with no protest. Unfortunately, he didn't see she was injured and took her back to the den. He knew where she lived because he had seen the young foxes playing in the ditch when he drove past them.

Poor Foxy had to repeat the slow, painful trip to the man's house on three legs. It took her all night to return to his porch, where he found her when he went out to get his paper in the morning. She was sitting in almost the same spot by his door. This time, the man saw her dangling, obviously broken front leg. He put her in a box and brought her to me; again, she allowed him to handle her with no protest. That in itself was extremely unusual because fox pups old enough to eat solid food are usually as aggressive as they can be, considering their size, toward anything they consider a threat, including people.

Foxes are highly intelligent, but I have no idea how Foxy figured out that a human could or even would help her. Possibly she hoped to be fed. She was extremely hungry, so food rather than help for her leg could have been what she was seeking. It amazed me that she had been able to travel with a broken leg all the way from the den to his porch twice without being killed by a larger predator. I am used to intelligent animals and what they do, foxes being especially well-endowed with common sense. However, for such a small puppy, her intelligent approach to getting help, in addition to her stubborn persistence, seemed quite out of the ordinary, even for a fox.

The kind man apologized several times for not bringing her the first time he found her. He had thought taking her back to her parents' den was the correct thing to do, as it would have been if Foxy had just been lost. It is always best to leave young mammals of all kinds with their parents or where their mother can find them, unless they are obviously hurt or starving. In Foxy's case, and that of any young animal who is injured, the best thing to do is immediately take it to a wildlife rehabilitator.

After hobbling three quarters of a mile twice in two days without food or water, poor little Foxy was dehydrated and emaciated. Before I did anything else, I gave her liquid electrolytes with the two cell salts, which she quickly lapped up. Then I gave her several pinky mice (hairless newborns which are easy to digest) from the freezer, thawed and mixed with Gerber® strained chicken baby food. Foxy gobbled it all up hungrily, topping it off with more electrolytes.

Meanwhile, I was finding tape and trying to determine how to splint her broken leg so it would remain completely immobile when she moved around. The humerus on a canine is up against the body, so it is impossible to actually put a splint around it. After checking her all over for ticks, I wrapped Foxy's broken leg tight to her body with vet wrap, completely immobilizing it especially in the area of the fracture. She made no protest, not once growling or snarling, nor did she try to bite or escape, as most wild foxes her size would have done. That allowed me to handle and treat her without wearing thick leather gloves, making the process much faster and easier for both of us.

When I had finished wrapping the front part of her body in pink and purple vet wrap, Foxy looked like a little clown puppy. I put her in a large plastic dog kennel in our house where it was warm. A thick blanket made a soft bed over a heating pad under the back corner of the kennel. Being small and emaciated, she required the extra heat to stay warm enough, especially during the night. Since the heating pad was only under one corner of the carrier, she had the option of sleeping where it was or in a cooler area.

94

I kept Foxy supplied with a bowl full of pinky mice mixed with chicken baby food and a bowl of electrolytes or plain water, so she could eat and drink anytime. I renewed the cell salts in her water four times a day, so she ingested the electrolyte combination whenever she drank. I also mixed the two cell salt tablets into her mouse pieces and puppy food whenever her food bowl needed refilling. After two days of eating all she wanted several times a day, she had visibly grown but was still surprisingly tame and cooperative. Like most young canines, Foxy liked to have her ears scratched and acted more like a domestic puppy than a wild fox pup.

By afternoon of the second day, she had filled out somewhat, causing the vet wrap around her body to become too tight. I cut it and put pieces of tape across the gap, letting me loosen the vet wrap without removing it or allowing the leg to move. I had to do the same on the third evening and again on the fifth day. By then, Foxy was gobbling down five to seven large mice a day. I always cut mice into bite-sized pieces for small carnivores like fox pups so they can easily chew them. Sometimes she hid a few mouse pieces in a corner of the kennel. Hiding extra food is a common practice if foxes have more food available than they can eat.

When I loosened the vet wrap on the fifth day, I felt the fracture area of her humerus. I was happy to find the bone had solid calcification where the break had been and new bone completely encasing the shattered bone pieces. With her leg stable and finding no movement in the break area, I completely removed the vet wrap. Foxy favored that leg, indicating it was still tender by limping a little for the rest of that day. By the next afternoon, she was walking on her healed leg with no limp at all.

After her leg was well, as she became older and more mature, Foxy became increasingly timid around humans, with behavior more like a typical wild fox pup. I limited my contact with her to cleaning her kennel and giving her food and fresh water, deer bones to chew, and rag balls or feathers with which to play. She continued to eat from six to eight mice each day, with an occasional snack on dog food mixed with egg yolk, helping her grow quickly.

I released Foxy in our riparian area when she was nearly fully grown, putting out food for her each night until she quit coming to eat it. Foxes learn to hunt quickly if they are released where there are plenty of grasshoppers, voles, and mice. Not long after she had learned to find her own food, Foxy left our area, possibly driven away by the resident foxes, who are usually quite possessive of their territory. Hopefully she survived to find her own territory and a mate; raising her own pups far away from roads and vehicles.

She owed her life to her ability to communicate her desperate needs to the kind man who brought her to me for care and to her willingness to completely cooperate with her rescuers. Foxy showed amazingly high intelligence for such a small pup, even a fox pup.

**Its intelligence
helps a fox to survive in
many habitats.**

Foxy was a fox pup who went to people for help when her leg was broken by a vehicle.

SECTION TWO: THERE IS NOTHING LIKE A BEAR

**Golden rain clouds creep
across steep green mountain sides,
hiding feeding bears.**

CHAPTER 9
CINNAMON

One of the first bears we received for care after moving to the Bitterroot Valley was a young female Black Bear (*Ursus americanus*). She came to us after her mother was accidentally killed in their den, which was under a brush pile in the forest. In late March, when the brush was being moved with a bulldozer, the adult was crushed to death. Her body protected her tiny cub, so the cinnamon-colored baby wasn't injured. The bulldozer operator discovered her beside her dead mother after hearing the baby's cries. He put her in a box and left her by the door of the Forest Service Office in Lincoln, Montana, where she was found the next morning. No one told us whether he left her there all night or on his way to work that morning.

The Forest Service called the Montana Fish, Wildlife and Parks office in Missoula and they contacted the Warden Captain. Fortunately, he just happened to be at the Blackfoot-Clearwater Wildlife Management Area near Ovando, along with all the other wardens from Montana including Bob, who were attending a firearms practice and requalification day. After the Missoula Warden Captain received the call from his office, he drove the 27 miles to Lincoln to retrieve the cub. He took her back to the game range and gave her to Bob, so we could care for her until they found a permanent home.

Because she was so young, they said she would have to live in a zoo. At that time, human-raised bears in Montana weren't released back into the wild, even after they were grown. It was believed cubs required at least a year with their mother to learn how to find food and survive. The mother and cub hadn't even come out of hibernation, so the little bear hadn't had the opportunity to learn very much more than how to suckle and play in the den.

By the time Bob arrived home with the cub, her loud cries indicated she was extremely hungry. I quickly fixed a large cardboard box for her with blankets covering the bottom, placing a heating pad under one corner where I made a small den with another blanket. After the hungry cub drank a bottle of warm milk, she went quickly to sleep in her warm, blanket cave. She was still tiny, about the size of a newborn Labrador puppy and so cute that just watching her while she slept gave us both that proverbial Awww moment. Her soft baby fur was a pretty reddish-brown color, so we named her Cinnamon.

Cinnamon was fairly easy to care for when she first arrived. As she was still a young baby, she slept most of the time between feedings. Upon waking, she let out a loud cry to tell me she was awake, making it clear she wanted her bottle immediately, if not sooner. After slurping down her milk, she was ready for a good grooming with a soft brush, similar to being licked by her mother's tongue. She quickly fell asleep again after a bit of rough and tumble play with my hand.

Because she was fed as much milk as she wanted, on demand day and night, in about a month Cinnamon had grown enough to be in the covered 6-foot by 13-foot outdoor kennel. We had built it about 50 feet to the east of the basement door, so I didn't have to go far to feed young animals kept there, making it especially convenient for night feedings. It had a warm house with hay in it where she could sleep and much more room for her to romp and play with her toys. Almost every day, I put a collar on her and took her for walks on a leash so she could explore the world outside the kennel.

Soon after she became familiar with the leash, Cinnamon became a model for the local Grizzly Stove Company, manufacturer of a line of wood stoves. She posed in the door of their newest stove design while a photographer took photo after photo. Amazingly, off leash and with her collar removed, Cinnamon stood perfectly still in various positions, looking baby-bear adorable while the camera clicked repeatedly. One of the cutest photos was featured on a new stove's advertising brochure. I don't know how many stoves Cinnamon helped sell, but the company made a generous donation to the Bitterroot Audubon Wildlife Rehab Fund, which is used to pay for food and medical expenses for injured and orphaned wildlife that rehabbers in Ravalli County receive for care.

Cinnamon also began accompanying me to schools when I gave educational programs with the unreleasable birds. As expected, the children loved her. On leash, she followed me up and down the rows of desks, affording all of the children a chance to see her up close and personal. If the schoolyard had a large enough tree, we all went outside, where she demonstrated how Black Bears are able to quickly climb to escape danger. The cubs especially need this ability when they are young, since many large predators, including wolves, grizzlies, and male black bears, will kill and eat cubs. With the leash, I kept Cinnamon from climbing high enough to escape my reach. I didn't want to have to sit under the tree and wait for her to become hungry enough to climb down.

When I let Cinnamon free to climb the large pine trees at home, she sometimes played up in the bigger branches for several hours before hunger brought her to the ground. If I was outside working, she found me and ran to me, crying to tell me it was time for her bottle. If I was working inside, I went out to check on her every 15 or 20 minutes. When I called her name close to her feeding time, she answered back, climbed down the tree she was in, and ran over to me expecting to be fed. After she had her bottle, I put her back into the kennel so she could take a nap, which she usually did after eating.

I wasn't certain whether a zoo would actually be found to take her or if she might eventually be released. Either way, I thought she should have the opportunity to practice climbing trees and playing in the branches, like bear cubs in the wild do.

Sometimes at schools, Cinnamon protested loudly when I detached her from the tree after she had climbed as high as the leash allowed. The children and their teachers thought she sounded a similar to a human baby crying when she objected to being taken down. I always put her back at the bottom of the tree trunk a few times, allowing her climb again to the limit of her leash before putting her into her travel kennel. She loved to climb and everyone seemed to enjoy watching her bound up a tree.

Years later, young people came up to me in stores and said, "Aren't you the person who brought Cinnamon to our school?" Then they told me what a thrill it had been to have the privilege of seeing a live bear cub up close. Many people seem to relate to bears more than other wild animals, somewhat like they relate to their dogs because, similar to canines, when you look into a bear's eyes you see a thoughtful, intelligent individual looking back. Also like canines, bears have incredible memories and the ability to quickly learn new things. Of all other mammals, bears are most closely related to canines such as dogs and wolves, having diverged from them around 38 million years ago.

Cinnamon playing with her rag toy.

School children had always called me the "bird lady" because I showed them live birds. I was a bit apprehensive they might begin calling me the "bear lady," a nickname with potentially two meanings when spoken. Their parents might have become upset if they thought a nudist was giving talks to students in public schools.

Not long after school let out for the summer, the Montana Department of Fish, Wildlife and Parks found a zoo in Albuquerque, New Mexico, that offered to take Cinnamon. A game warden took her to the Wildlife Rehabilitation Center in Helena, Montana, and from there she was taken to her permanent home.

Several years later, while traveling in New Mexico, we went to the Albuquerque Zoo to see how Cinnamon was doing. By that time, she was a beautiful, full-grown adult. She was with two other adults in a large pen with a swimming pond, flat rocks to lie on, and trees to climb. It was an excellent zoo with large enclosures, and all of the animals appeared to receive good care. They even had a small wolf pack who lived together in a large natural enclosure. We were extremely pleased Cinnamon had been sent to such a nice home.

It was especially beneficial to her well-being that she had two other bears as friends with whom to interact. Because she was a single orphaned cub, she didn't have a sibling or mother bear to play with when she was young. From what we have observed over the years, bears do like to have fun. Depending on their age and sex, they are much happier and healthier when they have a mother, siblings, a friend, or their own cubs with whom to play.

**Each step defying
death, mountain goats traverse cliff
walls like level ground.**

ENCOUNTER WITH A BLACK BEAR

With short legs pumping rhythmically,
The young black bear bounded
Up the grassy mountainside
Straight toward where I waited,
Disguised by a weathered tree stump,
Breathlessly wishing him closer.
His nearsighted eyes did not warn
Him of the intrusion of a stranger,
But the evening breeze, sliding gently
Around the shoulder of the mountain,
Went like a friend to warn him.
With a startled huff, he suddenly froze.
His searching nose pulled him to full height.
A black silhouette carved out of the sunset,
Sniffing audibly, locating danger with
His nose his eyes could not find.
Suddenly, he turned and ran,
A black shadow weaving like smoke
Through darkening tree trunks.
Too soon he was gone,
But he left me a memory.

CHAPTER 10
YOGI

Sometimes in the fall, mother bears bring their cubs down into the valley in search of food to fatten up for hibernation. If they damage beehives or break into garages or barns to get at stored grain, some disgruntled property owners kill them, even mothers with cubs. Cars frequently hit bears in late summer and fall when they try to cross highways while foraging. Hunters also occasionally kill mother bears during the fall hunting season, even though it is illegal to shoot females with cubs. Most years, one or more orphaned bear cubs are seen and reported in fall or early winter. Bob, in his job as game warden, would set his small bear trap with irresistible-smelling bait nearby and quickly catch the cub.

That is how we came to know Yogi, a small male, black in color. In fall 1993, he was seen for several days in a yard near Hamilton. The hungry cub entered the trap the first night it was set and Bob brought Yogi home to live in a 13 by 26-foot covered kennel we had set up for orphaned bears. At that time, cubs who were kept in captivity for more than a month or two were nearly always sent to zoos. Yogi was too small to release that fall, even if we could have gotten him fat enough to hibernate, so he stayed with us through the winter. He was a cute little guy. His size was important because, with no mother to take him to a den and hibernate with him, he would have no chance of survival if released.

Black bear cubs remain with their mother for more than a year from the time of their birth in late January or early February, learning from her what to eat, and hibernating with her in late fall. When they leave the den the next spring, the one-year-old cubs remain with their mother for a few more weeks before she leaves them to find a mate and begin a new family. After a gestation period of seven and a half months, the cubs (most commonly twins) are born. Occasionally, black bears have three or four at a time, and sometimes only one. More than three is unusual in Montana because less food is available here than in states with ecosystems which provide more high calorie and high protein foods, including a wider variety of fruits and berries, acorns, fish, frogs, etc. Mother bears have six teats, but having more than four cubs at a time is highly unusual, even in states with large amounts of calorie-rich food available in the fall.

Yogi quickly settled into his routine of eating, playing with his ball, swinging tire, and other toys or, when he was tired, sleeping in his insulated doghouse. Morning and evening, Bob fed Yogi three cups of high protein dog food topped off with a donut. A local bakery generously donated leftover items to us each day as treats for bears who were staying with us. Often, apples or other fruit were provided by a local grocery store. They usually discard fruit if it develops soft spots, but a bear doesn't care if the fruit is imperfect.

We were amazed at something interesting that happened two years after Yogi was released, when Bob fed peaches to a different bear cub. He had to trap the yearling who was reported to be hanging around homes without his mother. The brown-colored bear was extremely thin and smaller than a healthy yearling should be, so wouldn't have survived the winter without our help. A couple weeks after Bob caught him, he gave the cub a dozen or more over-ripe peaches from the box he had gotten from the store that day. The next day, there were several piles of droppings scattered around in the bear's pen, each containing hundreds of white intestinal worms. The only new food the bear had eaten was the peaches. We had removed the pits, which contain cyanide, so the only thing we could think of that would kill so many intestinal parasites at once was insecticide residue on the peaches.

The bear's feces contained many worms for several days, making it obvious why he was so emaciated. He was unable to eat enough to feed all the worms in his intestines, let alone nourish himself. Fortunately, whatever killed the worms didn't seem to harm the little bear. He gained weight much faster after his unintentional deworming. We didn't receive any big boxes of peaches when caring for Yogi, though there were usually two or three in each box of discarded fruit when they were in season. We never noticed any intestinal worms in his feces, but he might not have had many, being only half as old as the skinny yearling.

Each feeding time, Bob went into Yogi's kennel to collect his droppings in a shovel. Then he placed the food in Yogi's food dish, the dog food first, then apple slices and other fruit, and a donut to top it off. While Bob was doing all that, Yogi went to a corner of the kennel, sat down, and politely waited. After he became used to Bob and knew the routine, Yogi sat closer to Bob where he could better see as his food was placed in the bowl. By spring, he sat very near, patiently waiting until Bob finished with the food and took the shovel full of droppings out of his enclosure. Bob always padlocked the kennel door when a bear was the tenant. They are intelligent escape artists who can easily open a chain link gate if it is simply latched.

Yogi was especially interesting to me because he stood straight up and walked on his hind feet much farther than other cubs for whom we had cared. Since we had been told he would be placed in a zoo and he seemed lonesome, I frequently stopped by the kennel to talk to him. Instead of running into his doghouse cave when I spoke, he often stood on his hind feet by the side of the pen nearest me with his front paws on the wire. He always appeared to appreciate the attention. Sometimes he stood up on the far side and walked on his hind feet to the kennel wire that was close to me. He put one paw on the wire for support while he listened to me talk about whatever came to mind. He didn't seem to care what I said but seemed interested in the sound of my voice. I found it fascinating how far and how well he could walk on his hind legs before reaching the wire or dropping to all fours.

In June, Bob was asked to take Yogi to the Montana Department of Fish, Wildlife and Parks wildlife rehab facility in Helena. Their plan was to find a zoo that would give him a permanent home. Fortunately for Yogi, there were a large number of orphaned bear cubs in other states that year, so they were unable to find a zoo that wanted a black bear. He spent the summer eating and growing at the Fish, Wildlife and Parks facility.

By late fall, Yogi was fat, sleepy, and ready to hibernate. The wildlife biologists decided to place him in a den in the mountains, hoping he would wake up and learn to be a wild bear the next spring. He would be the first young cub raised in captivity to two years of age who was released in that manner in Montana. They anesthetized him to put a radio collar, designed to send signals for more than a year, around his neck for tracking. With it, they would know when Yogi left the den after awakening from the anesthesia. They could follow his signal to see whether he went back into the den to hibernate, as well as tell whether he went near where people lived. If he didn't survive after coming out of hibernation, they would learn that when the signal from the collar stopped moving the next spring. They wanted to be able to go where the signal came from, determine why he died, and retrieve their radio collar.

Yogi did leave the den to drink from a nearby stream after he recovered from the anesthesia, which always makes an animal thirsty. He went back into the den but came out several more times to explore the surrounding area and likely to drink more water. Then he returned to the den and settled down for his long winter nap. In the spring, he did exactly what a bear is supposed to do after hibernation. He ate natural foods all summer while avoiding human habitations. In late fall, Yogi returned to the same den to hibernate. The collar eventually stopped sending signals when the batteries went dead. Although Yogi had a large black number tattooed on the inside of his left hind leg, he was never reported as being shot by a hunter or livestock owner, nor was he recaptured by the MDFWP.

Hopefully, Yogi lived a long, full life, perhaps eventually fathering a new generation of black bears. He was nearly three years old when the biologists lost contact, so was well on his way to reaching adulthood. Few bears raised by their mothers survive their first two and a half years. It was fortunate the Montana Department of Fish, Wildlife and Parks biologists decided to release Yogi and track him to determine whether a bear raised in captivity could survive in the wild, an ability Yogi proved to their satisfaction. Perhaps most important, he did it without ever getting into trouble by approaching humans or their property.

As a consequence of Yogi's success, many other young black bears captured as cubs have been released rather than being placed in zoos, often by putting them in a den in the fall as they did with Yogi. Also, Bob released a number of young bears in the spring after we overwintered them. Many either had tattoos or ear tags, allowing us to receive information about them. None of the bears Bob released were reported killed by hunters or were recaptured by Montana Department of Fish, Wildlife and Parks. Most importantly, none were captured or killed because they became troublesome bears who damaged people's property.

Intelligent and resourceful, Yogi proved bears could learn to live in the wild after being in captivity for a fairly long period. Yogi just wanted to roam free in the mountains where he was supposed to live. He was a pioneer, so to speak, who made it possible for many other bear cubs born after him to live free, instead of being sent to zoos or euthanized. That was Yogi's gift to other bear cubs and his legacy.

**Polar bears will need
to grow flippers when the ice
in the Arctic melts.**

CHAPTER 11
OPENING DOORS

After we finished our log home in the Bitterroot Valley in 1980, we bought several chain link kennels. One was fairly small, six-foot by six-foot, with a panel for the top so it was completely enclosed. There always seem to be at least a few winter days in western Montana with really frigid temperatures, so we put the covered kennel in a basement room to provide a warm place for animals when needed. Over the years, we used the kennel for numerous young mammals and birds of all ages, including coyotes, mountain lions, deer, bear, a badger, eagles, hawks, owls, and others.

One late fall day in the early 1980s, the Montana Department of Fish, Wildlife and Parks tranquilized a small brown-colored black bear who was fairly high up a tree in Missoula, Montana. When the bear fell, he missed the net intended to cushion his fall, crashing to the ground after bouncing off several branches. When they loaded him in the bear culvert trap to transport him out of town, they found he had a badly broken right tibia, the larger of two bones between the knee and ankle. The little bear was taken to a veterinarian, who, after anesthetizing him, placed a metal splint on the leg with screws directly into the bone to hold it in place. Because the splint held the fracture together and immobile, the bear was able to walk while the bone was healing.

After the splint had been put on, the cub was brought to us for care. We called him Brownie, not a very imaginative name but he soon learned to respond to it. As the nights were quite cool, especially for a bear with metal screws through his leg, we decided to keep him in the small kennel in the basement. The six-foot cage in a fairly dark, quiet room seemed ideal for his recovery.

We scattered a bale of soft grass hay throughout the inside of the cage. When the wardens arrived with Brownie, he was still unconscious. Ours is a daylight basement with a door directly into it at the back of the house. They were able to carry Brownie into the kennel and place him carefully on the thick bed of hay. We checked him for ticks and rubbed a light dusting of flea powder into the thick fur on his back and neck. I had tied a small bucket of water to the side of the kennel, so he couldn't knock it over. Bears are often quite thirsty after being tranquilized and we wanted him to easily get a drink. We left him alone to recover from the anesthesia after padlocking the kennel gate. Bears are so intelligent that even doors with two latches always have to be padlocked to prevent escapes. We didn't consider it a particularly good idea to have a large bear cub running free in our basement.

We checked on Brownie several times to make certain he was waking up on schedule and regaining his coordination. We also wanted to observe how well he could walk on his steel-splinted leg. By early evening, he was up and walking around, so Bob fixed a bowl of food for him. When we went into the kennel room, we carefully closed that door before unlocking the padlock to open the kennel. If Brownie happened to escape from the chain link pen, Bob didn't want him to get out of the room into the rest of the house. There is a dark corner on the far side of the cage, where we thought he would run to hide if he did manage to escape.

Brownie quickly learned his feeding routine. Each morning and evening, Bob fixed a bowl of dog food topped with apple slices. Before placing the food in the kennel, he used a long-handled shovel to remove the feces that accumulated during the night. When needed, Bob cleaned and refilled the water bucket. After the chores were finished, the pan with Brownie's food was set inside the door and he was left alone to eat.

One morning, about a week and a half after he arrived, Brownie decided it was time to leave. When Bob was reaching across the cage with the shovel to scoop up a pile of bear droppings, Brownie ran past him and out through the kennel door. Apparently, Brownie had been observing closely what Bob did each time he entered and left the room. He didn't run into the dark corner as we expected; instead he ran directly to the door of the room. Then Brownie did something totally amazing. He stood up on his hind legs, one of which was splinted with metal and screws, grasped the doorknob with both front paws, and gave his best effort to pull the door open. Fortunately, his hairy paws slipped on the rounded metal so he was unable to grasp the knob tight enough to unlatch the door. Obviously, he was trying to pull the door open, as he had watched Bob do at least twice a day during the time Brownie had been in the kennel. When he couldn't get the door open, Brownie dropped to all fours and looked to see where Bob was.

Bob had remained still, watching Brownie's whole performance, so interested in what the bear was doing that he didn't try to interfere. As soon as Brownie was standing on all four feet, Bob used the shovel to guide him away from the door. Having a human pushing him around with a shovel was scary, so he quickly ran back into the kennel, apparently considering it a safe haven. Bob then gave the little bear his breakfast and closed the kennel door. That was the only time Brownie tried to escape.

When he had been with us over a month, I noticed some drainage around the area where the screws went into his leg, indicating the bone might have become infected. We placed our bear carrying box into the kennel, I held the sliding door to the box open, and Bob herded Brownie inside. When he was completely in, I pushed the door of the box down. We loaded it into the back of our pickup and drove him to Missoula so the veterinarian who had put on the splint could check the leg for infection. We left Brownie at the clinic while we did our shopping. They said they would tranquilize him to check his leg and we would be able to pick him up in about three hours.

With our shopping complete, we returned to the veterinary clinic. I had a bad feeling as soon as we walked in. The receptionist, looking concerned, said the doctor would be out shortly to talk to us. He soon called us to the back room to tell us the Montana Department of Fish, Wildlife and Parks head warden had decided to have Brownie euthanized because the leg was not healing as fast as it should have. Unfortunately, that was long before I had learned how to use homeopathic cell salts to stimulate bones to heal quickly. If I had known back in the 1980s to give Brownie the Hyland's Calc. Phos. 30X®, this story would likely have had a much happier ending. The tiny pill is an electrolyte that does an impressive job of stimulating cells to uptake calcium and, if given at least twice a day, results in broken bones completely healing in one half the time doctors or veterinarians expect it to take. I didn't learn about cell salts (also called tissue salts) until almost 15 years later.

After the veterinarian told us several times how sorry he was, we loaded our bear transport box and went home. There was no way to know whether Brownie's leg would have eventually healed. I think he should have been given more time, as he didn't appear to be in pain. He was a highly intelligent bear who would not have had any problem surviving after being released in the wild if his leg had properly healed. The saddest aspect of rehabilitating animals is that there is not a happy ending for every animal, but each one teaches us new things. Brownie, as did many of the bears we cared for, opened another door to reveal how intelligent bears can be, even cubs less than a year old. For Bob and me, there is nothing like a bear because of their amazing intelligence, charming personality, and almost unbelievable adaptability.

Life flame flickers out,
amber eyes go slowly dim
when an eagle dies.

This Golden Eagle (*Aquila chrysaetos*) chick, whose photo was taken by Adele Lewis, was normal. The last 20 years, many chicks have had developmental defects, resulting in chick mortality. Adult Golden Eagles are often killed by ingesting lead, illegal shooting for feathers, being caught in traps baited with meat, flying into wind turbines, and by vehicle collisions. These factors may be responsible for declining Golden Eagle populations in the U. S.

SECTION THREE: WISE OWLS

**Wise owls should embrace
night with soft silent wings, as
night is their best friend.**

CHAPTER 12
MONTANA'S FIRST FLEDGLING FLAM

My acquaintance with the first ever fledgling Flammulated Owl (*Psiloscops flammeolus*) reported to be found in Montana began the morning of September 4, 1975. An owlet who was learning to fly had an accident on a street near the University of Montana in Missoula. The tiny fledgling appeared to have been hit by a vehicle during the night. In the morning, a caring person found it huddled under a bush beside the sidewalk and took it to the Missoula office of the Montana Department of Fish, Wildlife and Parks.

That morning, Bob and I went to their office to pick up some business papers Bob needed in his job as game warden. For the little owlet I named Whooly, it was good I was with Bob. It was sitting all fluffed up in a box on the secretary's desk, looking around with big dark eyes. When we walked in, the secretary said, "Oh, I was just going to call you. Someone left this little owl here earlier this morning."

Unfortunately, the secretary didn't ask the name of the person who found the owlet or the name of the street where it was found. Not knowing the street name would prove to be a problem when reporting the owl to the people who keep records of birds found in Montana. States are divided into rectangular areas called a latilong. All birds reported for state records are recorded for the quarter latilong in which they are found. Unfortunately, the line dividing two of the quarter latilongs ran directly through the area where the little owl was injured. Because we didn't know the street name, it was impossible to correctly report the exact location.

The owlet was easily identified as a Flammulated Owl (the first one I had seen), being the only small owl with dark brown eyes living in North America. The iris of their eye is such a dark color it is hard to tell where the iris ends and the black pupil begins. Their large dark eyes and animated toy-like appearance make them extremely appealing. They are usually called flams for short, likely because it is somewhat incongruous for such a tiny owl to have such a long name. Male flams are only five and one-half inches long when fully grown. Whooly's tail feathers were still growing, so he was less than five inches long.

When I looked up Flammulated Owls in the Montana Bird Distribution book, I found there had previously been only three adults observed and reported in Montana. There was no evidence that Flammulated Owls had ever nested or raised young in the state. Flams are difficult to see in the wild because they are so diminutive. They weigh between two and five ounces, depending on whether they are male or female, with females being up to one third larger than males. Most importantly, they are well-camouflaged to look exactly like pine bark. With those characteristics, it wasn't surprising that flams had gone almost unreported here. Also, at that time few people in western Montana even knew Flammulated Owls exist. Many people still think any small owl, especially one with ear tufts, is a baby Great Horned Owl.

Whooly was the first fledgling flam found and officially reported. He was also the first evidence of breeding by flams in Montana. After I called the University of Montana to report I had an injured fledgling Flammulated Owl, found on a street in the University area in Missoula, an ornithology professor returned my call to insist that no Flammulated Owls nested in Montana. It was assumed the three adult flams who had previously been reported were what are called transient birds, those who do not nest here but migrate through an area or are lost, wanderers, or blown off course by a weather front.

It was obvious to me that many generations of Flammulated Owls had been hatched and fledged in Montana. I thought it highly likely they had been living and nesting in the forests of western Montana for thousands of years. It was also likely Whooly's parents had made their nest in a hollow tree in Missoula. Because Whooly's wing and tail feathers were not fully-grown, he wasn't yet able to fly well, which likely contributed to his hitting or being hit by something and being injured. It was evident he couldn't have flown far from the nesting cavity from which he fledged. If flams were indeed nesting near the University of Montana, they were nesting right under, or more correctly right over, the noses of the very ornithologists who insisted Flammulated Owls do not nest in Montana. I found that prospect quite humorous. It also may have been the reason the ornithology professor didn't want to admit Flammulated Owls were nesting there.

At that time, because it was assumed they didn't nest in Montana, no one had tried to find them. As soon as owl researcher Vida Wright began looking for flams in the early 1990s, she found several colonies nesting in western Montana. A colony is a group of several pairs. Unfortunately for the Flammulated Owls who do nest in Montana, according to a Forest Service biologist I consulted, by the early 1990s, 90% of the old growth ponderosa pine forests in western Montana had been clear-cut. There is no way to assess how many Flammulated Owl colonies there might have been before the clear-cutting of nearly all the old growth forest necessary for their nesting colonies.

Because they live in colonies or groups of nesting pairs, flams have to have an adequate number of large ponderosa pine or Douglas fir trees in their nesting territory. Each pair requires an unoccupied cavity in a fairly large tree for their nest. The owls can't make their own nesting cavity, so they have to use holes made by various woodpeckers. It takes many years and an old growth forest for woodpeckers to have drilled enough nest holes to accommodate a Flammulated Owl colony.

Trees grow quite slowly in western Montana due to lack of rainfall and relatively short growing seasons. A ponderosa pine usually takes 150 years or longer to become a sufficient diameter fairly high up on the tree to accommodate a nesting cavity large enough for small owls to use. One of a Flammulated Owl's main food sources is the pine moths that lay their eggs on ponderosa pine trees. For successful nesting, a colony of flams needs abundant nesting cavities in the same area where there is a plentiful supply of adult moths to provide a continuous food source for their owlets, features usually found only in old growth forests.

Most Flammulated Owls who nest in Montana begin to migrate south to their wintering areas by the end of September. Sometime around December, they reach the pine-covered mountains in Mexico and Guatemala, where they spend the winter. In March, they begin the long trip back to nest areas in Montana, other western states, and some Canadian provinces. Another important factor affecting Flammulated Owl nesting is they usually don't arrive at their nesting areas in the north until after mid-May. By that time, resident cavity nesters have already claimed many of the suitable holes in large trees.

Fledgling Flammulated Owls look like adorable animated toys.

In spring 1975, in and around Missoula, there was an unusually large hatch of pine moths. Clouds of them circled the streetlights, especially on the east side of Missoula and in the University area. There were also many old trees with cavities for nesting in the University area, although not all of the trees with nest holes are pines. A small colony of flams may have taken up residence in the old trees in the residential neighborhood near the University of Montana to utilize the abundant pine moths to feed their owlets. Other insects Flammulated Owls like to eat, such as beetles, grasshoppers, crickets, caterpillars, spiders, and other moth species can also be found in residential areas.

Flammulated Owls have long, curved, needle-sharp talons, like most owls and other birds of prey. Thus, they are capable of catching mice and small birds and often do. One of the first Flammulated Owls observed in Montana, an adult female, was seen in December holding a dead bird she had caught. Males may have more difficulty killing small mammals because, as with other owl species, they are only about two-thirds the size of females.

Both sexes of Flammulated Owl have feathered legs, like most other owl species, but the feathers stop just above the foot. The foot is covered with soft flexible scales but has no hair-like feathers on the toes, as do all other Montana owl species. The bottom of a flam's feet and toes have small bumps to help hold the insects they catch, so the captured insect can't slip out of the owl's grasp. A male owl has to supply food to his mate while she is brooding the eggs. When their young are newly hatched, he must bring additional food for her to feed the babies, as well as finding food for himself. When feeding young, male flams often have to provide food for a total of five or six owls, although the tiny owlets can't eat very much at a time. Between May and September, nesting season for flams, a constant supply of insects is usually available. By hunting mostly insects, especially the normally abundant, night-flying moths, flam parents don't have to compete with other birds of prey for rodents or small birds during the season when all owls and hawks are attempting to find food for their voracious young.

The Flammulated Owl gets its name from the rufous or "flame-colored" feathers along the scapula, the area just above the wing on the shoulder. Flams are mainly grayish brown on the back, having a light whitish breast with dark patterning. Rufous coloring also occurs on some feathers throughout the plumage and on the flat feathers surrounding the owl's eyes, called the facial disc. The markings and coloring make flams look much like pine bark, providing excellent camouflage.

It is my opinion that Flammulated Owls are one of Montana's prettiest owls, with short rounded ear tufts that disappear when the owl's head feathers are raised or fluffed. The ear tufts are most pronounced when the owl is trying to be inconspicuous. Flams are shy and freeze when approached, making themselves as long and slim as possible. This makes the light-colored breast feathers less obvious so they look even more like a piece of bark. Except for females brooding eggs or young while hidden in a nest cavity, flams have to find a concealed place to rest during daylight hours. Perched near the trunk of a ponderosa pine while roosting, their plumage is so well camouflaged and blends so completely with the color and texture of the tree's bark, they are difficult to distinguish from it, making them nearly invisible. Also, they usually close their eyes to narrow slits so their eye shine does not give them away. These characteristics make it hard to see a Flammulated Owl, even when you know exactly where it is. Flams can see well both in daylight and at night, but for safety they prefer to hunt during the period beginning at complete dark and ending just before any morning light appears.

Whooly's mother and father likely arrived in the Missoula area the last week of May or early June. The male would have found an unoccupied hole in a tree and claimed the surrounding area as his territory. During this time, male owls are quite vocal. The mating call is low and mellow but carries long distances. It is repeated over and over with little or no variation, sounding somewhat mechanical. It is often a two-note call, repeated several times, sounding like whoo-WHOOT, with a strong accent on the second note. From a distance, it sounds like only one whoot. They also make a one-note call, a low whoop, whoop, whoop, whoop, repeated many times. Whooly often gave the two-note whoo-WHOOT call.

After the male finds a suitable nest cavity, the female does some housekeeping, lining the bottom of the cavity with small wood chips and feathers. After copulation, she lays from two to four small round white eggs and begins to incubate immediately after the first egg is laid. Incubation takes about 26 days. Around the first of July, Whooly's siblings would have pecked their way out of the shells, with Whooly possibly being the last to hatch, two to five days after the first of his siblings, depending on the number of eggs laid. That he was the youngest and smallest owlet in the owl family was likely. Unless the parents were unusually late in nesting, Whooly should have been flying prior to the end of August, if he had been one of the first in the clutch to hatch.

After the tiny owlets hatch and dry from egg fluids, they look like marble-sized balls of fluffy down, with big brown eyes and wide hungry mouths. The mother owl remains with the young to protect them and keep them warm. If there is a threat, such as some kind of predator, both male and female are aggressive in the protection of their nest and young. That year, there were thousands of pine moths around the street lamps every night, so finding food for his family should have been fairly easy for Whooly's father. His young owlets, being well fed, would have grown fast.

By mid-August, the first hatched of the fledgling flams would have ventured out of the nest hole to partly fly and partly hop from branch to branch, behavior appropriately called branching. After permanently leaving the nest cavity, young owls hide during the day and practice flying from branch to branch during the night to develop their flight muscles and coordination. Although still down-covered, except for their wings and newly grown short tails, they are able to fly quite well for short distances.

As the youngest fledgling, Whooly wouldn't have begun branching until around the end of the third week of August. By that time, his older siblings were flying around the treetops at night, remaining hidden in thick evergreen branches during the day. Owlets are dependent on the adults for food for several weeks after they begin flying. They need that time to learn hunting techniques, and what to hunt, by observing their parents.

Flam fledglings must learn their survival lessons quickly to be ready to begin the migration south soon after mid-September. Their departure from northern states depends partly on weather and availability of insects. The owls likely migrate as a family group, so the young can learn where to go. They also must learn where to find safe daytime roosting places and food sources on their trip south. With habitat constantly being disrupted and changed by human activity, it is a wonder they can successfully migrate for such a long distance. Besides finding enough food, the tiny owls have to avoid being caught and eaten by mammal predators and birds of prey. They also have to avoid being hit by vehicles and hitting man-made objects. From Montana to where they spend the winter in the mountains of southern Mexico or Central America, is a very long, perilous trip for such a small owl. In spring, they have to make the equally long, dangerous trip back to Montana.

Migrating flams are especially affected by the spraying of insecticides that kill the insects upon which they depend for food. In addition, constant exposure to the combination of many pesticides (umbrella term including herbicides, insecticides, fungicides, and others) used to kill weeds, fungi, and insects affect the nervous system of birds and their ability to maintain heat and energy, seriously compromising their ability to fly.

The clear-cutting of large areas of old growth forest that used to occur in mountainous areas in the United States and Mexico has destroyed much of the habitat Flammulated Owls need for survival. Just imagine flying all night, expecting to find a forest with a place to rest and food to eat. When you finally arrive, tired and hungry, there is nothing but a forest of new houses, no trees and hardly any insects because everything has been sprayed with insecticides. That is not a good prospect for long-term survival for Flammulated Owl populations.

Upon their return to northern states, they often find their nesting areas adversely affected where either logging or forest fires have depleted the number of old, large trees with nesting cavities. It would be similar to returning from a trip or a vacation to find your home and entire neighborhood completely gone. The nesting process can also be disrupted by encroachment by off road vehicles and other human activity into areas where there are nesting colonies. The spraying of any type of herbicide or insecticide in, near, or even far upwind of the nesting area can be disastrous to the young. Most commonly used pesticides are hormone or gene disrupters that can adversely affect developing owlets.

Whooly was still not well coordinated by the first week of September. Young owls often have trouble controlling their landings. Whooly had obviously hit or been hit by something fairly hard. He was a bit bruised, especially his left wing. The tip of his upper bill had broken off by striking an object even harder than the bill, the blow causing him to be somewhat dazed. That impact changed his life. Whooly went home with us that day and remained with us until spring. By the time his bruised wing healed and the tip of his bill grew back, it was too late for him to migrate. Without his parents to teach him, he wouldn't have known where to go or how to find and catch food. So, while his parents and siblings had to make the dangerous migration to Mexico and back, Whooly was able to fly around in a big, warm room all winter, with all the food he could eat provided for him.

We designed a room in the basement of our house as a flight room for small birds. I strategically placed branches and a small fir tree a neighbor had cut down around the room, so Whooly could fly from branch to branch or from tree to branches. After Christmas, I collected several discarded Douglas fir Christmas trees, made stands for them, and placed them around the room, so Whooly had a small forest to live in for the rest of his stay with us. There was also a table in the room where I placed his food, consisting of grasshoppers, crickets, mealworms, mouse livers, and mouse hearts. He didn't like the rest of the mouse, only the liver and heart. Since I also had other raptors in care, I removed the hearts and livers for Whooly, giving the rest of the mouse bodies to the others.

On nice days, I put jesses on Whooly's legs. A lightweight line attached to the jesses allows a bird to fly for quite a long distance, while remaining under the handler's control. Whooly could fly from my hand to a branch or post top without being able to escape. Jesses are used by falconers to control their hawks or falcons until the birds are released to fly free and hunt. A falconer's bird is taught to return to the arm of the falconer.

Whooly in his room posing for photos on a Douglas Fir tree.

Carrying the line while flying from my fist to a post or branch built up Whooly's flight muscles. He soon became accustomed to the jesses. Hunting on a long line proved a good way for him to practice catching grasshoppers and other insects when spring came. By late September, when he had recovered from his injuries and could fly well, it was quite cold outside, so no insects remained available for him to catch. I had frozen nearly a gallon of large grasshoppers I caught soon after Whooly became our guest. He had a varied diet of mealworms and crickets from the pet store, in addition to thawed grasshoppers and an occasional live moth, all of which he readily ate.

A couple days after Whooly came to live with us, when I talked on the phone with an ornithologist at the University of Montana, I asked him if

Flammulated Owls were common nesters in our area and if he knew what they eat. I explained the owl, a small fledgling just out of the nest, was found on a street in the University area and that he had been injured. He told me Flammulated Owls eat mice and insects like other small owls but do not nest in Montana. I suggested flams must nest here since a fledgling who was just a brancher and couldn't yet fly well was found in Missoula. He stated someone must have found the owl in California or some state in which they nest and released it in Missoula.

The ornithologist called and asked about Whooly several times in September and the first part of October. He sent six different students to our house to photograph him but never came himself. Whooly was likely the most photographed Flammulated Owl ever. I took several rolls of film of him, as did several friends who photographed wildlife, and each of the six students.

In one of our phone conversations, the ornithologist stated he needed another Flammulated Owl study skin and suggested I give Whooly to him. To my horror, he wanted to kill the little owl. He claimed Whooly would have to learn to catch mice and would not survive in the wild if released. Whooly acted like he was afraid of live baby mice and he wouldn't go near a dead adult mouse. It was unlikely he would kill a mouse, even if he found one. Whooly strongly indicated he most definitely didn't want to eat mice, other than the hearts and livers I gave him. He only wanted to eat insects; I thought he should know better than anyone what he preferred to eat. I found early in the spring that he especially liked the live Salmon Flies I caught for him.

I quickly learned that Whooly knew much more about Flammulated Owls than ornithologists did, including those who had written about flams in books. At that time, very little was actually known about their natural history. As for surviving in the wild, I thought Whooly deserved a chance to try. I was definitely not in favor of him becoming a study skin. I told the ornithologist I was going to release Whooly, saying if someone brought me a Flammulated Owl who didn't survive or was unreleasable and had to be euthanized, I would give him the dead owl. He was not happy with that proposal. He still didn't think Flammulated Owls could be found in Montana. I believed there was likely a significant population of them, which would be found if someone actually looked for them during nesting season.

By October, it was below freezing outside, so Whooly had to remain in his room. During the day, he roosted on a favorite limb on one of the

Douglas fir trees or on one of the dead tree branches I had placed in his room. Whenever he decided he wanted a snack, he flew down to the table, picked up an insect in his right foot, and flew back to one of his roosts. He brought the insect up to his beak headfirst and ate it like a child eating an ice cream cone. He was undeniably one of the cutest little guys I had ever seen, especially when he was eating.

In the evening, around dusk, Whooly went to his feeding platform, ate an insect or two, and then flew around and around the room, as if he had someplace to go. He almost made me dizzy to watch him. Occasionally he perched on one of the branches for a rest stop. He hooted with a one-note whoop, whoop, whoop for a few minutes, then off he went again. It appeared he had a strong urge to migrate. Whooly's behavior indicated the migrating family group likely stays in contact by occasionally hooting, but since he was alone, there was no other owl to answer him. By mid-December, he stopped his continuous flying and remained quietly perched on his favorite branches, except when he flew to the table for food. Apparently, it was time to stop migrating.

I wanted to know more about Flammulated Owls, so I spied on him every night when I had time, especially in early evening. I often watched him through the basement window; after putting on layers of warm clothes and wrapping myself in an old blanket, I sat outside looking in through the basement window of my own house. The way neighbors and people driving on the highway past our house looked at me, they obviously considered that to be extremely strange behavior. I had to spy on Whooly through the window because, when I went into the room with him, he didn't act in a normal manner. He perched in the top of his fir tree and just sat there looking at me. He didn't hoot or fly around when I was present. To see what he did naturally, I had to watch him from outside his room. If I sat very still, he didn't seem to notice me.

All through January and February 1976, Whooly spent his nights flying from tree to tree, or perched on top of one of his new, recycled Douglas fir Christmas trees. He occasionally went down to snack on some of the insects I always left on the table for him. Or he found and picked them from the fir branches, where I hid some of the larger grasshoppers to make it more like finding his own food.

One day in March, I had to serve on jury duty. Because it was a traffic violation, I didn't think it would take long to determine guilt or innocence. I normally gave Whooly only enough food to last until late afternoon, supplying him with fresh insects in the evening to eat during the night.

121

The case was against a woman charged with drunk driving. Her test showed a high blood alcohol level and she testified she was driving the car. She and her boyfriend were both in the car and drunk. She was so incapacitated she reportedly drove off the road into the river. The State Patrol Officer who responded to the accident gave her a ticket for driving under the influence. She was positively guilty as far as I was concerned.

Oddly, only three of the 12 jurors, two others and myself, voted guilty. Some who voted not guilty said they had driven under the influence of alcohol and didn't think she should be fined. Three of the men said they had been in accidents and switched seats with their wife or girlfriend since they had already received tickets for drunk driving. For insurance reasons and because they would receive a larger fine than the other person, they let the other person take the blame. They thought the woman was likely covering for her boyfriend and he had probably been driving. Consequently, we had a hung jury for a long time. Talk about a jury of your peers. Most of them sat there and admitted getting away with violations of the law much worse than those for which the woman was on trial.

Finally, at about 8:00 that night, I was the only one voting guilty, all the other jurors were mad at me, the judge was mad at all of us, and I was becoming concerned about Whooly not having any food. Normally, I would have stubbornly remained there all night, because when a person drives drunk, they are endangering all other people on the road. That is not excusable by any stretch of truth or justice. Of course, all the scofflaws on the jury disagreed with me. It would have been a long night or a hung jury, except for Whooly. I needed to feed him, so I voted not guilty and we all went home. I still wonder if those two people ever killed anyone else or themselves while driving drunk again. Fortunately, people have become more concerned about drunk drivers. The change in attitude came at a terrible price. People driving while under the influence of alcohol or drugs have been responsible for the permanent injury or death of many innocent people in Montana, including a large number of children.

In mid-March, Whooly began making his two-note hoot. As in November and December, he spent long periods flying around the room without stopping. Every night throughout the rest of March, all of April, and well into May, he circled the room fairly continuously, stopping occasionally for brief stints of hooting or to eat. Finally, he stopped the constant flying, and remained perched in his fir trees, hooting his two-note mating call almost continuously. Apparently Whooly considered his migration back to Montana to be completed and was trying to attract a mate.

Studies conducted in Colorado by Dr. Richard Reynolds, showed Flammulated Owls return to the same nest tree and have the same mate for at least as long as five years, suggesting the owls mate for life. Being a young male, Whooly would have to find a nest cavity and an unattached female to be his mate. He would likely have returned to the same area where he was fledged if he had been in the wild. Whooly constantly gave his mating call when he was continuously flying around the room. That suggested migrating male flams may actually court migrating females, so the pair is established and ready to begin nesting when they arrive back in their northern nesting territories.

As soon as the snow melted, on warm afternoons I began taking Whooly outside again to practice flying on the long, lightweight line. I put snap-on jesses on his legs just before taking him out of his room and removed them as soon as I took him back. I never leave permanent jesses on birds, especially owls, because the feathers on their legs can be damaged by them.

By May, many live grasshoppers, daddy longlegs, salmon flies, and spiders were available for Whooly to practice catching. When the salmon flies began hatching along the banks of the nearby river, I caught a few to see if he liked them. The way Whooly gobbled them up, they must have been flam candy. Fortunately, there was a large hatch in spring 1976. I caught and froze nearly a gallon, which provided him enough to last until early June, when he would be released.

When we were outside, I put a live salmon fly on the ground in front of us. Whooly flew from my hand down to the insect and grabbed it in his right foot. Holding it head first up to his bill, he tore it into small pieces, swallowing each piece as he pulled it from the salmon fly. The last small part of the abdomen was gulped down whole. I had him hop up onto my hand as we looked for other insects or spiders and daddy longlegs. If he spotted something he liked, he flew down, caught it in his right foot, squeezed it briefly, then ate it.

He soon learned to fly back up to my hand without my putting him there. Maybe he found it was a good vantage point from which to spot insects, or he felt safer when he was off the ground. I wound up the long-line carefully so it would unwind without tangling. I didn't want it to tighten on his legs when he flew downward and forward to catch an insect. That would have thrown him off balance, causing him to miss catching the insect or even resulting in him landing on his chest, possibly injuring him. For as long as salmon flies were available along the banks of the nearby river, I released live ones in his room. By the end of May, Whooly was highly proficient at catching live prey. It was time to say goodbye, but the first three days in June were cloudy and rainy, not the best weather for releasing a small owl.

The fourth day of June was warm and sunny. In late afternoon, after making sure he had eaten his fill, we took Whooly up to the old growth pine forest half a mile northeast of our house. I placed him on a pine branch, close to the trunk. We took some photos, wished him a long and happy life, and walked away. We never saw Whooly again, but my neighbor, who had seen him many times when I was carrying him around catching insects, thought she saw him hunting in her yard at dusk about three weeks after we released him. I am certain she did see a Flammulated Owl, but there was no way of knowing whether it was Whooly.

In July 1986, 10 years after I released Whooly, the first actual nest cavity containing multiple Flammulated Owl young was discovered in Montana. The man who found it was working on a logging operation when he felled a pine tree with the nest in it. In the hollowed-out section of the tree trunk, he found three hatchling owlets, which he gave to a friend who brought them to me. I reported the nest to the ornithologist and to Denver Holt. During the logging operation, an area of many acres was clear-cut, effectively destroying all the Flammulated Owl nesting habitat. As no other young flams were brought to me during the tree cutting, there may have been only one pair nesting there, rather than the usual colony consisting of several pairs. The other possibility is that nests were not found so the young in the nests died.

The oldest of the three owlets I received for care was a female. She had a birth defect with two carpal joints, equivalent to our wrists, formed on both wings, rendering her unable to fly. The smallest and youngest owlet, a male, was about half grown and downy. The malformed female and the older male were nearly full grown but still downy, with wing and tail feathers just beginning to emerge. The older male had a broken right leg as a result of the fall when their nest tree was cut down. I splinted his leg and it healed straight and strong. Like Whooly, all three lived through the winter with us in a room with trees and branches. At that time, we lived in our house in the Bitterroot Valley. The young flams had no parents to show them the migration route or how to catch live prey, so couldn't successfully be released until spring.

The next spring, after the two males had practiced catching live insects in their room and on the long line, I released them the end of May. They deserved a chance to have a life in the wild, to find a mate, and hopefully produce young. I put the flightless female on my education permit. In 1987 and for eight more years, she traveled to school classes and to other educational presentations with the unreleasable birds I used for education at that time. One day she suddenly fell over dead. I gave her to the ornithologist, who finally had his Flammulated Owl study skin, although it was an unusual one with the wing deformities. Since then, I have necropsied many birds and animals who died suddenly, similar to the female flam. Their hearts were malformed, with the right ventricle being obviously enlarged. I couldn't necropsy the malformed flam because it would have made her body unusable as a study skin, so I never knew for certain why she died.

After several years and much research of pesticide symptoms, it became apparent the spraying in forests of an insecticide, endrin, for spruce bud-worms at the same time that 2,4,5-T, an herbicide, was used on forests and wheat fields for weed control, was what likely caused the many birds, including ducks, hawks, owls, and songbirds, to hatch with serious bill, eye, and limb malformations between 1981 and 1986. Fortunately, both endrin and 2,4,5-T were banned in 1985 by the EPA. After 1986, no more malformed birds were brought to me for 10 years, until 1996, when I received a Western Meadowlark with a short upper bill and consequent crossed bills. USGS researchers are working on determining what has been causing malformed limbs and bills on individuals of many species of raptor and songbird since 1996 in Canada, Alaska, and the rest of the United States.

After observing Whooly all winter and researching the literature to find what was known about Flammulated Owls, I wrote an article for the Montana Department of Fish, Wildlife and Parks magazine, *Montana Outdoors*, about Whooly and the natural history of Flammulated Owls. During the next 10 years, as I predicted, I received several more of the small owls for care, both fledglings and adults. Because of my data on those owls, our internationally famous local owl researcher, Denver Holt, published what is called a short communication in the autumn 1987 *Journal of Raptor Research*, titled "Occurrence and First Nest Record of Flammulated Owls in Montana." The article reported the dates of observation for all the Flammulated Owls who had been found in Montana at that time. All but three adult flams and all the young owls discussed in the paper were ones I had received for care and for which I carefully recorded location and other data. The owls included three hatchlings, two fledglings, and several adults. I was listed as a co-author on Holt's paper, as was Philip Wright, a University of Montana professor who, ironically, was the ornithologist who had wanted to turn Whooly into a study skin.

The official report on Whooly and the other hatchling and fledgling flams helped me to finally convince the ornithologists and Forest Service biologists that Flammulated Owls actually do nest in Montana. They certainly needed to be considered in land management plans concerning timber cutting on public lands. The Forest Service hired a young woman, Vida Wright, to conduct research to determine approximately how many Flammulated Owls nest in western Montana and what type of habitat they prefer. I gave her the locations where the flams I had received were found. She found nesting colonies in the areas I described that had not been destroyed by clear-cutting, and also in several new locations. Most of the colonies were in old growth ponderosa pine mixed with Douglas fir.

On August 20, 1988, 12 years after we released Whooly, a woman's dog found a small fledgling Flammulated Owl under a bush in her yard, approximately a quarter mile from where we had released Whooly on June 4, 1976. She brought the small owlet to me because she thought it might be injured. The youngster was completely healthy but not old enough to fly well. It was at the uncoordinated age when owlets are called branchers, the same age as Whooly was when I got him. The woman explained that each spring, she and her husband had heard small owls hooting in the trees on the ponderosa pine-covered mountainside behind their house. I made the whoo-WHOOT call I had learned from Whooly. She said that was exactly the way the owls sounded. Her report of what they had heard each spring strongly indicated Flammulated Owls had been nesting for many years on the mountainside close to where we had released Whooly.

I checked the little owlet from head to toe, then gave it several mealworms and three grasshoppers, which it readily ate. After giving it a few drops of water to drink, I sent it home with the kind woman who agreed to take it up into the pine forest where the owls lived. She put the owlet up in a pine tree at dusk, so its parents could find it. She agreed to keep her dog inside or on a leash for several days, giving all the little fledgling owlets (there likely were others) a chance to learn to fly without the dog bothering them.

There is no way to know for sure, but I like to think the tiny owlet might have been one of Whooly's descendants, possibly his grandson or great-grandson. If Whooly found a mate and successfully raised young after his release, he could have had many descendants after 12 years. It is not known how long Flammulated Owls live in the wild. Likely not many years, considering all the dangers they face daily, especially during migration. Maybe Whooly beat the odds, survived several migrations and fathered several families of young flams. It is also possible that Flammulated Owls had been nesting for many generations in the exact area where we released Whooly. Hopefully they will continue to nest there for many, many more.

**Ignoring species
until habitat destroyed
is a human trait.**

THE FLAMMULATED OWL

**Silently he flutters, then glides
Through the branches and trees,
Catching moths and insects
To feed young owlets, guarded by
Their mother safe in a cavity
Carved by a woodpecker high up
The trunk of an old gnarly pine.**

**Insects beware of keen brown eyes.
From quick feet you must hide,
As he flutters through branches
Snatching pine moths in flight or
Plucking hoppers from grass stems
In the meadows between the trees
That grow on the mountainside.**

The flame-touched owl is coming
To dine, to end his fast, which
Lasted the day while hidden,
Camouflaged by sprinklings of light
To mimic a loose chunk of bark,
While perched on a branch close by
The trunk of the old gnarly pine.

Snowy Owls will fly
silently away over
disappearing snow.

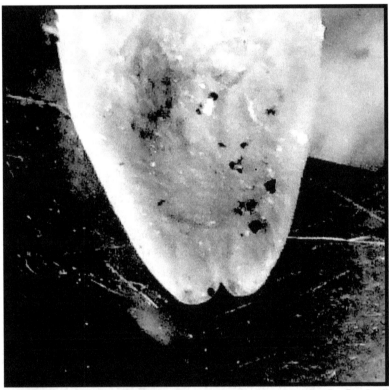

The tongues of most owls, like this Great Horned Owl (*Bubo virginianus*) tongue, have slightly bifurcated (divided) tips.

CHAPTER 13
NIGHTWING AND WOODSY

This is the story of a small male Great Horned Owl (*Bubo virginianus*), named Woodford G. Owl (Woodsy for short) by the people who raised him. It is also the story of Nightwing, a female Great Horned Owl brought to me as a downy hatchling in late spring 1989, who became his mate.

If a pair of owls cannot find an abandoned Red-tailed Hawk's nest or other large nest to use, they occasionally build their own. Those nests are often quite flimsily built near the top of an evergreen or hidden in a hollow in the top of a large, broken-off cottonwood snag. The old snag where Nightwing and her two siblings were huddled, sheltered from the blowing rain by their mother's body, came crashing down in a violent wind storm. The mother owl flew out as the snag fell. Nightwing was thrown clear, landing on soft grass. Unfortunately, she was the only hatchling to survive the fall; the tree trunk crushed her siblings. Nightwing was found on the ground the next morning by the landowners while cleaning up the downed trees, and brought to me.

She was old enough to eat by herself, so all I had to do was give her water and keep her supplied with mice, up to six or eight per day. She grew to be a beautiful, light-phase Great Horned Owl. Her goldish-grey color made it easy to distinguish her from other darker owls after she was released. As soon as she could fly well, I freed her in our back yard. We have a half-mile of Willoughby Creek on our land with our house located on the south edge of the riparian area along the creek. Our property on the east side of the Bitterroot Valley is in a dry region that receives little rainfall. Located between two mountain ranges, we are in what is called a rain shadow. Due to lack of rain, most of the deciduous trees and deciduous fruit-bearing bushes that grow in our area live near streams.

During the day, owls prefer to roost where they can't be seen in thick trees along streams and rivers. Nightwing always roosted in one of the large ponderosa pine trees in the riparian area near Willoughby Creek. She could easily hear me and came for her late dinner of mice each night when I called her name. By the end of November, she was hunting and catching wild rodents so didn't need more than a daily supplemental mouse or two. By January, she was finding all of her own food. The hay field next to the riparian area was filled with meadow voles, providing adequate prey for her to hunt each night. Often in the early morning, I could hear her distinctive hoot.

Right after the new year began, during the first week of January 1990, the Montana Department of Fish, Wildlife and Parks brought Woodsy to us, after taking him from the people who raised him. He was approximately the same age as Nightwing, but because the people had illegally kept him in captivity, he didn't know how to find or catch live prey. I wasn't told where the people had obtained Woodsy or why they had him. He may have been found on the ground after the same windstorm that orphaned Nightwing.

Woodsy appeared healthy but a bit underweight and small, even for a male. The people had fed him hamburger and raw chicken meat. Young owls require whole rodents or birds for enough nutrients to promote good health and normal growth. Hamburger has very little nutritional value, with few vitamins and minerals and too much fat to be good for owls or other meat-eating birds. Young birds need sufficient protein, vitamins, calcium, trace minerals, and other vital nutrients during their fast growth period as hatchlings to enable them to develop muscles, bones, and feathers.

I put Woodsy in a flight room and gave him all the mice he could eat. After two and a half weeks, he had gained weight, looked much healthier, and appeared ready for release. He was tame so came to me when I called to him in the flight room. After being released, human raised owls will come when called, if they have been trained to come for their mice while in captivity. Owls have excellent hearing, so they can recognize their name being called from over two miles away.

I released Woodsy on Saturday, January 26. On Sunday evening, I called his name from our back deck before putting his mice on a large square board. The board gave released owls a place to look for their food whenever they come to eat. It also kept the deck clean and prevented mice from falling through gaps in the floor. Soon after I called him, Woodsy flew down from the pine trees behind the house, first landing on the deck railing, then going down to the three mice I had left on the board. After he swallowed one, he flew up into a tree across the creek behind the house where I could clearly see him. Another owl, who sounded like Nightwing, began hooting from a thick pine tree close to the house. It hadn't taken them long to find each other.

I wasn't too thrilled with Nightwing taking an inexperienced, newly-released male for her mate, but there was nothing I could do about it. Young owls like to have the company of other youngsters, and with her living in our creek bottom, it was inevitable they would meet. Hopefully, accompanying Nightwing on her hunting excursions would help Woodsy learn to catch prey faster than by trial and error on his own. This would help ensure his survival and more quickly teach him to become a competent mate.

Later in the evening, I went out on the deck to see if the mice remaining on the board were frozen. Woodsy was sitting on a white mouse to warm it so he could eat it, so I went back into the house for more mice. After thawing several in warm water to replace the frozen ones, I went out to the porch, walked up to Woodsy and handed him a warm mouse, which he took from my mittened hand with his beak. He quickly swallowed the mouse. Then I tried to pick up the two frozen mice left on the board, so I could put the four warm mice in their place. Woodsy grabbed my mitten with the talons on his right foot to stop me from taking them. After pulling my mitten out of his grasp, I replaced the frozen mice with thawed ones, with Woodsy closely watching. He immediately walked over to the thawed mice, picked up one with his right foot, put it into his mouth, and swallowed it head first. He soon had eaten all of the mice. Then he flew to a branch near the top of a big pine in the back yard and began to hoot. He was still sitting in the tree hooting, when I went out later. Nightwing was perched in a nearby pine tree, hooting an answer each time. I left another warm mouse on the board and went to bed.

Early the next morning, the mouse was gone. Two Great Horned Owls were hooting about three fourths of a mile to the south on our neighbor's land. I didn't think Woodsy and Nightwing would be that far away so believed it was probably the pair who had nested in our neighborhood for several years. They had been hooting every morning for some time before Woodsy's release. I was a bit worried they would try to chase Woodsy and Nightwing away, since older pairs often push youngsters out of their nesting territory.

That night, I was late in putting mice put out on the deck. It was completely dark, so I couldn't see the owls, but I could hear Woodsy's food call coming from trees to the east of our house. I decided to walk down to where he was calling to try to locate him with my flashlight. I started down the path that leads north down the hill to the creek. When

131

Woodsy saw me, he flew down from the pine tree directly to me, veering off just before colliding with me. He landed on a low branch nearby and sat there scolding me with his food call that sounded like the squealing of an old rusty hinge. I put a mouse on one of the tines in a stack of weathered elk antlers piled at the edge of the yard for decoration. As soon as he saw the mouse, Woodsy flew down to the antler pile, picked it up in his foot, and put it into his mouth headfirst. He remained on the antler pile and let me walk up to him to give him two more mice, which he quickly gulped down.

The next morning, two owls were hooting back and forth from the ponderosa pines in the big gully to the north of our house. I recognized the voices of Woodsy and Nightwing. Woodsy's hoot was especially distinctive for the rusty hinge sound he always made before the main hooting sequence. I saw him several times during the day, so took some mice out to the board on the deck earlier than usual, a little after five o'clock. Owls were hooting across the creek to the north of the house, so I called Woodsy's name. He immediately flew to the deck, quickly eating two mice. He kept watching behind and above while he ate, especially whenever the other owls hooted, as if he was afraid. It must have been one or both of the adult pair, as he was not afraid of Nightwing. Woodsy flew back to the thick branches of the pine trees as soon as he ate his mice and didn't return for the additional mice I left on the board just before I went to bed.

For the next five nights, Woodsy didn't come to eat his mice. Both pairs of owls were hooting almost every day at dusk and dawn. I could hear Woodsy and Nightwing in the pines in our big gully and at the same time, two other owls were calling a half-mile to the southeast in our neighbor's trees. I called Woodsy, but he was apparently too busy courting Nightwing to respond. Since he wasn't coming to eat the mice I put out for him each night, it appeared he was learning to catch his own food.

On the evening of February 4, Woodsy was hooting from a tree near the house. When I called his name, he came in a silent glide down to the deck, almost landing on my foot. I handed him a mouse, which he took in his bill before flying up to a branch in a pine tree. A little while later, he flew down to get another mouse from the board on the deck. I walked over to him and picked him up to check his condition. He seemed to be in good weight, with his chest muscles nicely rounded. While I was checking Woodsy, another owl, who sounded like Nightwing, flew to a tree near the back of the house hooting continuously. She seemed quite disturbed by what appeared to be the capture of her mate. After my examination, I set Woodsy on the deck, giving him two more mice. He ate one and took one with him, carrying it in his beak to a tree branch. He ate it while repeatedly making his rusty hinge call. Nightwing continued to hoot not far away. I left mice on the board in case either of them wanted more. Males usually offer mice to their prospective mates during courtship. It is critically important to a female Great Horned Owl that her mate be a good provider.

At dusk the next day, Woodsy was making his rusty hinge food call from the trees by the creek. I said "Hi, Woodsy." Upon hearing his name, he flew toward me, then glided straight up, landing on the roof. I took the mice down to the antler pile where he could see them from his perch. He flew down, eating two and carrying the third with him when he flew off into the dark. The next morning, he was hungrier than usual, flying down to land at my feet as soon as I walked out into the yard. When I reached down with my mitten, he closed his beak on it and wouldn't let go. I picked him up and again checked his condition. He still seemed in good weight. Since he was acting so hungry, I put him in a small room with a deer heart cut into strips. The heart was large enough for him to eat as much as he wanted in one meal. When he had eaten all he could hold, I picked him up on my gloved hand and carried him outside. After a brief look around, he flew up onto a branch in a nearby ponderosa pine to digest his dinner.

In the creek bottom, we had built a hack box, which had a large feeding platform on its flat roof. A hack box is a small room made of wood to house a hawk or owl for several days before releasing them. It had two by six-inch wood posts on each corner to raise it well off the ground away from small mammal predators. After being released, the birds would return to eat food I put on the flat roof of the hack box.

Being full from his large evening meal, Woodsy skipped breakfast the next morning but arrived promptly at dusk for his supper. After landing on the branch of a dead cottonwood across the creek from our house, he gave his squeaky-hinge food call. I had put the leg of an accident-killed deer fawn on the feeding platform, along with one mouse and some strips of the deer's heart. I put a second mouse on the antler pile after showing it to Woodsy and calling his name. He came gliding down, landing directly on the mouse. He spent a couple minutes snapping his bill and talking to me in owl language, a cross between squeaks and hoots.

Eventually, he picked up the mouse and, as always, swallowed it headfirst. I walked over to the feeding platform to show him the mouse and deer leg that were there for him to eat whenever he was hungry again. He watched intently but remained on the antler pile.

I went to the house and watched through the window to see what he would do. He sat and stared at the food on the platform for a while, then flew to it, gulped down the mouse, and ate several pieces of deer heart. After finishing his supper, he flew up the creek. Sometime during the night, either he and Nightwing or the other owl pair ate the rest of the deer heart and a good bit of the deer leg. Woodsy didn't come at dawn for breakfast so he must have gotten enough to eat during the night. That evening at dusk, he was back on the hack box feeding platform, eating the mice, deer heart, and pieces of liver I left for him. I didn't see him the next morning but heard the two owls hooting to each other about half a mile up the creek east of the hack box. That evening, when Woodsy came to eat, I was busy so didn't see him.

On February 9, Woodsy was late for his supper, not arriving until nearly 10:00. By that time, the mice I had put out earlier were frozen solid. I took out some newly thawed mice, handing them to him one at a time. He gulped them down before flying back to join Nightwing. Woodsy or possibly both owls returned before morning and ate some meat from the partially frozen deer leg on the feeding platform. Just before daylight, all four owls were hooting, sounding like they were in the trees along the creek to the east of our house. When I called Woodsy, he came to eat his breakfast. He gulped down three mice and then began nibbling on the deer leg. The next two nights, he came when I called him, eating five mice each night.

On February 12, it began snowing in the evening just before I put Woodsy's mice on the hack box. He didn't come to eat until sometime during the night. By that time, the mice were covered with snow. The next morning, all but one of the mice remained under the snow on the hack box. Woodsy had found only one for his evening meal. Still, he wasn't hungry enough to come when I called him in the evening. Again, he didn't show up until later, after I had gone to bed. Just before I fell asleep, I could hear the two owls hooting behind the house. They were still hooting the next morning in the pines in the large gully north of the house, continuing their serenade until after sunrise.

Early that evening, just before dark, Woodsy and Nightwing began hooting again just west of the feeding platform. Then suddenly they flew

134

to the northeast over the ridge above the creek. The female of the resident adult pair of Great Horned Owls began hooting from west of the hack box, the same area where Woodsy had been a few minutes earlier. Her mate answered her from north of the creek, and both flew together toward the east. I was worried the adults would find Woodsy and Nightwing and possibly attack them. Eventually, Woodsy returned to eat all three of his mice. I was relieved the youngsters had once again evaded the older owls.

For the next two days, owls were hooting from several directions in the creek bottom and to the north up the big gully. Both days, Woodsy came for his mice, appearing unharmed. Then for two days the mice were not eaten. I had to retrieve them from the hack box each morning just before daylight to save them from being eaten by the resident magpies. I feared the older owls might be keeping Woodsy and Nightwing away. I was thrilled to see Woodsy glide down to eat his mice the evening of February 20. For several days after that, he came some nights and skipped others.

On February 27, I went out at 10:45 p.m. to listen for the owls, hoping to determine which were in the area. Woodsy was on the hack box eating mice I had put out earlier. We had a nice conversation, with me talking to him in English and Woodsy doing his rusty-hinge, squeaky hoot vocalization back to me. The next night when I went out to check on the owls, Woodsy was again on the hack box; we had another visit, but he only ate one mouse. He must have finally been learning to catch a few mice and meadow voles for himself. After a few more days, he completely stopped coming to eat the mice on the hack box.

Woodsy and Nightwing began roosting in the pine trees along the driveway about 150 yards to the west of our house. At first, I wasn't sure why. I saw them each morning when I drove my four-wheeler down to the old buildings to feed the birds who were in flight rooms and pens there, and to feed and milk the goats. One morning, I saw Nightwing sitting on a flimsy nest that looked like it was made of a few sticks piled in the thick pine needles at the very top of one of the tallest pine trees beside the driveway. The swaying tip of a pine seemed a precarious place to lay eggs. After searching with my binoculars, I found Woodsy watching me from a high branch in the next pine to the west.

As the main supplier of food for the pair, while Nightwing was sitting on eggs, Woodsy had to take her some of the mice and voles he caught. He also needed to hone his hunting skills for when the eggs hatched, when Woodsy would have to catch enough prey for baby owls, Nightwing, and himself.

135

All during March, I saw the pair each time I went down the road: Nightwing sitting on the treetop nest and Woodsy perched nearby. They didn't seem to mind when people drove by or even if we walked on the road under their nest tree. From his high vantage point, Woodsy followed with his eyes the cars or anything else on the road, but except for a slight turning of his head, he never moved.

Early one morning in mid-April, when Nightwing was off the nest, I finally saw the tops of two downy little heads above the sticks in the treetop. Three days later, during the night, there was a violent storm, with beating rain and wind that broke branches from several trees not far from the house. As soon as it was light enough to see, I rushed down to the owl nest. I was afraid the little owlets might have been blown out and fallen to the ground. I thought the nest must have been destroyed when the strong wind tipped the top of the pine sideways. It was hard to believe but the nest, still containing both little owlets remained tucked in the treetop branches. It was apparently much sturdier than it appeared from below. Nightwing and Woodsy were perched nearby, drying their feathers in the morning sun. Nightwing must have been on the nest holding the owlets firmly in place during the storm. Riding out such a wild wind and rainstorm in the top of a violently swaying pine tree had to be frightening. It scared me just thinking about what could have happened.

Fortunately, there were no more wind storms and, with lots of voles supplied by their parents, the owlets grew fast, eventually outgrowing their nest home. One morning, when I went by the nest pine, both owlets were standing on branches below the nest. For several days after that, with a bit of searching, the two adults and two downy youngsters could be found perched in the thicker middle branches of one the pines bordering the road.

It wasn't long before the owlets were flying from tree to tree each evening, practicing their flying techniques. After I observed some blotched landings, it was clear that landing on branches was a skill requiring quite a bit of practice by fledgling owlets. About a week after fledging, the two owlets were flying quite well and the owl family no longer remained in the area of the nest. They were hard for me to keep track of after that. Nightwing and Woodsy had to hunt a larger area to find enough prey for themselves and the full-grown youngsters. The adults also had the important task of teaching their owlets how to hunt. Just in case they needed extra food, I continued to keep a fresh accident-killed deer leg on the feeding platform, but only the magpies brought their young ones to eat it.

We have seen and heard owls often each year since Woodsy and Nightwing's owlets fledged and I have released several more young ones I raised. After the four owls left the area of the nest tree, we didn't know if it was Woodsy, Nightwing, or one of their offspring we were seeing when we caught brief glimpses of Great Horned Owls. For several years, I tried to always have deer meat on the feeding platform for the resident magpies or any other hungry meat-eating bird who came by. Eventually, the hack box fell apart and we recycled the wood. No owls ever nested in the pine trees along the driveway again, but Great Horned Owls often hoot from the pines along Willoughby Creek and nest in the large pines in the creek bottom.

An owl's eyes are like
a pair of binoculars
in cartilage tubes.

Many of the Great Horned Owls received for care by rehabbers are about this age or slightly younger. From this age until they can fly well is when they are the most likely to get into trouble.

CHAPTER 14
KNOCK, KNOCK, WHO'S THERE?

When Zachary came to me in a box carried by a concerned rancher, he was a downy baby with feathered wings, just old enough to leave the nest and begin branching. A young Great Horned Owl's mottled brown and tan flight feathers grow into beautiful broad wings long before the feathers on their bodies have finished growing. With feathered wings and short-feathered tails on their hefty bodies, young Great Horned Owls can have problems while practicing their take-offs and landings. Zachary had fallen from a branch of the tree straight into serious trouble not long after leaving the nest where he was hatched.

Zachary's dilemma was not actually his fault. His parents had laid their eggs in an old Black-billed Magpie nest woven into the branches of a large cottonwood growing near the middle of a cow pasture. Both eggs hatched and, after several weeks, the fledglings left the nest to explore the many branches of the tree. Just before dawn one morning in May, Zachary was practicing flying from branch to branch when he miscalculated his landing and fluttered clumsily to the ground. The cattle who lived in the pasture had eaten or rubbed all the branches from the lower part of the tree trunk, leaving no ladder for the young owl to use for returning to safety in the tree. Zachary's undeveloped wing muscles were not strong enough to lift his chubby fledgling body to the branches far above his head. As the sun came up, the frightened owlet huddled tight against the tree trunk for protection.

When a small herd of cows came over to rest in the shade and chew their cud, Zachary fluffed up to make himself as large as possible, doing his best to frighten them away. Spreading his wings out wide, he snapped his beak in loud claps at the large, scary monsters who surrounded his tree. Unfortunately for Zachary, his valiant attempts to scare them backfired, causing one cantankerous old cow to become aggressive. She began pawing at him, trying to stomp on him with her front feet.

The other cows were standing in a circle around the tree watching the strange little creature snap his beak and flap his wings while trying to dodge large hooves striking at him. Fortunately for Zachary, the rancher noticed his cows were acting strangely, all looking intently at something at the bottom of the tree trunk. Curious as to what might be the center of their attention, he hurried to the tree to investigate. By then, the vicious cow had succeeded in stomping on both of Zachary's legs. She was about to stomp him into an owlet pancake when the rancher intervened. Gently picking up the injured owl, the rancher hurried back to his house. Sadly, both of Zachary's downy legs were broken by the cow's sharp hoof. In addition, his right leg had the skin separated at the top of the drumstick and all the skin from his leg was hanging down around his ankle like a loose sock.

His rescuer placed him on a clean towel in a box and brought him to me as quickly as possible. Because the wound was so fresh, I was able to clean the exposed flesh of his leg, pull the down-covered skin up over the exposed muscles and tape it in place. I put temporary splints on both broken legs, gave him electrolytes, and fed him several small mice. After dusting him with delousing powder to kill the usual contingent of lice and feather mites, I made him as comfortable as possible by propping him up with soft rags. The rag nest held him upright with his legs hanging straight below him.

Zachary came to me on a Sunday, so I had to wait until the next morning to take him to the veterinarian, Dr. Donald Buelke, who had kindly helped me save wildlife for several years. To our surprise, the skin had already healed to the muscle, so we left it taped in place. Dr. Buelke put round plastic splints on both legs to put a slight traction on the bones, preventing the broken ends from overlapping. Propped up by his rags, Zachary could almost stand on his splinted legs.

Being a young bird has its advantages. Their broken bones heal amazingly fast, usually in a week or less. Because Zachary had two breaks to heal, I left the plastic splints on for 10 days to be sure they were healed, then replaced them with a lightweight Styrofoam splint on the outside of each leg to support some of his weight while he learned to walk again. At first, he was a bit uncoordinated, occasionally almost falling over as he practiced moving his legs forward one at a time. After several days, Zachary walked quite well on his newly healed legs. The torn skin on the right leg had healed completely. Already, pinfeathers were beginning to show in the new skin that had grown over the three-fourths inch gap running around the leg where the skin had not quite come together. In 10 more days, Zachary had recovered complete use of his legs and feet. It would have been impossible to tell he had ever been hurt except that his left leg was a little crooked making his foot toe in slightly. This caused him to walk in a slightly bowlegged cowboy swagger even more pronounced than that of other young owls I had raised.

Zachary could soon walk, perch, and fly as well as any fledgling owlet, so I placed him in a large flight room. He ate his fill of mice each day and practiced flying. Soft brown feathers soon replaced the down on his body and head. After several more weeks, he was covered with beautifully mottled brown and tan feathers, with long ear tufts on each side of his round head. It was time for Zachary to be released.

Young owls remain with their parents for two or three months after leaving the nest, learning from them how and where to hunt. The adults provide their fledglings with food until they become proficient hunters. Young owls I have raised and released returned each night to eat mice I put out for them. They have to learn to hunt by trial and error, so without benefit of their parents' tutelage, my released owls often come for handouts until December or January. By that time, they prefer the fresh, warm mice they catch themselves. Also in January, our resident pair of adults begins attempting to drive all young owls from the area, claiming our land as part of their nesting territory.

While owlets are in the flight room, I call their name as I put their mice on a piece of plywood. After they are released, I place the plywood on the ground or on our back deck, depending upon the individual owl's preference. I call their name at dusk and they fly to the plywood to eat their mice.

Zachary preferred the back deck of our house for his rendezvous site. He was completely tame since I had had to hand feed and handle him while his legs were splinted. He was always ravenous by dusk, so when I called him, he usually came immediately. Snapping and squealing his food-call, he glided through the trees to our deck from his daytime perch in our riparian area.

Willoughby Creek, where Zachary lived, runs from east to west through the middle of our land. The more drought-resistant ponderosa pines grow anywhere there is enough moisture, including riparian areas like this one. Many of the big ponderosa pines were young trees when Lewis and Clark came through the Bitterroot Valley in 1805. Near Willoughby Creek, Black Cottonwoods grow large, providing nesting places and roosts. Several species of owl, including Great Horned Owls and smaller ones like Saw-whet and Western Screech Owls, prefer their day roost and nesting sites in riparian areas where places to hide are plentiful. We have documented all three of those species nesting on our land near the creek.

Each evening when Zachary arrived for his supper, he landed on the deck, swaggered over to me, and hopped onto my right foot. Looking up at me with enormous yellow eyes, he squealed his baby owl food call incessantly until I gave him his mice. He looked like an adult owl, but he certainly didn't sound like one. Zachary usually came when I called, but when he didn't, I left his mice on the plywood and he came to eat when he was ready. This arrangement worked until early October, when the mice began to freeze before Zachary arrived to eat them. After that, Zachary devised a new plan for getting warm mice directly from me. He walked over to the door leading from the deck into our house and sat on the doormat until I brought mice. If I didn't get there soon enough, he knocked on the door with his beak to gain my attention. He learned to show up before 10:30, my bedtime, after going hungry a couple times. He must have figured out I was available to feed him only if the lights were still on.

If Zachary was exceptionally hungry when I went out to feed him, he walked to my right foot, hopped onto my shoe, looked up at me, and squealed his baby food call at the top of his lungs. As soon as I dropped mice on the plywood, he hopped off my shoe and walked over to them. I gave him five or six, which he picked up one at a time with his right foot. Placing the head of the mouse in his mouth, he gulped it down whole, as do most Great Horned Owls. Zachary usually ate all the mice except one, which he carried in his right foot to the pine trees near the creek. He had a favorite branch on a big tree where he usually perched to digest his mice. He always sat on the mouse to keep it warm until he was ready to eat it. When enough of the mice he had previously eaten digested to make room in his stomach, he ate that last one.

Owls do not have crops. Their stomach is made up of two parts, a proventriculus and a ventriculus, or gizzard. There are no digestive glands in the gizzard. The proventriculus begins the digestive processes with acid, enzymes, and mucus. The gizzard filters out the indigestible parts of their prey like bones, fur, feathers, and teeth, which remain in the gizzard for several hours while being squeezed into an oval shaped pellet. The digestible food goes to the small intestine where food molecules are taken up by the cells. The pellet goes from the gizzard back up into the proventriculus where it remains for several more hours. When the owl is ready to eat again, it regurgitates the pellet before hunting for new prey.

I continued to feed Zachary whenever he came for food until late January. The first part of that month he began coming for mice every three or four days rather than each day, indicating he was successful in catching some of his own food. When he wanted me to feed him, he walked to the door after landing on the deck, and knocked with his beak. The last week of January, he came only once for mice; then he stopped coming. I am never sure something hasn't happened to a young owl when it stops showing up for handouts. I always hope they have gone to find a territory they can claim as their own. Young owls sometimes must travel as far as 30 miles to find suitable habitat not guarded by other Great Horned Owls. I had no way of knowing where Zachary had gone. Often, I never see young owls again after they leave our area.

The next year, a little after dark near the end of March, about 13 months after I had last seen Zachary, Bob heard a knock on the door leading out to the deck. He opened the door and looked out, seeing no one there. Then, hearing a raspy sound, Bob looked down and said, "What are you doing here?" Curious, I went to learn who was there and, to my amazement, saw Zachary standing on the doormat. As soon as he saw me, Zachary began squealing his baby owl food call at the top of his lungs, I stepped out and said "Hi Zachary, are you hungry?" He promptly hopped up on my foot and sat there squealing even more urgently.

I picked him off the toe of my shoe and took him into the house so I could examine him thoroughly. I didn't find any injuries, but he was covered from head to tail with lice of several sizes, many of which began searching me for new territory to colonize. I took him back outside and dusted him with delousing powder, then placed him in a large cardboard box while I thawed eight large mice in a pan of warm water.

Except for being somewhat gaunt and covered with lice, there was nothing wrong with Zachary. I set him on the porch and put his mice on the mat by the door. He promptly ate all except the last one, which he picked up in his foot like he always had when he was young. With it dangling in his talons, he flew to his favorite perch in what I called Zachary's pine tree. He sat there with the mouse still gripped in his talons, looking content and obviously happy to be stuffed to capacity. Before going to bed, I went out to look for Zachary. He was still there but had eaten that last mouse. Since the temperature was above freezing, I thawed two more mice and put them on the mat by the door. He didn't come for them right then, but they were gone in the morning.

The next evening, certain Zachary would return, I had six mice thawed and ready for him. He arrived just after dusk and knocked on the door to let me know he was there. Apparently, he was managing to elude the resident owls. They were busy tending their newly hatched young, so the female was at the nest at all times, leaving only the male for Zachary to avoid.

Zachary came for food every night for three weeks, knocking on the door to let me know he had arrived to eat his mice. His weight was back to normal and he looked healthy and fit. He was noticeably heavier when he hopped onto my foot and his food call was no longer incessant when he sat there looking up at me. I had deloused him again to kill any lice that may have hatched from eggs remaining on his skin.

Toward the end of the third week, he ate only four mice each night, leaving two on the mat. I knew he would soon go back to his own territory. At the end of April, he stopped coming and I never saw him again. Many young owls die from accidents or starvation the first year they are on their own. With a bit of help, Zachary had made it through his first critical year. I hoped he would find a mate, father many babies, and live to be 30 years old, the life span of a wise Great Horned Owl. Zachary had shown he was highly intelligent. He exhibited cause and effect reasoning and flew back to where he knew he could get food and help when he needed it. He even remembered to knock on the door to get our immediate attention and the mice he expected to receive.

After catching vole,
an owl swallows it head first;
tail last to go.

144

CHAPTER 15
LILY AND HOOTY OWL

Lily and Hooty Owl were two more hatchling Great Horned Owls I raised and released, who were quite amazing in their behaviors. I received them several years apart but both showed impressive intelligence after they were released.

Lily was released in 2003 after being raised similarly to other Great Horned Owls I received for care while rehabbing wildlife. She was fairly young when she was brought to me because she was found on the ground over two weeks before she was old enough to be out of the nest. There had been a strong windstorm during the night, which either blew the nest down or blew her out of it. She was the only owlet found. After I released her on our back deck, Lily came when she was called to get mice each evening. She continued to come for mice all fall and through January, like other young owls who came in as hatchlings in the years before her.

One unusual aspect of Lily's behavior after her release was that when I called her, she made her loud food call while flying from wherever she was to our back porch. Many of the released young owls food called *after* they arrived where I was waiting with their mice. Lily was the only one who gave a repeated, loud, squealing food call all the time she flew from where she was perched to where I was. She could hear me call her name when quite a long distance away. I could tell from which direction she was coming and determine about how far away she was when I called her because of her loud call.

Lily was usually fairly close when I called her, so I didn't know she was sometimes going off our land. One evening just at dusk, a neighbor who lived up on the top of Sunset Bench about a mile and a half to the north of our place, called to tell me a huge Great Horned Owl was sitting on the roof of their barn, watching her domestic rabbit. People often think Great Horned Owls are much larger than they really are. Since they only weigh from two and a half to a little over three pounds, I don't consider them "huge." I knew the rabbit was quite large, likely much too big for a novice hunter like Lily to kill or carry. I was more worried about Lily than the rabbit. Most of our neighbors have guns and little hesitation when it comes to killing wildlife, even protected bird species. One person told me straight out that it is only illegal if he gets caught.

My neighbor told me I needed to come up to her place immediately and get that owl away from her rabbit. I told her to watch the owl and said I would be off the phone for a couple minutes. Back then we only had a wall phone, so I couldn't take the phone with me. I went out onto the back deck where I fed Lily, and yelled her name three times as loud as I could while facing toward the neighbor's house. Their place can't be seen from our house, so after calling her name, I remained on the porch listening for about a minute. I soon heard Lily's loud, squeaky food call coming toward me. Her calls sounded like they were floating down the hill, coming closer and closer with each call. As it was almost dark, I couldn't see her until she landed on the deck railing.

I went back inside, picked up the phone, and asked the neighbor if she could still see the owl. She said, "No, it suddenly flew away toward the south." I knew Lily was sitting on the deck railing food calling loudly to tell me that she had arrived and wanted her mice. I told the woman the owl was sitting on our deck and held the phone up to the open window so she could hear Lily's squealing call.

My neighbor asked, "How did you do that?!"

"I called the owl's name and she flew home. She comes when she is called much better than most dogs."

My neighbor indicated she didn't believe me, which I thought was quite funny. She could hear Lily talking to me over the phone. At least, since the owl wasn't any longer perched on her barn, she was satisfied her rabbit was safe.

I had taken mice out to thaw just before the neighbor called because it was getting dark; Lily usually came to eat at dusk. By then the Black-billed Magpies had gone to roost, so it was safe for a Great Horned Owl to come out in the open without being mobbed by our dozen or so resident magpies. I told the neighbor I needed to go feed the owl, thanked her for calling, and hung up the phone. I took Lily's mouse dinner out to the board on the deck. Lily immediately landed on the plywood and ate all of them. She then flew back to the porch railing and sat there for about half an hour before flying back to the trees in the creek bottom.

Like the other owls, Lily came for mice each evening until nearly February and then left to find her own territory. Lily never returned in subsequent years to get mice like Zachary and a couple of the other owls had done. One, a female I called Hooty Owl, did return each year during

146

winter for three years in a row, more than any other Great Horned Owl I released while rehabbing.

Hooty Owl was brought to me in 2005. She was found on the ground uninjured after a windstorm but wasn't old enough to perch on a branch. Apparently, the nest was destroyed or at least the people who brought her couldn't see it in the tree under which she was found. Like other owlets I raised, after she was old enough to begin flying, I put her in a flight room to strengthen her wings and practice flight and landing skills, calling her name each time I took mice to her.

When she could fly well enough, I released her in our back yard. She quickly learned to come to me for mice when I called her name. By the time I received Hooty Owl for care, we had several raccoons living in the creek area. They sometimes came up onto the back deck at night, apparently looking for food. I couldn't leave mice on the deck because the raccoons would eat them. I was also afraid an adult raccoon might be able to catch Hooty Owl when she was on the deck. Raccoons like to have birds for dinner, and not as guests.

Bob attached a small wooden platform big enough to hold six or seven mice on top of the T bar pipe holding our three song bird feeders. Hooty Owl soon learned to come to the bird feeders and land on the pipe to eat her mice. She almost always came to the T bar when I called her name. Each night, I waited until about 9:00 to call her and give her mice. She stopped coming in January and I didn't see her again until the following November (2006) when we noticed an owl sitting on the T bar. Figuring it must be Hooty Owl, I quickly thawed some mice in hot water and took them out to her. I provided mice for her every night until she left again in February 2007.

I didn't think I would see Hooty Owl again, since she was two years old and had spent about nine months on her own before coming to mooch for mice during the second winter. I was wrong. The next fall, late November 2007, Bob was looking out the window just as it was beginning to get dark. He told me a Great Horned Owl was sitting on the T bar of the bird feeder so I quickly thawed some mice. The owl remained on the T bar until I went out the door. When I walked toward the bird feeder, she flew off into the nearby trees.

After placing the mice on the T bar, I backed slowly away from the feeder and called "Hooty Owl" twice. Almost immediately the Great Horned Owl flew out of the trees, landed on the T bar, and began eating the mice. I was still standing fairly close to the feeder on which the owl landed, but she wasn't at all concerned about my presence. There was no doubt Hooty Owl had again returned for her winter handouts.

Each night through the end of December, Hooty Owl came to eat the mice I placed on the small platform. This resulted in my coming up with a devious plot to report the first bird for 2008 on the Montana Outdoor Birding website. In 2007, some people who reported the first bird sighting on January 1 became somewhat overly aggressive about getting to report the first bird for 2007 on the website. Some removed other people's reports and added their sighting because they claimed to have seen their first bird before the person who put on the original report. That naturally caused some hard feelings in the birding community. Hooty Owl showing up each night for mice whenever I called her almost guaranteed I could see and report the first bird for January 1, 2008, ending any first bird competition for that year. As long as it does no actual harm, it can be great fun to out-do others at their own game.

On December 31, at three minutes before midnight, I took Hooty Owl's six mice out and put them on the platform on the T bar. I waited a couple minutes and then called her name. She came flying down from the top of the pine trees and landed on the T bar, loudly squealing her food call to let me know she was somewhat peeved about the late service. I said "Hi" to her and watched as she ate her mice. Then I went inside and put one Great Horned Owl on the bird list for 12:00 a.m. on January 1. Obviously, no one else reported seeing a bird on that New Year's Day before I did. In fact, I don't think anyone ever put a bird on the list at 12:00 a.m before or after I did it, with Hooty Owl's help. Being first at anything usually takes teamwork, at least in that case it did.

Hooty Owl came for her mice until the end of February. Then the Great Horned Owls began courting each night. She likely found a male who brought mice to her to convince her to mate with him. The next winter, Hooty Owl again began showing up near the end of November. She only stayed around until the end of January, the last time she came for handouts. Even though I could have, I didn't call her in at midnight on New Year's Eve. I considered it someone else's turn to post the first bird for January 1, 2009.

For a Great Horned Owl to return only in winter and make certain she was observed in order to get mice delivered to her during the coldest part of the year seemed quite intelligent to me. She flew to the T bar and perched in plain sight before dark, so we could see her as soon as she first returned. After that, she came whenever she was hungry or if I called her

148

name. Obviously, she returned to live on our land each November and sat on the T-bar to get our attention because she expected to be fed. That is definitely cause and effect reasoning. Interestingly, for years many important ornithologists, avid birders, Audubon members, college professors, and others had told me birds are not capable of cause and effect reasoning. They must have forgotten to tell the birds, because the birds never failed to prove them wrong.

Intelligence shown
by recognizing an act
brings wanted effect.

TRIBUTE TO AN OAK TREE

The oak had welcomed ninety-three springs.
I know because I counted its rings.

In oak years, that isn't very old.
That's why its story must be told.

To grow so large took many a year.
It withstood storms and sheltered the deer.

A nest in its roots was home to a vole.
A screech owl lived in a flicker's hole.

The flickers had raised a family there.
Acorns from the oak helped fatten bear

And helped keep the wild turkeys alive
Through the frigid winter of '85.

Branches that had begun to sag were
Young squirrels' favorites for playing tag.

A hollow branch made a fine bat house.
The fallen leaves hid the baby grouse

And chipmunks dashing out of their hole
Between the roots beneath the oak's bole.

Such benevolence we don't often see.
So many provided for by just one tree.

But the oak's good deeds weren't considered at all,
When it stood in the way of a shopping mall.

An aspen grove of
clones growing from single root
are stately siblings.

150

CHAPTER 16
OWLS ACTUALLY DO THAT

In a logging operation on the East Side of the Bitterroot Valley in 1992, a logger felled a large old ponderosa pine. He had noticed white owl droppings on the thick clump of dark green mistletoe in one of the nearby Douglas fir trees, so he knew owls lived and roosted in the area. What he had failed to notice was the owl-sized hole in the partially hollow ponderosa pine standing next to the white-streaked fir tree. The fir was a roost tree for the pair of Long-eared Owls (*Asio otus*) who had made their nest in the large hollow in the trunk of the ancient pine. The loss of a rare nest cavity large enough for Long-eared Owls to raise young was extremely unfortunate.

After felling the pine, the logger began cutting off the limbs and found the hole in the trunk. He turned off his saw to check the fairly large cavity. When he heard rustling noises coming from inside the hollow, he found a flashlight in his pickup and looked in. Six big yellow eyes looked back. A fourth owlet, the smallest and unable to stand, was lying face down with one of its siblings perched on its back.

One by one, he gently lifted the four babies from the cavity, placing them on a makeshift nest of old rags in the bottom of a box. After putting the box of owlets in the cab of his pickup to keep them safe, he went back to work. He had several hours of sawing left to do before he could leave.

On his way home, he brought the owlets to me. I didn't immediately recognize the down-covered hatchlings to be Long-eared Owls because they came from a hollow tree, an unusual nesting site for that species. Long-eared Owls usually nest in an old corvid or raptor nest or other stick nests built in protective thick brush such as spiny hawthorn bushes. Despite the unique home site, the size and shape of the downy gray bodies of the three larger owlets, combined with the size of their feet and bright yellow eye color, identified them as Long-eared Owl chicks.

When the man handed me the box, the smallest owlet was lying on the bottom of the box with the other three standing on it. It appeared to have been incapacitated for some time, resulting in a twisted leg and curvature of the spine. Its small body was weak and malformed, with the down partially worn off its back from being used as a perch by the older siblings. It was clear the little one needed special care and, even then, prognosis for survival was not good.

Owls begin to brood their eggs immediately after the first one has been laid, so the last baby to hatch can be several days younger than the first hatchling. Being younger and smaller than their siblings typically makes it difficult for the youngest owlets to compete for food brought by their parents. This often results in death from malnutrition. My smallest new patient wasn't quite dead but was extremely weak. Lack of nutrition had stunted its growth and had also affected the growth of its feathers. The primary feathers on the wing tips were only a quarter-inch long and still completely encased in the sheaths. Its body was mostly bare. The three much larger siblings were covered with thick down, with the primary feathers on the tips of their wings almost fully grown.

I immediately placed the little one in a box by itself, propping it upright with soft rags. I gave all the owlets electrolytes directly into their crop through a tube on a syringe. Because the larger ones could walk, I placed them in a big cardboard box with clean grass hay covering the bottom, giving them room to walk around or lie down in the hay to sleep. They were able to pick up and eat mouse pieces by themselves from a dish full of cut up mice. I continued to tube the little owlet with baby bird food and the electrolyte combination that quickly hydrates dehydrated animals. At first, it was much too weak to swallow solid food, even small pieces of pinky mice.

Because I had a large number of other injured and orphaned animals and birds in my care, I called another rehabilitator, Mary Gossi, and asked if she would take the smallest owlet for round-the-clock intensive care. Mary was a wildlife rehabilitator who specialized in caring for owls. She was especially good with owlets who needed a lot of attention, including physical therapy.

Mary originally named the little owlet Spock after the Vulcan man with long pointed ears on the popular television show called "Star Trek." Because of the owlet's small size, we at first assumed it was a male (female owls arc up to one third larger than males). As it grew to fledgling age, it became obvious by her size in comparison to her siblings that Spock and one of her siblings were females and the other two were males. When they were fully grown, the four owlets looked like two different-sized sets of twins when they were perched in a row. After we learned Spock was a female, Mary began calling her Spocklette.

I kept the other three unnamed owlets to care for at first, instead of giving them to Mary, because they could eat by themselves and only needed mice provided to them. Eating all the chopped-up mice dipped in water they could hold each day, they were soon fully grown.

It was apparent Mary would have to give Spocklette a considerable amount of physical therapy. Her spine was bent sideways to the left just below her shoulders, then bent back toward the right just forward of her stubby tail. Her left leg was twisted under her body, ending in crooked toes that could not grip. At first, Mary had to feed Spocklette with a tube as I had done. As she became stronger, Spocklette was able to pick small pieces of pinky mice off the tips of forceps with her beak, gulping them down as though afraid something would steal them before she could swallow. Mary fed her small pieces of hairless newborn mice (pinkies) dipped in water, day and night, whenever Spocklette squeaked her baby owl food-call.

With Mary's loving care, the owlet not only survived but was soon thriving. At least 10 times a day and each time Mary got up at night to feed the little owlet, she massaged the twisted leg and toes, and carefully straightened the owlet's back, holding it in place while she massaged it. As Spocklette grew, her back straightened and the massages enabled her to regain full motion of her leg and toes. After two weeks, she looked like a completely normal, healthy owlet, able to eat mice by herself, walk, and perch on branches Mary provided for her.

As soon they began trying to fly, I reunited the three older owlets with Spocklette in Mary's owl house. It consisted of a large flight room with bars on the east side to let in the morning sun. There they could exercise their wings and develop the necessary coordination to become hunters. It is important for owlets like Spocklette, raised alone by humans, to be placed with other individuals of their species as soon as they are fledglings. Interacting with her siblings would help Spocklette understand she was an owl. Because she was raised alone and very small when orphaned, she had imprinted somewhat on Mary. Spocklette knew her name and responded when called. She could distinguish Mary from her husband Mike, who never fed her but whom she saw routinely, and both from other people, vocalizing her special food-call to Mary whenever she saw her.

The fledgling owlets were soon interacting as if they had never been separated. The four Spocklettes, as Mary called them, spent a great deal of time playing. They pounced on the pine cones, sticks, and feathers

Two of the Long-eared Owl chicks I kept until they were old enough to be placed in the owl flight room with Spocklette.

Mary gave them for toys, threw them around, or practiced killing them with their talons. They did the same with the extra dead mice left after they were through eating their fill.

Fledgling Long-eared Owls eat four or five wild mice or at least three of the larger meadow voles each day. A pair of adult owls with four or five fledglings to feed are extremely busy parents. They also have to catch several mice or voles for themselves daily, maintaining their health and strength so they can care for their young. Fortunately, many rehabilitators have a source of clean, frozen domestic mice from area scientific laboratory breeding colonies.

Mary taught the young owls to catch live prey by furnishing grasshoppers to chase. The owlets watched the grasshoppers crawl or hop around with the intense stare that characterizes owls. Suddenly, they dropped from their perch onto their prey, often missing at first. When the owlets had become fairly skilled at grasping grasshoppers, a few live-trapped mice were released in the owl house. The owlets quickly learned mice can scurry around, making them much more interesting than dead ones lying motionless on a board.

When the owlets could fly well and were fairly skilled at catching live prey, Mary released them the evening of a night with a full moon. Bright moonlight made it easier for them to see while becoming acquainted with the forest in the area around the owl house. At that time, Mary and Mike lived at the base of the Bitterroot Mountains, where thick-timbered areas of ponderosa pine and deciduous bushes are interspersed with open grassy meadows. The mountainside goes upward to the west of their land into U.S. Forest Service land, perfect habitat for Long-eared Owls to set up territories.

The next night at dusk, Mary stood in front of the owl house and called "Spocklette", "Spocklette." The four young owls came flying to her from the nearby pine trees. Spocklette fluttered around and around Mary's head, making her special call in her baby owl voice. She nearly landed on Mary but opted instead for a nearby pine branch where her siblings were waiting. Mary left their mice on the ground in a large open area at the edge of the yard. All the owlets fluttered down as soon as she returned to the house. In the bright moonlight, Mary was able to watch them pick up and swallow the mice.

This ritual was repeated each night for several weeks while the young owls learned to hunt and catch their own meals. Warm, fresh mice are much preferred by most owls. One by one, Spocklette's siblings ceased to appear for thawed mice when Mary called. Eventually, Mary found all the mice remaining on the ground in the morning. Even Spocklette had stopped coming for handouts. The young owls had hopefully all become proficient hunters, successfully finding their own territories. With luck and skill, they would survive, find a mate the next spring, and raise young of their own.

In late summer 1994, almost two years after the four owls were released, Mary was working in her flower garden at dusk. A Long-eared Owl suddenly appeared and began flying around her head. Mary was astounded to realize it was Spocklette, calling repeatedly with her unmistakable baby owlet food-call. Amazingly, she was still using that same vocalization to communicate with Mary, even though she was a two-year-old adult. After recovering from the surprise of Spocklette's totally unexpected appearance, Mary hurried to the house and thawed several mice. Meanwhile, Spocklette flew into the nearby pine trees. Mary heard food-calls coming from what sounded like several places in the tops of the pine trees into which Spocklette had disappeared, but no owls were visible.

Mary carried the thawed mice to the same spot where she had fed Spocklette and her siblings two years earlier. As she put the mice down, Mary called "Spocklette", "Spocklette." An adult Long-eared Owl came flying toward her, with four young owlets following. The young ones were still showing fluffy down poking out between the new feathers on their bodies, indicating they had recently fledged. Spocklette again flew around Mary, incessantly making her special food-call. As soon as Mary returned to the house, where she could watch the action from the window without disturbing the owls, Spocklette landed and ate several of the mice. Mary immediately began thawing more mice, putting out five or six per owl. Spocklette and her brood were obviously extremely hungry. All the mice were gone by morning.

We surmised something must have happened to Spocklette's mate, since no adult male was with the owl family. Owl researchers insist the male Long-eared Owl, not the female, feeds the young and teaches them to hunt. Owls do what they have to do to survive and that often does not include following the rules scientists make up for them.

As a single mother, it had been impossible for Spocklette to catch enough mice to feed herself and four hungry youngsters. Becoming desperate, she was intelligent enough to return to Mary for help. She knew mice magically appeared when she sounded her special food-call for Mary and especially when she flew around and around Mary while calling. Because she acted in a manner that attracted Mary's attention and communicated her need for food, Spocklette was not disappointed. Mary made mice appear as she always had. Spocklette's actions also positively identified her. Not being able to catch sufficient food to feed herself and her four hungry fledglings, Spocklette decided to take her young ones "home" and ask Mary for help in feeding them, a conscious and intelligent decision showing cause and effect reasoning.

As soon as she had watched Spocklette and her young owlets eat the mice, Mary called me to share her surprise and excitement over the homecoming. Mary was especially happy to see that Spocklette was a mother, saying it was one of the most exciting and rewarding moments of her life. It made all of the work of rehabilitating wildlife seem worth the effort, even dragging herself out of bed several times a night to feed emaciated youngsters, as she had for Spocklette. I definitely agreed.

I had raised several Great Horned Owl youngsters who returned after a year or more of being in their own territory, so I understood Mary's unbounded pleasure at seeing Spocklette again. That she had returned with four fledged owlets was the most amazing part. No other returning owl I had observed had brought young home with them. Mary called Spocklette's owlets her "grand-owlets" and joked about being a proud grandparent. Spocklette and the four young owlets remained in the immediate area of the Gossi's land, eating all the mice left out for them each night. I made special evening trips to see Spocklette and her young, but none came down from their perches in the nearby pine trees when I was in the yard. I could hear them calling to each other but it was too dark to see well-camouflaged Long-eared Owls in the thick pine branches. As soon as I left, they all came soaring down to eat their mice.

After accepting handouts for almost a month, all five owls left and the young ones were not seen again. Spocklette didn't return for help until 1998, six years after her release in 1992 and four years after she brought her first fledglings home. She obviously never forgot where to go if she got into trouble and needed food.

In spring 1998, the U. S. Forest Service conducted a prescribed burn in a steep drainage approximately two miles southwest of the Gossi's home. Because of a temperature inversion, the smoke remained near the ground, becoming so thick that for several days visibility varied from a few feet to less than a football field's length. The light of the sun was so severely blocked that even at mid-day, it was like evening dusk. Worst of all, breathing was severely affected. A Great Horned Owl pair was forced to leave their nest on the Gossi's land. Fortunately, their young owlets were able to fly from tree to tree and hopefully made it to where the smoke wasn't so thick and the parent owls could see to hunt for them. The resident Red-tailed Hawk pair abandoned their nest containing eggs. They completely left the area and didn't return.

Just after noon on the second day of the extremely thick smoke, Mike was inside the house and Mary was in a nearby town. Mike suddenly noticed an adult Long-eared Owl calling from a pine tree by the front door of the house. He went out the front door and saw an owl fly away through the smoke. He ran out and called "Spocklette, Spocklette." He was answered with an adult Long-eared Owl's distress calls, including a yowling, catlike call, a barking call, and another call, which sounded like a rusty gate. The owl flew toward him and landed in a pine tree about 50 feet away.

The Gossi's didn't have any frozen mice at the time so Mike called Mary, who drove the six miles to my place on her way home from town. I gave her a large sack of frozen mice, so they would last for as long as Spocklette needed handouts. Mary thawed several mice in warm water, walked with them in hand to the owl feeding spot in their yard, and called "Spocklette." The owl immediately flew to within 20 feet and landed on Spocklette's favorite branch in her tree in the front yard. She began to food beg, using the baby owl food-call she had always used to get Mary to make mice appear. The owl was definitely Spocklette, but this time she was alone. Mary put the mice down and Spocklette flew around and around Mary's head still making her baby food-call. Then she landed on the mice and began picking them up and swallowing them one by one as fast as she could get them down.

Spocklette didn't stay long. She came to eat the mice Mary put out for the next four nights, eating all of the mice she could hold each evening, then stopped coming. We all hoped Spocklette was not too badly affected by the thick smoke, which caused a lot of people to be hospitalized and seriously affected many kinds of wildlife and domestic animals.

Remembering where to get handouts of mice and knowing her name six years after being released definitely indicates owls possess the capacity for long-term memory. It is not surprising to those who have known owls personally that Spocklette returned to and remembered her old home and her favorite perch. However, returning home to get food from Mary, after the length of time Spocklette had been on her own, was somewhat amazing even to me. I was used to owls returning for food, but none had returned quite that long after being released or had ever returned four years after their previous visit home.

Spocklette also proved, contrary to popular belief and current teaching, that being so-called "imprinted" on her human caretaker didn't adversely affect her ability to thrive in the wild, mate, and raise young. Her close connection to her human caregiver was extremely beneficial to her survival and to the survival of her first four fledglings. It has also been essential in the survival of many of the other owls raised and released by rehabbers. Using imprinting as a reason to not release a rehabilitated young owl is *not* for the benefit of the owl.

Interestingly, I have also had several people tell me in no uncertain terms that owls don't do that, when I told them about Spocklette seeking help six years after being released. That Spocklette used the tactics she did to attract her human caregiver's attention when she needed food was extremely surprising to ornithologists who were told about her behavior. According to reports from rehabilitation centers, many owls have been observed to exhibit similar behavior after being released. Most owls raised by humans quickly learn to come when they are called by name and often return for food after being released. So yes, owls really do that.

Long-eared Owls have a comparatively large vocabulary when communicating with each other. Spocklette did her best to make Mary understand what she was trying to tell her, even as a baby owlet. What was unique about Spocklette's communication was that she used different techniques to gain attention. She came flying right up to Mary when her name was called and flew in close circles around Mary, making her baby owl food calls. When Spocklette returned to seek help, she perched on her favorite branch in her preferred tree. Both times she needed help, she did everything she could to get immediate attention. She even sat in the closest tree to the house and hooted at mid-day, extremely unusual behavior for a Long-eared Owl in normal circumstances.

I have never understood why some people insist owls are stupid. Even people knowledgeable about birds have stated that to me, but they never say why they believe owls lack intelligence. The rehabbers I know find owls to be charming, intelligent, fascinating individuals, each with his or her unique personality. Spocklette may seem more intelligent than most other rehabilitated owls because she learned to effectively communicate with Mary in ways they both could easily understand. Hopefully, Spocklette and her three siblings produced many young. The Long-eared Owl population in Montana appears to be in decline for some reason, according to long-term research by Montana's owl expert, Denver Holt. Therefore, every surviving Long-eared owlet contributes to sustaining a viable population.

Tragically, a year after Spocklette's last visit home, Mike Gossi succumbed to lung cancer and Mary moved to a different area of the Bitterroot Valley. If Spocklette ever ran into trouble again or needed a helping hand, there was no one available who could understand her if she returned for help. Spocklette is still fondly remembered by those who knew her. I personally will always be indebted to her for proving the naysayers incorrect regarding all the things they claimed owls aren't intelligent enough to do. Spocklette proved "owls actually do that!"

Furtive owls can glide
silently through black night. Stealth
was their invention.

A Pygmy Owl (*Glaucidium gnoma*) often hunts during the day because its primary prey is small birds. Its bright yellow eyes are much smaller (similar to a small hawk's eyes) than those of owls who hunt mainly at night. Photo by Eugene Beckes.

CHAPTER 17
PYGMY OWL PARTNERSHIP

It was the sixth day after the first big snow in winter 1996-97. Several more inches had fallen since, covering the ground with 30 inches of fluffy snow. Snow usually falls vertically here in western Montana, so all of the ground was evenly covered. Freezing rain had formed a crust on the snow, making it difficult for birds of prey to catch mice and voles. The rodents could scurry around in their tunnels under the snow in relative safety. Small owls, like the Northern Pygmy Owl, are left mostly dependent for food on songbirds, who are fast and difficult to catch. Without sufficient food, hypothermia takes its toll, often killing overwintering small owls. They have to hunt day and night to find and catch enough food to survive, with many failed attempts using already limited energy.

Northern Pygmy Owls often hunt during the daytime, so I wasn't surprised to see one hunting sparrows at dusk. I first noticed it sitting on a two by four, silhouetted against a light pink cloud. The two by four had been pointing toward the sky on the south end of our old log barn since heavy, wet snow had caused the roof to fall several winters before. The little owl, with its tail also pointing upward, artfully repeated the basic shape of the fallen barn.

A tail-up posture in a pygmy owl is a sign it is seriously hunting, so I stood still and watched. Nothing seemed to be happening. The House Sparrows were already safely in their night roosts under the eaves of the tin-roofed shed. There are likely thousands of those introduced sparrows for every Northern Pygmy Owl in the Bitterroot Valley, so I decided to help the hungry owl catch a much-needed meal. If the sparrows were flushed, I thought the owl might be able to catch one. I walked around to the west side of the shed and pounded on the side of it. A half-dozen sparrows flew out and over the shed right toward where the owl was sitting high up on the two by four.

I peeked around the corner of the shed to see whether my efforts had produced results. All the sparrows were hiding between the extra kennel panels leaning against our big kennel. The pygmy owl was sitting on top of the panels flicking its tail with agitation. Suddenly, it made a dive at the sparrows, but they slipped through the small wire diamonds formed by the chain link fence wires. The owl, being too large to fit through the spaces in the wire, was unable to reach any of them. After the unsuccessful attempt, the owl flew several yards to the south and lit on a branch of a large elm tree, where it could watch the sparrows.

I flushed the sparrows out from the wire to give the owl another chance at catching one. They zipped back over the top of the shed like little brown rockets, straight to their safe havens under the roof. By this time, it was becoming quite dark. If I could get the sparrows to fly out from under the eaves of the shed once more, the owl would have the advantage, since sparrows are not able to see nearly as well in the dark as the owl. I again pounded hard on the side of the shed, much to the consternation of the wild Rock Pigeons living inside. This time, only four sparrows flew out from under the eaves. The rest remained hidden, wisely refusing to leave the safety of their dark hiding place between the metal and the wood on the roof of the shed.

Three of the sparrows flew low into the Russian Olive trees that edge the east side of the road. The fourth flew high like it was going to go over the shed in exactly the same flight path the flock of sparrows used the first time I flushed them. When it was almost over the top of the shed, the sparrow turned suddenly and flew down to where the others were hiding in the thick thorny branches of the olive tree, with the small owl just inches behind it. Again, the owl was unable to grab a sparrow in its talons. Catching supper was proving a difficult task.

Because it was almost dark, the sparrows were becoming visibly anxious to go back to their roosts under the eaves. Slowly, so I wouldn't scare the owl, I walked around to the north of the tree to encourage the sparrows to fly back to the shed. They did, with the owl right on their tails. The owl went under the eaves after a fleeing sparrow, hitting the wooden side of the shed hard enough to make a soft thud. Again, it had missed. It made a mid-flight recovery and flew across the road to a post where it perched and looked back to watch the sparrows trying to squeeze into the space under the eaves. One wasn't quick enough. Making a dark streak against the snowy background, the owl flew from the post to snatch the unlucky sparrow out of the shallow space. They fell together to the snow with the owl on top. The sparrow struggled briefly then lay still. I watched as the hungry owl ate its hard-won meal, tearing off small chunks, swallowing feathers and all.

With its meal finished, the sated owl flew to the top of a birdhouse on the side of the shed, where it could rest and digest its dinner, protected by the overhanging roof from the freezing rain that had again begun to fall. I went to feed and water my livestock in the dark, wishing for owl eyes. It had been a short but successful partnership.

Though they share night and silent flight, little owls and large moths are not friends.

While moth species don't get much attention from people, they are an extremely important food for many species of fish, bird, reptile, amphibian, and even large mammals, especially grizzly bears. Most moth species are extremely important pollinators so are also helpful to people. This handsome moth is an Alfalfa Looper Moth (*Autographa californica*).

A Burrowing Owl (*Athene cunicularia*) like this one is occasionally seen in the Bitterroot Valley. Many used to live here; those who nested in the Flathead area and Canada once used the Bitterroot Valley as a migration route when flying south for the winter. This owl was found unable to fly on top of the continental divide near Lost Trail Pass between Montana and Idaho in fall 1992. It had become emaciated and dehydrated during migration and, after being rehabilitated, was released in better habitat for a Burrowing Owl than the top of a mountain range. Few of these owls have been observed by bird watchers in Ravalli County in recent years. However, a nesting pair was found at their burrow in 2017, the first nesting pair observed here in many years.

CHAPTER 18
A BOX FULL OF SAW-WHETS

Bob was sitting on the porch, enjoying the April 2002 concert of bird songs, when the antics of a red squirrel caught his attention. The squirrel was looking with great curiosity into the hole on the front of an old flicker house Bob had nailed fairly high on the trunk of a dead ponderosa pine tree. After looking in the hole, the squirrel turned and scurried away as if it was frightened of something in the box. Wondering what could have frightened it, Bob picked up his binoculars and focused on the entrance hole. Suddenly the head of an adult Northern Saw-whet Owl (*Aegolius acadicus*) was framed in the irregular-shaped hole. She watched the squirrel retreat, continuing to stare until it disappeared into another group of trees, then looked all around as if to check for more intruders. After a few minutes, her head dropped out of sight as she settled back down on her eggs.

An energetic Northern Flicker had broken the board to the right of the hole Bob had drilled in the front of the standard, flicker-sized bird house, making the hole large enough for a pair of saw-whet owls to use the box for their nest. Bob told me about his exciting discovery, so we both began watching for the owl to again peek out of the hole. One or both of us saw her several times during the next week.

Northern Saw-whet Owls were an enigma to the first ornithologists who came to the North American continent from Europe. The fledgling owls looked so different in feather color from their parents that, when the ornithologists initially observed them, they thought the owls were two different species. Once that was sorted out, the pretty little owls were given the name Northern Saw-whet Owl because the ornithologists thought the food calls of the fledglings sounded like a saw being sharpened and whet means to sharpen. Bob and I were excited we would be able to both see and hear fledgling saw-whet owls if and when the eggs in the nest box hatched and the young grew to be fledglings.

On the morning of April 22, we discovered the top of the birdhouse was missing. During the night, it had been ripped off, as it was lying on the ground several feet from the tree. There had been no windstorm, so we surmised a raccoon had raided the owl's nest for the eggs or hatchlings.

We decided to repair the house quickly in the remote possibility that the owl and her mate had been able to protect their family from whatever had taken the top off the birdhouse. Bob cut a board for a new top and put a screw in each corner. While he was doing this, a Black-billed Magpie flew down to the roofless house and looked in. After a short examination of whatever was inside the house, it flew away. We couldn't tell by the magpie's reaction whether there was anything remaining in the box so Bob started climbing the tree to replace the missing roof. He hadn't gotten very far up when the little owl stuck her head out of the hole, peering down at him as if to say "Now what?" We were extremely happy to see she was still on the nest. Deciding it would be best to wait until just before dark to replace the top of her house, Bob climbed down from the tree. We were concerned the owl would fly out while the roof was being replaced. She would be vulnerable to harassment by the magpie who had looked into the box and its friends who were always around in the daytime.

At dusk, Bob started up the tree with a screwdriver and the new board. When he had climbed almost up to the box, the owl flew out of the top and landed on a branch about 10 feet away. She watched closely as Bob looked in the box. He counted five tiny owlets. Then he put the board in position, quickly tightened the four screws and climbed down to watch what the mother would do. She remained on the branch intensely observing him as he walked back to join me on the deck, where I was watching with binoculars. After looking around for a short time, she looked back at the nest box, flew to the hole and went in. After waiting a little over an hour to be certain she was comfortably settled, we put a large piece of sheet metal entirely around the base of the tree to obstruct any more tree climbing nest raiders.

Occasionally in the days after repairing the roof and putting the metal deterrent on the tree trunk, we saw the female saw-whet peeking out of the hole. Finally, on May 4, Bob told me I should come out on the porch to see the young owlet who was looking out of the lopsided hole. Nearly every afternoon after that observation, we saw one or two little round heads visible for long periods, as curious owlets took turns viewing their surroundings. Near the end of the second week in May, Bob witnessed the coming out of the first of the fledgling saw-whets to leave the nest box. That evening, as many as three owlets looked out of the hole at once. As the light began to fade, the fledglings became visibly excited. Soon, one of the adult saw-whets flew down from the adjacent pine tree to alight on a branch six to eight feet away from the nest box. The owlets continued to bob their heads, while acting quite agitated. Suddenly, one of them came completely out of the box, hung by one foot from the hole for about 15 seconds, then dropped down to a branch four feet below the nest box. The adult flew down to the fledgling owlet, likely to feed it, but it was too dark too see exactly what they were doing.

The next night two more fledglings left the box. The night after that, the fourth one joined its siblings in the branches of the nearby pine trees. One roosted for two days during daylight hours in a small bush at the base of the pine closest to the nest tree. This made it easy to observe and get a close look at its beautiful juvenile plumage of chocolate colored wings and back with bright yellow ocher belly and startlingly white "eyebrows." Large yellow eyes stared at us from beneath the white eyebrows, but the small bird didn't move or seem at all disturbed by our presence.

By the evening of May 14, International Migratory Bird Count Day, when birders attempted to count all the birds in Ravalli County to determine which species are here at that time of year, there were four brown and gold owlets food-calling from nearby pine trees. The fifth owlet was still in the nest box where it had remained by itself for three days. I went out after dark to count as many of the saw-whets as I could see for the official bird count. The littlest owlet was peeking out of the box, its adorable brown head framed by the irregular hole. Even though it could hear its siblings making food calls from a nearby pine tree, it didn't seem quite ready to venture out into the huge scary world beyond its small sanctuary.

It was soon obvious what made the world so scary to the small owlet. The adult owls were hooting frantically while swooping and diving angrily at a half-grown raccoon climbing the pine tree next to the tree with the nest box on it. Earlier, when it was daylight, I had seen at least two of the owlets hiding in the thick needles of that tree so I was quite concerned for them. Fortunately, all of the fledged owlets could fly quite well. One by one they flew to a nearby tree where they resumed telling their distracted parents they wanted to be fed as soon as possible.

I was somewhat indebted to the raccoon, since it attracted the adult owls into the light of my flashlight, so I was able to count both of them. Previously we had seen the male only once. The air show those two adults put on, swooping back and forth past the raccoon's head, was spectacular and their bravery was inspiring. Saw-whet owls are tiny compared to a raccoon, even a young raccoon. It was an amazing owl-watching event

A fledgling Saw-whet Owl shows off its brown back and wings with cream-colored belly and white eyebrows, much different than the feather colors of an adult Saw-whet Owl.

for me and provided a record number of seven Northern Saw-whet Owls for the bird count, two adults and five young. By the next morning, the youngest owlet had flown out of the nest box, joining its siblings in the thick branches of nearby pines. The raccoon had climbed down to go about its business of finding food that was easier to catch than flying owlets.

The rest of May and all of June, the five owlets could be heard after dark, food calling to their parents from various trees. During the day, with a bit of searching, they could often be found in one of their favorite day roosts in our backyard trees and bushes. We could look at them for as long as we wanted, even as close as three feet away, without appearing to bother them. They opened their eyelids a bit, peeked out to see what was there in front of them, and then went back to sleep. There were usually at least two together and often three, perched side by side on the same branch. They unknowingly posed for two professional photographers, who often sold photographs to be used in magazines and calendars.

Eventually, the owlets learned to hunt mice and insects and dispersed to find their own territories, or perhaps they migrated to a warmer area for the winter. If I searched hard enough, I could sometimes find a parent owl in one of their roost trees, but we no longer saw or heard the young ones. The adult pair of Northern Saw-whet Owls began using a larger box on a ponderosa pine across the creek, so we were unable to see them from the porch. No owls ever used the old flicker box again. Occasionally since that summer, I have unexpectedly seen our fledged owlets peering out at me from magazine pages or from cover photos, bringing back pleasant memories of our box full of saw-whets.

An owl's mellow hoot,
like an exclamation point
coming at days end.

A Short-eared Owl (*Osio flammeus*) likes to listen for mice and voles from a post or other perch over its grassy habitat. After hearing a rodent rustling in the grass (as much as 50 to 75 yards away), it takes off and flies silently to where it attempts to catch its prey. Photos by Eugene Beckes.

SECTION FOUR: WILD MAMMAL FRIENDS

**Endearing newborns
melt glacial hearts, causing a
flood of compassion.**

CHAPTER 19
BULLWINKLE

Bullwinkle was a moose (*Alces alces*) calf who came from Gold Creek Road south of Hamilton, Montana. He was reported to have been wandering around alone for several days so Bob brought him home. What happened to his mother was never determined. Either they became separated and mother moose was unable to find him or she was killed.

Fortunately, we had built two large pens in which to keep deer fawns several years before Bullwinkle was found starving. The smaller, 26 by 26 feet, was made of chain link panels. The large pen, 26 by 126 feet built around several trees, was made with five-foot high woven wire with two-inch squares. At first, I kept Bullwinkle in the smaller pen to make certain he would come to me for his bottle. Since he was over a week old, I thought he might be wild at first, but surprisingly, he wasn't frightened at all.

Most people think moose are homely, but I thought Winky, as I usually called him, was extremely cute. He was also extremely hungry. I was milking several goats to provide food for the three white-tailed deer fawns we had that spring, so fortunately I had plenty of goat milk for Winky. I had to find a domestic calf nipple and a large calf bottle, because he could drink a lot at a time. Even when he was small, he could push quite hard with his nose, so I usually had to hold onto the bottle tightly with both hands to prevent his knocking it out of my hands.

I always fed Winky before the little deer. He wasn't at all aggressive toward the fawns, who were much smaller than he was. Winky appeared to appreciate their company, following them around the large pen. He also followed me. He was always gentle and cooperative, behaving somewhat like a large puppy, including wanting to lick my face. He came immediately when called and, except for nose-bunting his bottle (apparently to make the milk flow faster), he was never at all aggressive.

With all the goat milk he could drink several times a day and once during the night, Winky grew fast. He soon weighed over a hundred pounds and the hump on his shoulders formed by the muscles required to support his fairly large head and eventually his heavy antlers was higher than my waist. I took him branches from willow trees and fresh-cut alfalfa from our field, and gave him and the fawns grain every day. At two weeks of age, I always taught fawns and other grazing animals to eat grain for supplemental food. Winky wasn't hard to teach; he liked to eat.

By the end of August, Winky was ready to be weaned. I slowly decreased the amount of milk I gave him but of course, continued to give him all the willow branches and alfalfa he could eat, as well as his supplemental grain. By then the fawns were permanently released. Until mid-August they followed us into the pen at night when they came for their supper. Winky was always happy to see his fawn friends when they came back into the pen and when they no longer came back each night, he missed them.

By mid-September, he was fat and healthy and no longer getting milk. After receiving permission from the refuge manager, we took him to the Lee Metcalf Wildlife Refuge in our Scout, which had a large area behind the front seats, with a screen to separate the two areas. Winky jumped into the back of the vehicle when I went in and called him. We released him near a large pond with a great deal of pondweed growing in it. As soon as we opened the back door of the Scout, Winky jumped down, looked around for a minute or two, and walked directly into the water. He immediately began eating the water plants, even though he hadn't had them before. A moose's large muzzle is designed to act like a valve, with their nostrils closing automatically when they put their head under water. The water pressure tightens the seal of the nostrils so they can keep their head or their muzzle underwater for over a minute while biting off underwater plants. The way Winky gobbled down those water plants, they must have been like moose candy.

The people who worked at the refuge kept us apprised of sightings of Bullwinkle in the pond eating pondweed. After several weeks, he was no longer observed eating in or near the ponds and wasn't seen on the refuge again. He may have gone west across the river and the highway and then up into the Bitterroot Forest. Because he appeared to be doing fine on his own for several weeks, he should have continued to thrive unless he was illegally killed.

In the late 1980s when we raised Bullwinkle, moose populations were doing well and calves were healthy. In the last 20 years, biologists have become concerned about significant declines in moose populations throughout the United States and Canada. They stated the huge drop in numbers indicates something is going on, but since there appear to be multiple factors, they don't know for certain what is causing the declines. Overall warming of year-around temperatures can greatly affect moose survival in multiple ways, so that is one factor being considered. In British Columbia, populations have gone down by 20% to 70% in recent years. In the United States, Minnesota used to have two distinct moose populations but one has nearly disappeared.

Here in Montana, moose on the Rocky Mountain Front are doing fairly well, even though some individuals have a high level of tick infestation. Adult moose in a second population in the Big Hole Valley near Wisdom are dying from high levels of arterial worm infection, causing that population to be in decline. Moose in the Cabinet Mountains in northwestern Montana lose the most calves to predators, but the adults appear to be doing well so the population seems to be remaining stable. According to Montana Department of Fish, Wildlife and Parks data between 2010 and 2013, there was a 52% drop in Montana's total moose population from what it was immediately prior to 2010. Interestingly, they reported a significant drop in elk calf survival in western Montana during the same time period. Elk calf survival is reported by Montana Fish Wildlife and Parks to be much higher since 2014, resulting in burgeoning elk populations and longer hunting seasons.

Other wild grazing animal populations in Montana appeared to increase beginning in 2014, with more of the young surviving. Between 2014 and 2017 the prevalence of underbite on white-tailed deer fawns of both sexes I examined went down by almost half what it had been in previous years, from 72% to 40%. Most importantly, far more female fawns were born and survived to produce their own fawns. Male fawns didn't fare as well. With the sex ratio suddenly highly skewed in favor of females, less than two-fifths of the fawns born from spring 2014 through spring 2017 were male. Having more females born and surviving to produce their own young obviously causes the population to increase. What is responsible for these abrupt changes is unknown at this time.

173

Hopefully the populations of moose, a valued member of our Montana ecosystems, will also begin to increase here and in other parts of the United States and Canada. I have cared for somewhere between six and eight thousand injured and orphaned animals since I began rehabbing wildlife in 1969. Bullwinkle, the moose calf was a unique and interesting youngster from whom I learned a great deal about moose. He also taught me to care deeply about the welfare of moose everywhere.

**Moose are considered
homely except by hunters
who want their antlers.**

Mountain Goats (*Oreamnos americanus*) spend much of their time on steep cliffs and ledges, where they eat grass, shrubs, and other foliage in addition to mosses and lichens. Although called goats, they actually belong to the subfamily *Caprinae* (goat-antelopes) and are the only living species in the genus *Oreamnos*.

CHAPTER 20
RAMSEY

In spring 2002, Montana Department of Fish, Wildlife and Parks brought us an orphaned newborn male bighorn sheep (*Ovis canadensis*) lamb I named Ramsey. He was so cute and precious it was impossible to not fall instantly in love with him. Ramsey was one of only two bighorn sheep lambs I have received for care. The other lamb, a newborn, was nearly dead when it was brought to me and I was unable to save it. Ramsey was a healthy nine pounds but hungry when he arrived. I fed him the usual goat milk formula with a tablespoon of whipping cream in it, along with the two cell salts to stimulate his cells to uptake the minerals they needed for growth.

I put Ramsey in the 26 by 26-foot chain link deer pen, but he didn't like being alone and I hadn't yet received any deer fawns that year. Bighorn sheep are highly social animals and Ramsey greatly missed his mother, running around the pen bleating at the top of his lungs. Fortunately, several goat kids had been born the week before I received him. I put a week old, similar-sized male kid named Marble, black with brown and white spots, in the pen with Ramsey, hoping he would calm down. Marble was mostly Nubian and old enough to be bottle fed. His mother gave enough milk to feed both Ramsey and Marble.

The two quickly bonded, acting like little brothers. They soon learned to come when called and to follow me. I often took them for walks in the field so they could experience the world outside the pen and learn to eat leaves from grasses and other plants as we hiked around.

When nature photographers Erwin and Peggy Bauer came to photograph birds and animals, I took Ramsey up on the ridge where native plants grow. He posed nicely while they took several rolls of 35-millimeter slide photos. I didn't take Marble on that excursion because he would have likely gotten in the way of photographing Ramsey. A goat kid is not really welcome in a wildlife photo. Ramsey kept looking around for his friend. After the photo session was over, he followed me down the hill and back to the pen where his buddy was.

Both Ramsey and Marble were healthy and grew fast, learning to eat grain to supplement their milk. I also provided fresh cut alfalfa from our hay field. When Ramsey was almost a month and a half old, the people at the Montana Department of Fish, Wildlife and Parks wildlife rehab center in Helena decided to take him to their facility. They said they would keep him until it was time to wean him and then release him with a bighorn sheep herd. I suggested they take Marble to keep Ramsey company, because they were such good friends and it was clear to me Ramsey would not be happy by himself. They said the lamb would be fine and

Judy and Ramsey posing for famous wildlife photographer, Erwin Bauer.

they didn't need to take Marble. They probably didn't want to have to buy goat milk for him or have to feed him several times a day. I put Marble back with the other goat kids. Even with his brothers and sisters for company, he wandered around the goat pasture, looking and calling for Ramsey for several days. Eventually he settled down and began playing with the other kids.

Unfortunately, Ramsey didn't fare well. Bighorn sheep are highly social, so keeping a young lamb by itself causes serious stress. I didn't find out what happened to him until several months later. As I feared, he became extremely agitated without his friend, Marble. He tried to climb out of their large, wood-sided enclosure, crying loudly all the time. After only a few days, they released Ramsey into a wild bighorn sheep herd. They said they planned to have someone go find the herd every day and feed him a bottle of milk. Of course, that plan didn't work, as the person wasn't able to find the herd. Also, when they took him from me, Ramsey was used to getting three large bottles of milk a day plus all the alfalfa he wanted and grain twice a day. After many days had gone by, they finally located the herd and Ramsey was still with them. He looked emaciated, but they couldn't get close enough to feed or to catch him.

The next time they went out to check, they found him dead of starvation. I don't really know what they expected to happen. Young grazing animals have to have milk for two months or more to have even a slight chance of surviving without their mother. Ramsey wasn't yet two months old when they released him on his own in a group of strangers, with no food, while he learned what plants to eat in the environment where he was released. The plants there were not the same as the plants here. Also, he still needed the protein and other nutrients milk provides growing mammal young.

When we received Ramsey for care in 2002, most bighorn sheep populations in our state were doing fairly well. Montana is home to about 5000 sheep, which are scattered throughout the state in 45 populations. Licenses to hunt bighorn sheep, especially the rams with massive horns and a good curl, are greatly sought by hunters.

The exact age of rams can be told by counting the segments on their horns. A ram with six horn segments is actually five and one-half years old because a male lamb grows his first horn segment by six months of age, his second by 18 months, and so on. Aging a female sheep using her horn segments can be less accurate.

One interesting population of 200 sheep lives on Wild Horse Island, the largest island in Flathead Lake in northwestern Montana. That population usually does well; sometimes sheep from the island are relocated to augment other herds that have declined. In 2017, the head from a ram that died of natural causes, was found by Montana Department of Fish, Wildlife and Parks biologists. The horns of that ram were measured and received a score of 216-3/8, considerably higher than the previous world record of 209-4/8 held by an Alberta Canada ram. The large horns on Wild Horse Island rams are likely the result of good management of the habitat on the island, providing good nutrition year around for the sheep there.

Current declines in bighorn populations are thought to be primarily caused by infections, especially a specific pneumonia bacterium bighorns acquire by contact with domestic sheep, which are carriers of the bacteria. Another factor for declines in the last 20 years is the high prevalence of birth defects, with underbite being the most concerning. Photos of female sheep who have been captured and fitted with radio collars clearly show many have a significant underbite.

In a 2011 study of facial malformations on big game animals in which I participated, we reported 53% of male bighorn sheep culled by MDFWP biologists in the 2009 pneumonia outbreak had an underbite, based on measurement of the bite on intact skulls. Oddly, one of the biggest mysteries is why researchers who captured and collared bighorns at that time and since have said nothing about the underbite.

Such a high prevalence of underbite seems to be an important factor in the health of bighorn populations. If adult males have a prevalence of underbite over 50%, the newborns likely have a higher prevalence, since birth defects in young vertebrates often cause mortality soon after birth or hatching. In addition, an underbite seriously affects the ability of bighorn lambs to obtain adequate nutrition, resulting in higher winter mortality from starvation. The resultant poor lamb survival would cause declines in bighorn sheep populations in all the states where they live, even without pneumonia.

Also, nearly all the dead newborn grazing animals I have examined had an underdeveloped, damaged thymus, which is the primary immune system organ in a newborn mammal. Without a functioning thymus, newborn lambs are highly susceptible to contagious infections such as the pneumonia bacteria that cause significant die-offs of bighorn populations. Several of the internal birth defects we observed and reported in examined newborns who were found dead often cause mortality soon after birth. All of them had an underbite because of underdeveloped upper facial bones. This birth defect is easily observed and can be photographed to document it. Most perplexing, I have never found underbite mentioned in any of the studies concerning the health of individual bighorn sheep or studies of the bighorn population declines that have been done in the last 15 years by the Montana Department of Fish, Wildlife and Parks or independent bighorn researchers.

In 2017, the Forest Service banned the use of pack goats in specific forests in Wyoming, because the goats might spread pathogens, like the pneumonia bacteria, to the bighorn populations in those areas. That was of interest because both Ramsey and Marble appeared to be healthy and growing well until Ramsey was released without any supplemental food. My goats were never exposed to domestic sheep, so most likely didn't have any of the type of pneumonia bacteria that kills bighorns. Even though he didn't have a long life, Ramsey taught me a great deal about bighorn sheep and things that should and shouldn't be done when raising bighorn lambs.

Bighorn sheep run straight up sheer cliffs that appear to be unclimbable.

An adult American badger (*Taxidea taxis*) is not very large, ranging from 20 to 30 pounds, with males being larger than females. Even a fairly small badger is able to fend off much larger animals like coyotes, wolves, and even bears. They often dig under the carcass of a dead grazing animal and eat on the underside while large carnivores are eating the top of the carcass. That way the badger doesn't have to fight to get its share of the food. Photo by Alan Carey.

CHAPTER 21
VALENTINE, A BADGER WITH HEART

Valentine was an unusual badger right from birth. She had the usual white stripe down her little black muzzle that all American badgers have, but her white stripe ended with a small white heart just above her shiny black nose. Her extra heart was responsible for her name and maybe for her extraordinary good luck, which seemed to play a large part in Valentine's survival.

Like all badger cubs, Valentine and her two siblings were born in an underground chamber called a den, dug by their mother in a grassy pasture near Seeley Lake, Montana. That particular pasture proved to be an unfortunate choice for a den.

All went well for the first week and a half after the three kits were born. The fields were teeming with large field mice called meadow voles and with Columbia ground squirrels, both a favorite food of badgers. The abundance of prey was the reason the mother badger had chosen the pasture for her den. She had easy hunting so she could provide the small, squirming kits with all the milk they could hold. She lavished affection on her babies, licking and nuzzling them, keeping them immaculately clean. In badger families, the mother alone has the job of raising youngsters and teaching them to hunt. After mating with the father of her young, she may never see him again.

Like kittens and many other small mammals, badger kits are born with their eyes closed. Though they are blind for the first three weeks of life, their hearing and sense of smell are both highly developed. Valentine's world, in the pitch-blackness of the den, consisted of the smells, sounds, and feel of the fresh earth, the soft, squirmy bodies of the other babies, and the warm body of her mother. The tiny, blind kits had to find by smell their mother's life-giving nipples, which provided the rich milk that was their sole source of food.

Valentine and her siblings were about a week and a half old when tragedy struck the badger family. The nursery den had been dug in a pasture that was irrigated by flooding. One morning when the mother badger came back from hunting, she found water pouring down the large hole into the den. She didn't have much time. She grasped one of the youngsters by the neck and hurried out of the den. She had dug another one on higher ground not far away. She ran to the second den, dropped her precious cargo into the hole, and hurried back for another. The chamber where the babies were was offset with several tunnels and chambers lower than the nursery chamber. These were fast filling with water, but the mother badger still had time.

She picked up another baby and dashed for the new den. She was nearly there when a bullet struck her, a fatal shot right through the heart. The mother badger died instantly, her baby dropping from her lifeless jaws.

The rancher who was irrigating his land had seen the badger running down into the lower part of the pasture, so he went to his truck to get his rifle. Taking careful aim, he pulled the trigger. Human motives are inexplicable. Thus, his motive for shooting the mother badger is unknown. She was ridding his pasture of grass-eating rodents, so was of great benefit to him.

When the rancher arrived at the body of the dead mother, he found the small sightless baby crying and trying to snuggle into her mother's fur. He could not bring himself to take her life too. He wrapped the baby badger with the tiny white heart on her nose in his coat. Then he took her to the nearest conservation officer who could take her to someone who would raise her.

The little badger, soon to be named Valentine, was the only one of the ill-fated badger family to survive. The baby who remained in the flooding nursery drowned soon after its mother was killed, so was saved a slow death by starvation. The baby who had been moved to the higher den suffered several cold, lonely, terrifying days of thirst and hunger before its life slipped from its tiny body.

Valentine, meanwhile, was accosted by many new sounds and scents, most frightening to a small, sightless badger kit. She crawled around in the cardboard box in which the conservation officer had put her, roaring her disapproval and loneliness in a loud growl that didn't at all match her small size.

She remained with the officer for two days before being brought to us. The man knew Bob, since both worked for Montana Department of Fish, Wildlife and Parks. He and his wife didn't like the sudden loud growls emanating from Valentine whenever she woke up, day or night. I doubt they fed her often enough or the correct formula. Most people give straight milk, which does not provide enough fat for a small mammal. Hence, they are always hungry, causing them to cry.

For me, it was love at first sight. Valentine was one of the most exquisitely beautiful babies I had ever seen. I gave her soft blankets to crawl into, with a ticking clock wrapped in an old, soft sweater for company. After she drank her fill of two parts goats' milk and one part whipping cream, with a drop of Karo syrup added, she curled up next to the sweater-covered clock and went to sleep.

I had always loved and admired badgers from afar, having grown up on the prairie of South Dakota where there were still enough badgers remaining that I saw one occasionally. As a youngster I often became highly distressed by the "shoot-on-sight" attitude most of our neighbors had toward badgers. Anyone who shot a badger or bragged about shooting a badger incurred my perpetual and extreme loathing. As a child, I loved all animals, most especially badgers, almost beyond reason. According to people whom I tried to dissuade from killing badgers, skunks, coyotes, Great Horned Owls, ground squirrels, snakes, and other animals I considered my wild friends, I was a most unreasonable child.

I was totally enthralled with Valentine, all six furry inches of her, from the tip of her little black nose to the end of her stubby tail. I sat beside her box for long periods, watching her even when she was asleep. She was unbelievably cute and cuddly. She greatly enjoyed being held and stroked. She also liked it when I rubbed her fur with a warm, damp cloth to clean it. It probably felt like her mother's warm, licking tongue.

Valentine's new life was mostly uneventful for the first few days with us. She slept until she was hungry. When she woke up, she waddled around her box roaring like a toy lion to inform me she wanted her bottle, and she wanted it *immediately*. After she drank her fill of the milk and cream mixture, she liked to play with my hands in a miniature knock-down, drag-out, baby badger fight. After the rough and tumble, I cuddled and pet her until she became sleepy. This was repeated several times day and night, according to Valentine's desires. If I failed to wake up quickly enough during the night, her lion-like roars became louder and louder, soon awakening me.

When Valentine was about three weeks old, I was asked to give a presentation on wildlife at a local elementary school with the unreleasable birds I kept for educational talks. I took Valentine along so I could feed her when she became hungry. I thought the children would consider her as cute and adorable as I did, so would greatly enjoy seeing her. With her eyes just beginning to open, her little face had become even more expressive and completely irresistible. Her behavior was exemplary at first and she made great progress in dissolving the myth that badgers are horrible, ferocious creatures who attack humans on sight. Considering that her eyes were only partially open and she had only two tiny teeth peeking through her gums, attacking, or even seeing very well, was quite unlikely. She mostly crawled around the floor grunting and sniffing, while looking delightfully cuddly. She seemed to enjoy the petting and attention.

All went well until I took Valentine to the kindergarten room. Of course, the children initially thought she was absolutely wonderful. They all crowded in a tight circle around her, in the middle of the schoolroom. I had just finished telling them how badgers growl ferociously to frighten away anything, including people, who happen to come near the den they dig down into the ground with their sharp claws. As if on cue, Valentine, beginning to feel the pangs of hunger, opened her mouth and produced a loud and most ferocious-sounding roar. She was only about eight inches long and two to three inches tall from the floor to the top of her back, depending on whether she was standing on her short, stubby legs or lying flat on her tummy. By the time she emitted another roar that would have done justice to a full grown African lion, not one child was left in the circle around her.

One second there was a tight group of five-year-old children, with Valentine in the center. The next second, children were everywhere *but* the middle of the room. They were on desks, under desks, under the table, and in the corners of the room, all looking with trepidation toward Valentine, who was still roaring for her bottle in the middle of the room.

After a startled look at Valentine, to assure themselves the lion-like growls were indeed coming from Valentine's tiny throat, all the teachers began laughing so hard they couldn't say anything. Recovering from my surprise at the children's reaction, I quickly placed the small nipple in Valentine's mouth. The sight of the baby badger sucking mightily on her doll-sized bottle brought squeals of delight from the children as they slowly ventured back toward the middle of the room, looking a bit sheepish.

All came out except the little boy who was cowering under the table. It took a good bit of coaxing and assurance that Valentine was all noise and no bite, before he would leave his perceived safe haven and return to the center of the room. When I suggested he hold the bottle for her, he bravely came forward and was soon grinning from ear to ear as he realized how privileged he was to be feeding a baby badger. Hopefully, when that little boy grew up, he also considered it a privilege to share his land with wild animals, rather than killing them just because they are there. I also hope his children will still be able to experience the wonder and delight of meeting a real live badger, and that people killing badgers just because they happen to see one doesn't cause badgers to eventually go extinct. A factor that is seriously affecting badger populations is the extensive use of new rodenticides that are deadly to wildlife. Studies have shown where rodenticides are extensively used, badger populations are less than half that in areas where no rodenticides are used.

While Valentine was small, I took her to all the other educational talks I gave on wildlife for school classes and adult organizations. She wanted her bottle fairly often so I had to take her and feed her on demand. Also, people seemed to thoroughly enjoy meeting a baby badger up close and personal. She was an excellent public relations representative for badgers, displaying both the badger's ability to bluff its way out of threatening situations, as well as their seldom-seen playful and affectionate personality.

People usually only encounter badgers who are in a defensive posture. Because the badger feels threatened when confronted by people, what the person sees is a growling, snarling, fearsome-looking animal who is making short, menacing charges at them. This almost always frightens the person, who usually retaliates by killing the "vicious" badger. Those who are more tolerant of wildlife are richly rewarded if they have the opportunity to observe a badger or a family of badgers from afar. They may be treated to observations of the badger's real nature, playful, inquisitive, and independent. In Yellowstone National Park, people-tolerant badgers go about their business while throngs of tourists watch. They are as popular in Yellowstone as the other wildlife, especially mother badgers with playful young.

Valentine made many friends, aptly demonstrating to everyone she met that badgers are truly unique and fascinating animals. The grownups and children we visited were thrilled to be able to see a baby badger. Valentine occasionally became frightened or hungry and let us know how she felt by roaring her disapproval. People never ceased to be amazed such a loud roar could come out of such a tiny animal.

By the time Valentine was a month old, she had sharp, white baby teeth. I had been supplementing the milk formula with small mice we receive frozen to feed birds of prey and other meat-eating wildlife. As

185

Valentine at one month old, sniffing at a hole beside a rock in our yard, shows off the white heart on her nose.

soon as all her teeth had grown in, she graduated to large mice. Valentine ate five or more large ones a day with such relish that, when watching her, I began to wonder if mice might be a highly underrated delicacy.

When Valentine was about six weeks old, I began introducing her to what was to her the much more exciting outdoors. Her home had been a large cardboard box, well-padded with old blankets, warm and safe but quite boring. In a six by 13-foot kennel, I built a warm den out of logs, complete with a soft bed of clean hay. Valentine liked being outside and spent the day playing, occasionally taking a nap in her den. I went out to play with her as often as I could. She had all the mice and milk she wanted for food. She drank both milk and water by lapping it up like a small puppy. At night, I brought her inside to sleep in her cardboard box, as night temperatures were too cold for her to be outside with no siblings or mother to keep her warm.

Once Valentine became accustomed to her outdoor surroundings, she was allowed out of the kennel to explore in our yard. Keeping up with a young badger is similar to baby-sitting a rambunctious child, only Valentine could run faster and longer. She could get into more kinds of mischief per hour than Dennis the Menace and Calvin combined.

She soon discovered that, besides eating and running around at top speed sniffing everything, digging was her main purpose in life. Most of the ground here contains gravel; digging in it during summer when it is dry is like trying to dig a hole in cement. Places soft enough for a small badger to dig were difficult for Valentine to find. After a bit of searching, she did find some, 15 of them to be exact. When setting out a row of tam junipers along the top edge of the slope that goes down into the creek bottom, we had removed gravel from the holes in which the junipers were planted. We replaced the gravel with soft soil packed around each small juniper bush, making 15 convenient places to practice digging. Doing an excellent imitation of a backhoe, Valentine unearthed nearly every bush, some more than once. We replanted them each time she dug them out. Amazingly, although they spent various periods of time in the hot sun with their roots exposed, all but one survived to become a wildlife haven, most of which remains along the edge of our yard.

Luckily for the tam junipers, Valentine finally tired of digging them up and turned her attention to digging a den for herself beneath the firewood we stacked under the deck. The soil there had been back-filled when our house was built just a couple years prior to Valentine's arrival in our lives. Digging in the soft soil occupied Valentine's attention for several days, giving the junipers a chance to recover. After she started on her den, she spent considerable time every day enlarging the tunnels and digging new ones. If we could have seen what the tunnels looked like under the woodpile, they may have resembled a small version of the Carlsbad Caverns.

When she wasn't digging, eating, or sleeping, Valentine liked to follow us around. She was extremely affectionate and loved attention. She came to us, stood up on her hind legs, and hugged one of our legs with her front paws. She was always begging us to play with her and played by the hour, if we had the time. She considered it a great adventure to follow us back and forth across our hay field when we moved irrigation pipes. With her short legs, she had a difficult time keeping up with us, especially in tall grass. She plowed through the vegetation like a miniature bulldozer, every once in a while standing on her hind legs and stretching as high as she could to keep sight of us. Often, she was sidetracked by finding a fresh burrow dug by a meadow vole, a small mouse-like rodent with a short tail. Sometimes her attention focused on the intense pursuit of a large grasshopper, a great delicacy for her. She soon learned to catch them herself but readily accepted them from either of us as fast as we could catch them for her.

At night, I put Valentine in her kennel for her own protection, as well as to protect our bushes and trees. I let her run free in the daytime when I could keep close tabs on her activities. She spent the hot summer afternoons either digging or sleeping in her den under the woodpile, which was on the north side of the house where it was always shady and much cooler than any other place near the house.

By the third week of July, she was nearly three-fourths grown and had remodeled her den several times since beginning it in June. Bob had also been busy. He had cut a big load of firewood and stacked it with the other firewood already under the deck, being careful not to cover Valentine's entrance hole. The soil under the firewood had apparently not had time to completely settle since being backfilled, with Valentine's digging causing it to be even more unstable. In the late afternoon, two days after the new firewood was stacked under the deck, I suddenly realized I hadn't seen Valentine for several hours. I checked her den. To my dismay, the entrance hole was completely gone. Even more alarming was that the firewood pile had settled several inches into the soft soil. It appeared that Valentine's whole system of tunnels and side-passages had collapsed. There was no sign of Valentine, so I could only assume she was trapped, buried somewhere under hundreds of pounds of firewood and several feet of dry, suffocating soil.

Before I could begin digging her out, the carefully-stacked firewood covering the area over the den had to be removed. I began throwing it out helter-skelter all over the yard, wherever there was room to put it. As soon as the firewood was out of the way, I began to search. Carefully digging a long trench into the soft soil took most of the afternoon. I had to stop occasionally to feed the other mammals and birds I was caring for at the time. When Bob arrived home from work, I told him the bad news and we both dug until it was time to move irrigation lines. After that was done and the other mammals and birds were fed again, we resumed digging. As fast as we dug it out, the soft, crumbly soil caved back into the trench. We were able to alleviate the caving somewhat by widening the trench. We also had to dig carefully, so we didn't hit Valentine with the sharp spades and injure her.

Valentine had dug a veritable maze of tunnels and side passages. We carefully followed these tunnel traces, hoping one would lead us to her. After so much time, I was sure we would find her dead from lack of air. I didn't see how even a bug, much less a half-grown badger, could get enough air to survive under all that soft dirt. Using flashlights, we dug until long after dark, to no avail. We found several of her caches, where she had stored dead mice left over from her dinners, but we could find no sign of Valentine, dead or alive.

We finally gave up for the night and, after a much-needed shower, crawled into bed. We were both exhausted but were up and digging again before it was even light. The trench-like hole we had dug was about 12 feet long, five feet wide, and between three and four feet deep. We made it even wider and deeper, moving carefully into new areas. The network of tunnels Valentine had created in less than a month was absolutely astounding.

We dug until a couple hours after daylight, when we had to take time out to feed the fawns and recovering injured birds in our care and move irrigation lines. There were over 50 40-foot irrigation pipes to move, so that took nearly an hour. Bob resumed digging while I fed the young birds again. I returned to help dig, as Bob had still not found any sign of Valentine. Soon it was time for the fawns' mid- morning feeding and to feed the young birds again. It was also lunchtime for us. After lunch we resumed digging, continuing all afternoon, with occasional breaks to again feed the young birds and fawns. Valentine had been missing and presumably trapped somewhere in her network of tunnels for between 25 and 30 hours. By then, I had almost no hope of finding her alive, but neither of us was ready to give up. The trench was much wider and especially deeper than we thought she would have been able to dig. We were completely mystified as to why we hadn't found her.

Way too soon, it was time to give all the animals their evening feeding. Then we had just enough time to move irrigation lines before dark. When we finally finished that chore, it was almost dark. I went back to the irrigation heads to turn the water into the pipes, arriving just as it was becoming too dark to see well. Soon after I turned on the water, the water pressure blew two of the pipes apart. I had apparently failed to fasten them properly. I had to turn off the water, walk to the end of the line, and refasten them. By the time I was finished it was quite dark. I walked back to the house, planning to go dig for a little longer using the flashlight.

By the time I reached our front yard, it was too dark to see where I was stepping. Suddenly something grabbed me around my right leg, tripping me and causing my foot to bump a soft little body. Simultaneously, I heard a familiar badger growl. I managed to keep from falling, looked down and saw Valentine's black and white face peering up at me as if to say, "Why did you kick me?"

I let out a whoop of happiness that was surely heard by all the neighbors. It startled poor Valentine and brought Bob on the run. Valentine began dashing back and forth between us, alternately whining and growling to tell us she was as happy to see us as we were to see her. Bob quickly brought her a bowl of water and while she was quenching her thirst, I thawed a handful of mice, her favorite food. She ate them all and asked for more. I put several more in warm water to thaw while I examined her to see if she had been hurt. Except for having fresh dirt on the top of her muzzle and some in her eyes, I could find no damage. I cleaned her eyes with a damp cloth and gave her the rest of the mice.

We sat beside her while she ate. When she was finished, she let us know how happy she was to see us by snuggling up to us and rolling over on her back so we could give her tummy a good scratching. After the reunion celebration, I made her comfortable in her kennel, with more food and plenty of water. I locked her in so she couldn't get into any more trouble during the night. Since she no longer had a den to retreat to, I was afraid the neighborhood dogs who often traveled through our land at night might attack her.

We had to wait until the next morning when it was daylight to see where Valentine had been trapped for all that time. We had come within about two inches of her nose when we stopped digging to move the irrigation lines. She had been in a tunnel off to the side near the bottom of the trench, which was over four feet deep. Her tunnel must have been long enough to contain adequate oxygen to sustain her all the time she was buried. After we left, she was able to dig herself out of her tunnel, into the trench. Then she had somehow managed to climb out of the steep-sided trench, coming around the house into the front yard just in time to meet me.

For the rest of the summer, I spent as much time as I could spare walking with Valentine in the field and the creek bottom. I helped her learn to find and catch live voles. She already knew how to catch grasshoppers, but badgers can't live on grasshoppers alone. Bob and I encouraged her to dig a new den in the bank down by the creek. We had back-filled the trench and restacked the firewood under the deck, but Valentine wisely never showed any interest in digging there again.

By mid-August, Valentine was nearly full grown. When we had company from out of state, I was so busy I didn't have much time to spend with her. Fortunately, she spent most of the time during the hot August days sleeping or digging in her new den. When it was cool enough and during the night, she explored the creek bottom and the sagebrush-covered hillsides, digging here and there whenever an interesting odor prompted her. She was becoming quite independent, and sometimes didn't respond when I called her.

One evening in late August, Valentine seemed especially restless and agitated. The next morning, she was nowhere to be found. I followed her tracks up the creek to the east for nearly half a mile. Beyond that I couldn't find her tracks or any other evidence of her, not even the small holes she often dug in the dirt looking for juicy insects to eat. She must have been traveling fairly fast, with no stops to look for food or inspect scents she detected. It is typical for young badgers to leave their mother's territory to find an area they can claim as their own. Or she may have just gone in search of others of her kind. Badgers were common at that time in the sagebrush drylands east of us. All I could do was hope she eventually found a safe territory in which to live and male badgers with whom to mate, so she could raise new families of pretty little badgers with white hearts on their noses.

Growling and bluff, a badger's main defense against other animals.

Tawny liked climbing on our brush piles.

A cougar kitten
plays, runs, bounces, tumbles, slides,
a spring wound too tight.

CHAPTER 22
HUGGING COUGARS

We have had several cougars (*Puma concolor*) to care for since we began rehabilitating wildlife. The first was a very young female cub we received in late winter 1980, soon after moving to our new home in the Bitterroot Valley. She was retrieved from the den where she was born after lion hunters killed her mother. Her eyes had just opened, so we speculated she was between three weeks and a month old. I named her Tawny.

Soon after Tawny arrived, we informed the person who worked at the Montana Department of Fish, Wildlife and Parks rehabilitation center in Helena that we had a female cougar cub. He was responsible for finding a home for young cougars who were orphaned or for some other reason had been separated from their mother. Young cougars have to remain with their mother for two years to learn from her how to survive, stalk prey, and kill large animals like deer and elk. If they get separated from their mother before they have learned those skills, they will die of starvation. It is nearly impossible to return an orphaned cougar cub to the wild, because they can't learn necessary survival skills without their mother to teach them. We were told Tawny would be sent to the Olympic Wild Game Park at Sequim, Washington. The head of the park claimed they trained young cougars to work in motion pictures.

When Tawny first arrived, she was quite small and still uncoordinated, with her eyes newly opened. At each feeding I gave her two ounces of goat milk with a tablespoon of Gerber's chicken baby food and two teaspoons of whipping cream added. She did well on that and was soon the size of a medium-sized house cat. At first, I kept her on blankets in a large cardboard box, but she quickly outgrew the box, needing more room to explore. We were in the process of building our house at the time, so I put soft blankets in the fireplace in what would eventually become our living room. Hoping Tawny would learn to use a litter box, I placed a box of kitty litter in the middle of the room. By that time, Tawny was eating pinky mice by herself as well as her bottles of formula. Her food dish and a shallow dish of water were near the fireplace, so she could drink or snack whenever she wanted.

We had finished the basement first, so we could live in those rooms while we added insulation and interior walls, and did the varnishing, painting, carpeting, and all the other jobs necessary for finishing the main floor. The fireplace had never been used, so was like a clean little cave. The walls of the entire main floor were still to be finished on the inside. The outer walls were tongue-in-groove logs and all of the windows and outside doors had been installed, so there was no way Tawny could leave the upstairs area. When left alone, Tawny slept in her cave-like fireplace, played with her toys, or sat in the sun on the ledge of the south-facing living room picture window. I put a raised bed made of a board across blocks of wood with blankets on it in front of the window. Tawny could either sit or sleep on the bed or jump onto the window ledge. After she was sent to Oregon, I stained the ledge and varnished it without sanding out the scratches she had made in the soft wood. I wanted to be able to see Tawny's signature for as long as I lived in our house. That has been 38 years and counting. Her scratches are still there.

Being nocturnal, Tawny played most of the night with her toys: balls; feathers; old socks stuffed with paper; and such things as bones and small pieces of hide. From all the thumping on the floor while I was trying to sleep, she was enjoying herself. I got up an hour early each morning to go upstairs and play with her. She had a great time chasing the balls I rolled for her or chasing me. If I crouched down and stared at her, she charged and pounced on me, then tried to dash away before I could catch her.

After it warmed up outside, I put on her collar and leash so we could go for a walk. I was actually not taking her for a walk; it was more like Tawny took me. She looked around, decided on a direction, and off we went, Tawny leading the way with her short but determined stride. I think maybe she thought we were escaping back to the mountains. She most often headed for the riparian area along the creek, usually wanting to go past the creek to explore deer smells on the steep, dryland hillside north of the creek. She coursed back and forth through the sagebrush and bluebunch wheat grass, eventually topping out on the ridge above the valley where our house is located. I liked to watch the antics of the birds in the morning, learning more about each kind of bird. Tawny and I sat together on top of the ridge, looking down on the riparian area where birds were zipping around catching insects and building nests. Being a cat, it is likely Tawny had her own motives for bird watching.

One of my top three wishes as a child had been to sit high on a mountainside with my arm around a mountain lion. The other two were to pet a whale and to hug a baby gorilla or chimpanzee. All were wishes I believed I had no chance of ever fulfilling, but I had already been able to pet an orca. The poor whale was in a small pool at a carnival and it seemed to enjoy being softly stroked. I have never had the pleasure of hugging a chimp or a gorilla. It is much better for them to be living free, rather than caged somewhere just so I might hug them. I have had my arms around several cougars, although some of them didn't consider my embrace to be particularly affectionate. Apparently Tawny did, as she always purred contentedly.

The bench top where Tawny and I sat each morning wasn't exactly a mountainside. And as cougars go, Tawny was more similar to a large house cat than to a mountain lion. Each morning as I sat on the ridge with my arm around that beautiful, softly purring cougar cub and looked down on mere mortals in the valley below, I felt an exhilaration I hadn't previously experienced. The closest memory of feeling that way was when, as a child, I rode my thoroughbred mare Flicka bareback at top speed across the South Dakota prairie. But even that experience wasn't quite the same, although much more dangerous.

For several weeks, Tawny played in the living room, slept in the fireplace, and kept me awake at night with her antics over my head. Too soon, the MDFWP said they were coming to take her to Helena. That last morning with Tawny, I got up at two o'clock to spend a few extra hours with her. I wanted some alone time with my friend before she left. I usually woke up at four o'clock to play with her, after which I fed all the young animals and birds. If I had gotten up at the usual time, by the time the feeding was done, it would have been time for Tawny's departure. Tawny and I thoroughly enjoyed our time together from two to five that last morning she was with us. At night, she had been like a windup toy that never ran down, beginning when she was old enough to walk well. By four o'clock, after two hours of intensive play, she was beginning to get a bit tired and I was really tired. By mutual consent we spent the last hour cuddling. I scratched her and brushed her soft tawny coat. She purred and licked me.

From Helena, Tawny was sent, along with three other cougar cubs in their care, to the game park in Sequim, Washington. What we weren't told by Fish, Wildlife and Parks personnel in Helena was they often gave the park several cougar cubs each year because the owner said he wanted them. I didn't find out until Tawny had been gone for three months that the park was selling cougar cubs to anyone who would pay $2000 for a backyard pet. They were likely being kept in small cages until they became too dangerous for the owners to handle. The park was not keeping any of them or training them to appear in films.

When cougars were full-grown and became dangerous or hard to manage, they were at that time often sold to game ranches. These provided canned hunts to people who paid a high price for the privilege of shooting a tame cougar. The adult cougar is placed in a large pen where the "hunter" can easily shoot it. In my opinion, this is unadulterated murder, since there is no hunting involved, just pulling the trigger. Those so-called mighty hunters then get to take home their trophy and hang it on a wall. How someone can claim bragging rights to killing a tame animal in a pen is a mystery to anyone with a heart. Looking at it from a cougar's point of view, being shot is likely a better option than spending its life in a tiny cage in someone's backyard, often without proper food and care.

A good friend of ours went to the Olympic Wild Game Park on his vacation about two months after Tawny was sent there. When he didn't see any young cougars in any of the cages, he asked one of the park personnel where they were keeping the little female cub from Montana. The person replied they didn't have any cougar cubs. Apparently, they had already sold all four of the cubs who were sent there from Montana that year. At $2000 apiece, the Olympic Game Park received $8000 with very little expense. I was never able to find out what exactly happened to Tawny after she was sent to Sequim. I wrote several letters to the owner of the Olympic Game Park, but he never answered any of them.

I sent the "Cougar cubs for sale" advertisement placed in a Los Angeles paper by the Olympic Wild Game Park to Montana Fish, Wildlife and Parks rehabilitation center personnel. I also told them my friend had found no cougar cubs at the game park when he stopped there to see Tawny. They agreed never to send any more cougar cubs to the Olympic Wild Game Park, but that didn't help poor Tawny.

We received another young orphan cougar cub several years later. Spirit was a tiny female who was supposedly abandoned by her mother when the mother was chased by hounds. Her eyes were still closed when Bob brought her home, indicating she was less than three weeks old. She was found in a den in a brush pile by the hunters' dogs. They called Bob because he was the game warden, told him what had happened, and asked him to come and get the cougar cub, which they had removed from the den. Unless they had killed the mother cougar, it is likely she would have returned to care for her cub if they hadn't touched it.

I fed Spirit the same milk, cream, and chicken baby food formula I had fed Tawny. As soon as her teeth were grown in enough so she could chew soft meat and swallow it, I also fed her pinky mice, as I had done with Tawny. Spirit grew rapidly and was healthy and robust. That this was in any way unusual never occurred to me.

Spirit was gentle and playful, just as Tawny had been – except when Bob or I crouched down, especially behind the stuffed chair in the living room. Spirit could not refrain from going into a full cub charge and pounce if either of us crouched behind that chair and peeked out at her. She came at a full run from wherever she was in the room, jumped onto the seat of the chair, then to the back of the chair, and down onto our back, if we didn't move. I usually just reached up and caught her in mid-air or simply stood up, so she slid to a stop on the chair. She also liked to play fetch with a stocking stuffed with rags.

Spirit was shipped to the Apple Valley Zoo in Minnesota when she was eight weeks old. She was first taken to the rehabilitation center in Helena, then put on an airplane to Minnesota. On the day Spirit was transported to Helena, I got up early in the morning and spent several hours of quality time with her, as I had with Tawny. I didn't feel bad about Spirit going to the zoo, because I knew they would give her a good home. They had a large enclosure for their cougars and took excellent care of their animals. Missing her was simply the price I had to pay for the privilege of caring for her.

The caregivers at the Apple Valley Zoo were amazed that Spirit was healthier and larger than other cougar cubs the same age who had been raised on formula by humans. Most zoos regularly weigh and measure young animals who are born to their zoo animals. I had weighed Spirit every week because I was curious to know how much weight a cougar cub would gain in a week. I sent Spirit's weekly weight chart to the zoo in case it might be helpful to the keepers.

One of the zoo's head keepers called me soon after Spirit arrived. He wanted to know what I had fed her to cause her to grow, as he stated, "at rates previously seen only in cubs fed natural cougar milk by their own mothers." I gave him my formula, telling him it worked well for all baby carnivores we have in Montana. This applies at least for all those I have raised, including foxes, coyotes, bobcats, and young of the weasel family, like badgers, long-tailed weasels, mink, and skunks.

An important item in the formula is the plain whipping cream. Neither goat milk nor cow milk are nearly as rich as most other mammal milk.

197

The secret of my formula is to use real milk from goats, not powered milk replacer, and making it rich with the extra cream, more like the youngsters' mother's milk. I also add meat in the form of strained chicken baby food to the formula for carnivores, and then offer thawed pinky mice (newborns that are easily digested because they don't yet have hair) as soon as the young carnivore is able to chew. Many people mistakenly use powered milk, two percent milk, or even add water to cow milk to make it less rich when they feed baby mammals.

Milk should never be diluted for any baby mammal. According to my veterinarian friends, diluting milk with water causes a toxin to grow in the baby's stomach that can be fatal. Even if it does not prove fatal, it usually gives them a severe case of diarrhea, which is certainly unhealthy for them. If a young mammal, including domestic cubs or puppies, must be bottle fed, cream (*never* water) should be added to goat milk (or cow milk if goat milk is not available). If a powdered milk formula must be used for carnivores, it helps to add a small amount of whipping cream and, as soon as their eyes begin to open, the chicken baby food. When their teeth have erupted, they can begin eating pinky mice. Chicken and pinky mice are especially important for providing the protein needed by fast growing young carnivores.

With small mammal babies, such as rodents or rabbits, the ratio of whipping cream to milk needs to be increased. The formula for those young ones is three parts goat milk to one part cream. This works well for all types of wild or domestic rodents, rabbits, and hares.

In subsequent years, we have also received several older cougar cubs for care. One six-month-old male who came to us in summer 1993 had a large cataract in his right eye. No zoo would take a flawed animal, so Fish, Wildlife and Parks euthanized him. Since he was extremely shy and didn't like being confined, that outcome was likely best for him.

I tried to take good care of the older cubs, giving them all the deer meat they could eat, goat milk, and occasionally some mice, in addition to toys such as wings from Rock Pigeons who died, rag balls, or other objects with which to play. Caring for older cubs didn't give me any opportunity to hug them. They didn't like a human invading their space.

The last cougar cubs we received who were still nursing when orphaned were a pair of siblings, a female, Kitty, and a male, Tommy. Obviously, I wasn't particularly creative at thinking up cougar names that year. In late winter 1994, a couple from Darby, Montana, brought the cubs to us. While snowmobiling, the man and his sons found them wandering around outside the den. They were emaciated, suggesting something had prevented their mother from returning to care for them. They were about a month old, with their eyes open but were quite docile because they were so weak and hungry.

As soon as the cubs had recovered and regained their proper weight, I began taking them to schools with me when I gave talks on wildlife with my unreleasable birds. The school children and their teachers were thrilled to see cougar cubs. Tommy was quite shy, much more so than Kitty, and was a bit aggressive if he was frightened. I put both of them in my large travel kennel so they could keep each other company but only took Kitty out to walk around the schoolroom on a leash. She was smaller than a house cat at the time. They both were very cute, as cubs are with their stubby noses and short legs. Their little cougar tails, fairly short and pointed at birth, were already quite long and round to the end.

The Helena Wildlife Rehabilitation Center had trouble finding a good zoo that needed cougars. It was twice as hard with two cubs to place. By the time school was out in June, the cubs had grown a great deal. We put them in a large pen made of a six-foot high chain link fence. The pen didn't have a top on it, but they were unable to climb the fence, so could not escape. There was a large doghouse in the pen with soft hay in it where they slept during the day. I provided goat milk in a pan, which they drank without a bottle by then, and a pan of deer meat I cut into small pieces. I also gave them several thawed mice each day. At night, the two cubs usually chased each other, played rough and tumble wrestling games, or played with their deer hide, deer bone, and rag ball toys, in between chewing on deer legs or playing with their mice before eating them.

By summer, the cubs were consuming large amounts of road-killed deer quarters, deer hearts or livers, and a few thawed mice for treats. Time passed and the young cougars had grown quite large. By late summer, I began giving them the entire opened carcass of any vehicle-killed deer fawns Bob picked up. Fall and winter passed and, with all the food they could eat, they were over half as big as they would be when fully grown. They were slightly over a year old and still no zoo had been found. We were allowed to keep the two cougars here because the Helen Rehabilitation Center was closed in winter. The cubs had grown enough by early spring that I was beginning to be concerned about them jumping over the fence. Cougars can jump long distances and quite high. Tommy, being a male, was noticeably larger than Kitty, so I was most concerned about him jumping the fence.

One morning in mid-April 1995, I went out to feed them and found no cougars in the pen. Both had jumped out. I chastised myself for not paying attention to my concerns. Since cougar cubs have to learn to hunt by watching their mother and practicing, I hoped they would come back when they became hungry. I left the pen door open so they could go in to eat the dead deer I provided. At that time, the riparian area along the creek was like a dense jungle, so the cougars were easily able to keep out of sight. I attempted to search the entire area but couldn't find them. I finally gave up looking and waited for them to come back on their own. Several days passed, then a week. No cougars appeared and they didn't go into the pen to eat the fresh deer Bob had brought home. I did hear thumping on the back deck a couple times, but when I hurriedly opened the door, nothing was there.

On the tenth day of the great escape, I was in the garden transplanting broccoli plants about half an hour before the sun was going to disappear behind the Bitterroot Mountains. As I was taking a small broccoli plant to a hole I had made for it in the broccoli row, I heard an odd noise. It was a ffiitttsssszz, fffiittsssszz sound, somewhat like a sprinkler going on and off, but no sprinklers were on at the time. I looked around for approximately 30 seconds, trying to find the source of the strange sound. I couldn't see anything, so I started to lean over to put the broccoli plant into the hole and nearly hit Kitty on the top of the head with my hand. She had silently walked up and sat down about six inches from my leg without my knowing it. Then I finally found the source of the strange sound. Tommy was nearby at the edge of the garden, hiding under the Nanking cherry bushes, making the hissing noise.

Seeing Kitty sitting beside me when there had been only me in the garden a minute before, gave me a start for just an instant, kind of like when someone sneaks up behind you and says boo. Then I briefly wondered how long two very hungry half-grown cougars had been watching me plant broccoli. Both Spirit and Tawny, as small cubs, went into attack mode and pounced on me if I leaned over when they were watching me. I had been leaning over to scoop up small plants, dig holes, and put plants in the holes for about a half hour. I didn't lean over again. I simply said, "Hi Kitty, it's about time you two came home." Kitty made her hungry cub sound, a cross between a squeak and a meow. Tommy was still sitting under the berry bush emitting his spitting sprinkler sound.

I walked slowly to the house where I knew Bob had a dead deer carcass in the bed of his pickup. When you are around cougars, especially

200

very hungry ones, running or even moving fast in any way is not at all advisable. Kitty followed right behind me. Tommy soon came out from under his berry bush and brought up the rear.

They were clearly hungry but not thin, having apparently eaten something during their 10 days in the wild. That they still considered me their mom was quite obvious, especially since they had walked up to me and asked for food rather than having me for lunch. It was likely they had not eaten for several days, since they expected me to provide something for them to eat, like a good mother cougar would.

First, I went to the door of the house and told Bob the cubs were back. He brought our largest dog kennel out of the basement and set it in the back yard, while I cut a hindquarter from the deer carcass. We tied the deer leg at the back of the kennel, putting a string on the door so we could pull it shut if either Kitty or Tommy went in to eat. We placed the kennel where we could watch it and pull the door closed when one of the cubs went in. That should have been a good plan. Each of the cubs went in far enough so their heads and shoulders were out of sight. Unfortunately, both their bodies were long enough so they could reach the meat without getting their back legs and rumps into the kennel far enough for us to close the door. After a couple of tries, in which the cub with its head in the kennel simply backed out when we tried to pull the door shut, it became apparent that plan A was not going to work. We quickly concluded we needed to devise a plan B.

After a brief discussion, we decided to try to bait the two cubs into the garage, where we could confine them. The plan was to catch them one at a time with our strongest long-handled capture net and manually put each of them into a transport kennel. We could put the kennels in the pickup to move the cubs the quarter mile to the barn area where our largest covered chain link pen was. It was built on cement so nothing could dig out and, being covered, the cubs couldn't jump out. But first, we had to catch them and that, as it turned out, would not be easy.

Bob drove down to the barn with the pickup to leave the rest of the dead deer carcass in the large covered 26 by 13-foot chain link pen, where we hoped to put the cougars. When he came back, he brought the bear transport box for one of the cubs, since we only had one large dog kennel for the other. That was the plan, but as the saying goes, the best laid plans often go awry.

After moving our van outside, we closed the large garage door. Then we tied the deer leg just inside the human-sized door that opened directly

201

into the garage from the back deck. We didn't want the cougars to pick up the deer leg and run out the door with it. After tying a lightweight nylon rope to the door handle to pull the garage door shut, we waited. The rope went into the house through our bedroom window, which looked out onto the back deck. We could see when a cougar came up onto the deck and into the garage to feed on the deer leg. If one did, we could easily and quickly pull the door closed.

Both cubs were sitting in the back yard trying to figure out what we were doing. I am sure they also were wondering why I didn't just give them the deer leg to eat. When we went into the house, Kitty, following the scent of the meat, went up onto the deck. Then crouching down, she stealthily snuck in through the door and down to the deer leg lying on the floor of the garage. We pulled the garage door shut with the nylon rope. Now all we had to do was net her and get her into the kennel. Just when I was thinking that our little adventure was like one of those animal capture episodes on Wild Kingdom, it became a whole lot more like the almost unreal Disney movies.

We went into the garage to net Kitty and put her into the kennel we had ready in the middle of the two-car garage. Bob had left the pickup outside when he went to get the carrying box. That left no place for Kitty to hide at ground level. As soon as we went into the garage, things became really interesting. Kitty took one look at the net in Bob's hands, jumped to the top of the work bench along the north wall, and with a leap and a scramble up the log wall, she was on top of the lumber we had stored in the rafters. We didn't want to net her up there and cause her to fall onto the cement floor from 11 feet up. I quickly opened the large garage door, so Bob could back the pickup into the garage, positioning the truck bed directly under Kitty. I closed the door and put the dog kennel in the pickup with a padding of blankets on the floor of the pickup bed. We calculated that was where Kitty would drop when we pulled her down from the rafters, if we could get the net over her.

When we were finally ready, we had trouble getting the net completely over her long body because the rafters were in the way. I decided to try a lasso, taping the noose onto a long plastic pipe that was in the garage. That enabled me to slip the noose over Kitty's head and pull it tight. Then I pulled on the plastic pipe, releasing it from the noose. With the rope, I was able to drag Kitty forward from the closed in area where she was crouched, making it possible for Bob to put the net completely over her. We both pulled slowly and carefully, causing Kitty to drop down into the padded pickup bed. Bob held her down with the net, while I grabbed her, sliding her out from under the net into the open door of the kennel. Bob pushed the door of the kennel closed as I pulled the lasso off her neck and we had one totally confused captured cougar. The bigger cat, Tommy, was still out in the backyard waiting to be fed and likely wondering why his sister had disappeared.

We opened the door leading to the deck so Tommy could get into the garage, where the deer leg was tied to the workbench. The light rope still went from the door handle to our bedroom window, so whoever was watching when Tommy entered the garage could pull the door closed. With Kitty in the kennel and the deer leg on the floor, we hoped Tommy would quickly be enticed into entering the garage. It was about 11:00 p.m. by the time Kitty was secured in her kennel and we were getting tired. The wooden transport box Bob had brought up from the barn was sitting on the floor of the garage, open and ready for me to push Tommy into it, if we could succeed in getting the net over him. We were prepared, but Tommy wasn't. He seemed reluctant to go through that door, no matter what goodies were inside the garage. We waited and waited, taking turns watching, ready to pull the door closed.

At 1:30 a.m., with hunger getting the better of his fear, Tommy crept slowly and stealthily up to the door and looked longingly at the fresh deer leg. Finally, after pausing at the door for what seemed like forever, Tommy slunk down to the deer leg on the garage floor, his belly nearly scraping the steps as he went. Once he latched onto that meat and began chewing off large chunks, he didn't pay any attention as we pulled the door closed. We both ran for the garage, with Bob carrying the net. I pulled on my heavy leather gloves and thick leather jacket to be ready to grab Tommy and push him into the carrying box as soon as Bob had the net over him. This time everything worked as planned. Tommy remained on the floor and Bob quickly placed the large net over him. He held Tommy down with the net, while I grabbed the fairly large cougar by the neck. We quickly but gently guided him into the transport box. As soon as I pulled the net off over Tommy's head, Bob pushed the sliding door closed, while I blocked Tommy from coming out of the box. We finally had two captured cougars.

Amazingly, neither of the young cougars had made the slightest attempt to bite or claw me as I grabbed them and pushed them into their carriers. Even though what I was doing could be considered attacking them, they made no move to attack me or fight back. Cats have 10 very sharp claws on their front paws and 10 more on the back that can do a lot of damage. Fortunately for me, the two cubs still considered me to be their mother and apparently, fortunately for me, it is against cougar rules to attack mom.

We quickly loaded the transport box containing Tommy into the pickup beside Kitty's kennel, with what remained of the deer leg and a bucket of water. When we arrived at the barn, we carried the kennel and the transport box into the large, covered pen. The deer carcass minus the severed hind leg was already in the enclosure. After putting a pan full of water and the hind leg in their pen, we opened the door of Kitty's carrying kennel. We completely removed the door of Tommy's transport box so it was like a small den where they could sleep if they wanted. After securely padlocking the gate on their covered pen, we were finally able to go back to the house and crawl into bed. It was 2:30 a.m. and it had been a very long day.

The two cougars had to stay in the large, covered kennel for nearly 10 more months before a zoo was finally found for them. They ate deer meat, cat food, and mice, played with each other, and slept. They sat and watched me when I cleaned up after them or put water in their water pan. If I asked them to move, they obligingly walked to the other side of the pen. Things were quite uneventful for the rest of their time with us. I am sure it was extremely boring for two playful, curious cougar cubs to have to live there, but the wait for a good home was worth it.

In March 1996, the cubs were finally sent to a place found for them by Steve at the Montana Fish, Wildlife and Parks Rehabilitation Center. The zoo, which was in Canada, had a large, natural cougar exhibition area containing rocks, trees, and bushes. The zoo's two other cougars had been neutered so they couldn't reproduce. Kitty and Tommy were also sterilized, reducing natural aggressiveness so all four cats could live together without fighting. The young cougars would at least have room to run around and explore a bit, as well as having the two other cougars for company and with whom to play. After caring for them for so long, we missed them a lot, but we were extremely happy because Tommy and Kitty would have a wonderful home for the rest of their lives. That is the best we could hope for with cougars, because human-raised cubs are never released back into the wild in Montana.

CHAPTER 23
SMALL RODENT FRIENDS

Bob and I have had many rodent babies of various species to care for during our years of rehabilitating wildlife. We raised or cared for deer mice, northern pack rats, golden mantled ground squirrels, chipmunks, red squirrels, fox squirrels, northern flying squirrels, Columbian ground squirrels, yellow-bellied marmots, muskrats, porcupines, and beaver. It was interesting to observe them as they grew up, learned how to find food, and eventually became completely independent. Some were tamer and interacted with us more than others. All individuals of rodent species who were tame came when called and most were quite affectionate.

The many squirrels we raised were great fun to watch, especially the baby flying squirrels. Young squirrels of all species we received as babies quickly learned their names. When I called them, they came to get treats for a long time after release. Wild mice are also interactive and affectionate, especially those I begin caring for at an age prior to their eyes opening. The eyes of young rodent species are sealed closed for one to three weeks after birth, depending on the species. Young who are orphaned after their eyes have opened are usually somewhat wild and often not as affectionate toward the person who rehabilitates them.

Two little rodents who brightened our lives and improved our yard on the east side of our house were baby Columbian ground squirrels (*Urocitellus columbianus*): Sunny, a female; and Bucky, a male. Sunny was quite young, with her eyes not yet open, when a person accidently dropped a small stock tank on her hind legs. The bottom of the tank had an edge that snapped the leg bones between what would be the knee and the ankle on a human. The person was very sorry about what had happened and brought the little ground squirrel to me to raise and release. Bent wires with Styrofoam padding made good, lightweight splints, enabling her legs to heal quickly. I was thrilled to see both legs had a full range of motion when I removed the splints. Sunny didn't even limp.

When she was fully grown, I released her in the woodpile under our deck, on the north side of our house. She immediately dug a hole for her den beside the basement door. It was quite convenient for me, since I didn't have to go far to give her grain, apples, and other treats. Soon after she was released, someone brought us a half-grown male Columbian ground squirrel. Bucky wasn't injured, so I kept him in a cage for only a few days before releasing him under the woodpile, near Sunny's den. He and Sunny lived together in her den for a while, until he had time to dig one for himself. The next spring, they produced four baby ground squirrels. Sunny lived by the back door for several years, having several babies each year. Those babies had babies and now, many years later, we have several colonies of Columbian ground squirrels on our land.

One group is in the riparian area north of our house. A small colony still lives in the yard on the east side of our house, a short distance from where Sunny dug her original den. We can watch the antics of those squirrels through our dining room window, which looks directly down on them. Each spring we wait with great anticipation for the active babies to come out of the dens; they tumble and play like tiny puppies. Columbian ground squirrels are pretty little animals, highly entertaining to watch. Their other attributes are that they keep the side yard grass mowed and eat many of the weeds that grow in our lawn. It appears dandelions are their favorite plant other than grass; with the squirrels eating dandelions, we wouldn't need herbicides on our lawn, even if we were imprudent enough to use them. I am extremely sensitive to herbicides, especially those usually used on lawns, such as 2,4-D and other organochlorine compounds, and to Roundup, which slowly kills almost any animal exposed to it.

The best and most amazing ground squirrel-watching times are during spring mating, when they almost need to be X-rated, and several weeks later, when the adorable babies begin peeking out of their holes to check out their above-ground world. The young ones spend much of the day in wrestling matches or playing tag while dashing in and out of their holes. They provide much better entertainment than television.

Over the years, we have also received several yellow pine chipmunks (*Tamias amoenus*) and golden-mantled ground squirrels (*Callospermophius lateralis*) for care. The chipmunk who was the most interesting and entertaining was Chippy, a female we raised from a small baby. She spent her first winter running around inside our house, hiding clumps of seeds in every conceivable place, including a few places I never figured out how she was able to access. Chipmunks glue the seeds together in a small ball with their saliva, hiding their caches for future snacks.

We kept her in a large cage when we were gone and during the night, but most of the time she could go anywhere she wanted in our house. She climbed up one of our legs and lay or clambered around on our knees when we sat in our easy chairs to watch television. She almost always came when she was called, unless she was busy hiding a food cache. I was concerned about one of us stepping on her, but she was extremely adept at avoiding large human feet. She was our only pet at the time, so she didn't have to avoid a cat or dog, just four human feet.

Chippy sitting on the edge of our porch after being released.

As soon as dandelions began blooming in the spring, we released Chippy outside. She quickly began dashing around our yard, hiding food everywhere, just as she had when she lived in our house. Fresh dandelion flowers quickly became one of her favorite foods. She still came to me for sunflower seeds when I called her name. Her main new home, where she took naps and slept at night, was in a rock pile under a small ponderosa pine tree in the yard just east of the house. She lived in the rock pile for at least the next year. Then she either moved to a different area, something happened to her, or she simply stopped coming when I called her. Several chipmunks still live in the rock pile where Chippy made her home.

Proving how adept chipmunks are at hoarding food, I often found Chippy's little round seed caches when cleaning closets, bookshelves, or other places she used for cache hiding places. For at least five years after she lived in the house with us, I found surprise presents from Chippy still tightly wrapped with dried chipmunk saliva.

**Chipmunks hide seeds in
interesting locations
for late winter snacks.**

A Columbian ground squirrel in our yard in 2016 was likely a descendent of Sunny and Bucky. They are very charismatic and entertaining to watch. They are also an important food source for hawks and eagles during nesting season.

CHAPTER 24
CHUCKIE

We have had several yellow-bellied marmots (*Marmota flaviventris*) who required care prior to being released. By far the most memorable was Chuckie. In spring 1995, two young boys from Bonner, Montana, found a baby yellow-bellied marmot and raised her on a bottle. Not knowing her gender, they named her Chuckie. When Chuckie was old enough to release, they called us to ask if the young marmot could live at our place. Since we had exemplary marmot habitat containing a large colony of marmots to keep her company, we agreed this would be a good place for her. Because she was tame, we could supplement her natural food with grain, fruits, and vegetables to help her fatten for winter hibernation.

They brought Chuckie to us the Sunday after they called. She was endearingly cute and completely tame. We released her in a large rock and brush pile where other marmots lived. We were confident she would find an unoccupied den where she could live temporarily. She could then make that den her home or dig her own winter den in which to hibernate.

When I called her, Chuckie came out of the brush pile for her grain and an apple or banana. She was especially fond of bananas. Since she wasn't yet familiar with where the creek was, I left a pan of water near the den for her. After a little over three weeks, she stopped coming out of the brush pile when I called. I hoped she had gone into hibernation and hadn't become dinner for the resident foxes, but I wouldn't know until the next spring.

On a bright sunny day in late February of the next year, as I was walking down the road, I stopped by the brush pile. I wanted to look for fresh marmot droppings, tracks, or other signs indicating one or more marmots had awakened. Before I could start my circle around the brush pile, a little marmot ran out, stood up, and put her front feet on my leg. It was Chuckie asking for treats. I rushed back to the house for grain, an apple, dog food, and a pan for water. When I returned, Chuckie was nowhere to be seen. I called her name and out popped a cute little marmot head, showing me the hole where her home was. I put the grain, dog food, and water by her hole so she could eat and drink without going far from shelter. She took the apple from my hand to eat first.

When Bob came home from work, I told him Chuckie was out of hibernation. Together, we walked down to see her, taking more food and water in case she had to share with other waking marmots. She remained at the brush pile by the road for about a month. Then one day, when I went to milk the goats, Chuckie was nearby waiting for me. Her new den in the barnyard was about 100 yards from the old one in the brush pile. I don't know how she knew where to go, unless she could see me doing chores from the top of the rock pile, which was near the road directly above her den in the brush pile. She stayed at the barn for the rest of her life, never moving back to the brush pile by the road.

Our barnyard has a great deal of flat cement poured between the buildings. There were pig sheds with pens built inside and on the cement pad outside the sheds when we bought our place. We removed the pigpens so we could use the sheds for parking our trailers and for storage areas.

Soon after we moved here, we brought and released several marmots from a place where Bob live-trapped them because they were not wanted by landowners. The marmots dug holes under the cement to make safe, cozy homes. With so much cement and a shed with a space under it, there were many places for marmots to dig their dens. We soon had quite a large colony of them. They did eat grass and forbs in our goat pasture, which is one reason they are not welcome on many people's land in western Montana. They also dislike the holes marmots dig. Unfortunately for marmots, a large number of people who have never known a marmot personally use them for target practice, simply killing them for no particular reason.

Marmots are great fun to watch, especially when they play. We didn't care if they made their dens under the cement, so they were no bother to us and provided hours of pleasurable wildlife watching while I cared for and milked my goats. I was pleased when Chuckie chose a hole under the cement by the hay shed near the goat pen to make her new den, making it easy to feed her. From her den, she could go directly out into the goat pasture to eat grass, a marmot's main food. Year around, I keep a pan full of water for the resident pigeons, skunks, and marmots living in the area around the barnyard, so that was near Chuckie's den. It is nearly a quarter mile from the creek, the closest natural source of water. For short-legged animals who are considered tasty by predators and neighborhood dogs, it is a dangerous trip.

Chuckie seemed to like her new den under the cement. She remained in that hole, where she raised many cute youngsters, for five years before making a new den even closer to the goat pasture. She lived there until she was nine years old, managing to avoid the occasional fox, coyote, and the neighbors' marmot-shredding dogs. She didn't go out onto the road that passes by the barnyard, so she avoided being hit by vehicles, one of the main causes of mortality to adult marmots in our colony. Unless Chuckie was hibernating, she always came to me when I called her. She often climbed up on to my lap to be petted when I sat down beside her. She would let visitors pet her and come out to greet groups of school children who came to see the unreleasable birds I used for educational presentations. Many of the children seemed to like Chuckie better than the eagles, hawks, and owls I showed to them. Hopefully, when they grow up, they will remember meeting Chuckie and won't kill marmots.

Because Chuckie wasn't afraid of people, her youngsters and several other female marmots became quite tame, though not tame enough to pet. They all ate together when I provided grain or dog food. Every morning, when I went to the barn to feed and milk the goats, I took a special treat of apple, carrot, banana, or potato for Chuckie. She came to me to take the fruit or vegetable out of my hand. I stayed by her, petting and brushing her while she ate so none of the larger female marmots would take her treats from her, although we did share the grain with her marmot neighbors.

Every day during spring and summer, Chuckie was there to greet me when I went to the barn. She sometimes followed me around when I had work to do in the area near her den. She was friendly and loving, like a little grass-eating puppy. When she was in hibernation, from late August until early March, it was rather lonely when I went to the barn to do chores, even though all the other animals were there. I could hardly wait till March arrived, bringing marmots out of hibernation, and Chuckie there to greet me.

In spring 2004, when she was nine years old, Chuckie was thinner than usual when she came out of hibernation. She had a persistent cough and didn't regain weight as quickly as in other years. She had only three babies that spring. I gave her and her young ones extra grain, along with dog food, apples, and vegetables all summer. I put a tablet of Hyland's Calc. Phos. 30X® and one of Hyland's Bioplasma® (homeopathic electrolyte tablets) in her slice of apple every day. Because the electrolytes help cells work better, they may have helped her survive through the summer. Even with the electrolytes, she didn't have her usual fat layer when she went into hibernation in late August. She was one of the last of the marmots to go into hibernation that year.

The last time I saw her, I went down to do some pen cleaning early in the afternoon. Chuckie came out of her den without being called and walked over to me as soon as I arrived. After putting down an apple and a pile of dog food for her to eat, I brushed her and scratched her head, telling her what a good girl she was. It was almost like she had deliberately come to tell me goodbye before going into hibernation. I sat by her until she finished her food, giving her a final head scratch before she went back into her den. Chuckie didn't come out of hibernation the next spring. She must have passed away in her den during the winter.

Chuckie had a fairly long life for a marmot, although there are records of yellow-bellied marmots living up to 12 years. What made Chuckie amazing was her never wavering affection and sweet personality. She was intelligent, inquisitive and, even as an adult, quite playful. Having Chuckie as my unusual friend for nine years was a special gift and a privilege few people get to experience.

Spring sneaks in to leave
tracks of awakened marmots
in new fallen snow.

CHAPTER 25
PEPPER'S UNUSUAL FAMILY

In spring 2001, a newborn female mule deer fawn (*Odocoileus hemionus*) was found, possibly abandoned by her mother near Hamilton, Montana. She had a fairly severe underbite and had gone for some time without food, indicating that, for some reason, her mother didn't or couldn't return to feed her. As soon as she arrived, I placed one Hyland's Calc. Phos. 30X® and one of Hyland's Bioplasma® under her tongue to jumpstart her cellular communication, hoping to cause her facial bones to grow to normal size, as we had done for other young animals with brachygnathia superior (usually called underbite). In about 10 minutes, her milk formula of six ounces of goats milk with two tablespoons of whipping cream was ready. Three minutes after that, the hungry little deer had a full tummy. I decided to call her Pepper because of the black hairs peppering her brownish-grey base color sprinkled with off-white fawn spots. Even with her protruding lower incisors, she had no trouble sucking milk from the long lamb nipple I used for fawns with underdeveloped facial bones, though she may have had difficulty with her mother's much shorter nipples.

Pepper was soon at home in the deer pen with Bambi and Angie, two orphaned white-tailed deer fawns whose mothers had been killed by vehicles. Pepper quickly learned to come for her milk when I called her name. Most mule deer fawns crave attention and are extremely affectionate. Unlike white-tailed deer, they often remain quite tame their entire life, even if their life is spent on their own in the wild. This makes it harder to find a release site where they will be reasonably safe. Until they learn what they need to know to survive, if there are people around, a human-raised mule deer will walk right up to them. Obviously, this is not safe behavior during hunting season in Montana, or even when it is not hunting season. Some people shoot deer at all times of the year, sometimes for no particular reason.

We learned that lesson the hard way with Pumpkin, the first mule deer fawn we raised. She came to us two years after we moved to the Bitterroot Valley. All the deer we raised that year, including Pumpkin, made it

213

Pepper was an orphaned mule deer fawn who was raised and set free to live her life on a ranch in the foothills of the Bitterroot Mountains.

through hunting season. In January, long after hunting season was over, Pumpkin was out exploring one afternoon, likely looking for browse to eat. Unfortunately, she made the mistake of walking through our neighbor's land on her way back to our place. The neighbor's teenage son shot Pumpkin through the lower jaw with his pistol, severing her tongue and shattering her jaw and many of her lower teeth. She came home in terror and excruciating pain. She would never have been able to bite off plants to eat or chew normally, even if her jaw could have been fixed. We had to euthanize her and she died in my arms.

I found out the teenager who shot Pumpkin went out each day to shoot at every wild animal he saw, killing or maiming many of them. When he took his girlfriend's family hostage at gunpoint and shot holes in several police cars in a standoff with Ravalli County sheriff's deputies, I was not particularly surprised. I have to say I didn't feel the least bit sorry when he was sent to jail for many years for those felonies. At least while in jail, he couldn't kill or wound any more innocent wild animals.

Not long after Pepper came to us, Allie arrived. She was a week and a half old white-tailed deer fawn from Pattee Canyon near Missoula. The man who brought her had seen her with her mother soon after she was born. He did what everyone is advised to do by wildlife experts: he left her alone until he was sure she was in trouble.

Allie looked like something conjured up in someone's overactive imagination, a real-life fairytale animal. She was roan in color, a white background with small red spots scattered throughout the white hair. At the top of her legs, the red spots were closer together, like a war paint Appaloosa horse. Her head was reddish-brown, nearly the same color as a regular fawn but with more white markings on her pretty face.

All four legs were crooked, turned in at the first joint above the hoof. On the side of each hind foot just above the hoof, she had worn holes through the skin from walking on the sides of her feet since birth. The top of Allie's back was somewhat rounded and she had a slight underbite. The strangest thing about her was that her lower incisors were round and cone shaped, with a sharp point on the tip. Deer incisors are supposed to be flat with a straight edge on top as on other grazing animals and humans. Her cone-shaped, pointed incisors and rounded posture were exactly like those of a prehistoric deer skeleton I had seen in the natural history museum at the University of Nebraska in Lincoln. Except for her malformed legs, she was a beautiful little animal, quite stunning to look at.

I splinted all four legs to hold them straight and began giving her the two cell salt tablets in her milk every three hours. I hoped the cell salts would help her underbite and crooked legs grow to be more normal, as they had on other young grazing animals with those birth defects. Allie came to us for care soon after Pepper arrived. Pepper was much younger than Angie and Bambi, and Allie was small for her age. According to her rescuer she had trouble standing and suckling her mother, which likely caused her to be malnourished. After a week of observing Allie, her rescuer realized her crooked legs were the reason she had trouble standing to suckle. He finally decided she had to be taken to a wildlife rehabber or she would die.

Allie and Pepper soon became best friends. Angie and Bambi had already formed a bond, so we had the equivalent of two sets of twins, one set being a rather strange-looking pair. Of the four fawns, all but Angie had underbite. All four received the two cell salt tablets in their milk at each feeding and the underdeveloped upper facial bones on Bambi and Pepper soon grew to normal, resulting in a normal bite. Allie's facial and skull bones also grew to normal size, producing a normal bite, but of course the unusual round, pointed shape of her baby incisors didn't change. She seemed able to easily bite off the leaves from grass and forbs with her pointed incisors, once her facial bones grew to normal. Depending on the severity of the birth defect, those with underbite may be unable to bite off foliage efficiently and obtain adequate nourishment after they are weaned.

All the fawns grew fast and in mid-July we let Angie and Bambi out of the pen during the day to explore our land and learn what plants were good to eat. Allie's legs had straightened so she could walk normally on her hooves. She no longer needed splints and the holes in the skin on her legs had completely healed. In August, we took Pepper and Allie to a ranch with over 300 acres of land, where we thought they would be safer than in our neighborhood. The people who owned the ranch agreed to continue feeding the two fawns their goat milk formula while they learned what to eat in the wild. There were other deer in the area, both white-tailed deer and mule deer. The ranch had a creek flowing through a large timbered area, with multiple meadows dotting the property. Pepper and Allie seemed right at home. They enjoyed running and playing in the meadows or browsing in the creek bottom. Pepper liked to wade in the creek; Allie wasn't so fond of the water and mostly stayed on dry land.

The ranch owners kept me up to date on their progress. Both seemed to like their new home and didn't wander too far from their main hideouts in the creek bottom or in the brush on the edge of the meadow. Everything went well until the end of October, when tragedy struck. A small pack of coyotes found Allie in her favorite area in the brushy creek bottom. They had eaten all of her by morning, except her lower legs and a small piece of her beautiful roan skin. They were hungry and she was just another deer to them, a deer they could catch. Unfortunately, her skull and lower jaw with her unusual cone-shaped teeth were eaten or carried away, as the rancher couldn't find them.

Pepper greatly missed Allie and, wanting company, she remained close to the ranch buildings and the humans who continued to care for her. She managed to evade fall and winter hunters, human and canine. By spring, she was a beautiful yearling doe. Pepper spent her spring and summer as a yearling mostly browsing and taking it easy. Yearling mule deer have a significant amount of growing to do, in addition to putting on fat so they can make it through the next winter.

That summer (2002) we had received two male mule deer fawns named Zeus and Apollo. The rancher suggested Pepper needed company and agreed to have those two fawns released on his land. When it was time, we transported the young deer to the ranch. As he did with Pepper and Allie, the rancher continued to feed milk to the two males until it was time to wean them. Pepper became their teacher and big sister and the three deer remained together all fall and winter.

When mule deer breeding season came, Pepper went on a "walk about" into the woods and wasn't seen in the meadow area for several days. When she came back, everything went back to normal, as though she had not been gone. The rancher thought she had likely gone looking for a male mule deer and as it turned out, he was right. She was pregnant with twin fawns. Unfortunately, when her fawns were born the next spring, both were stillborn for some undetermined reason. Pepper had to be content with Zeus and Apollo for company for another year.

By mid-summer, Pepper had gained back the weight she had lost during winter. She was two years old and nearly full-grown. Being somewhat larger than her white-tailed deer neighbors who shared the ranch land, she often chased them. She made sure all the other deer knew she was boss, including the yearling bucks, Zeus and Apollo. When fall came, she again went on a "walk about" to find a buck to father her fawn. Something must have happened the first time she was bred that fall, because the next spring she had only one fawn, born at the end of June 2004, nearly a month later than usual. The rancher said the fawn looked kind of strange when it finally showed itself, following Pepper out into the open meadow. After making certain Pepper and her fawn would be around, Bob and I went there to see what was strange about it.

Pepper's new baby was a female, with big ears like a mule deer, but most of the rest of her looked like a white-tailed deer. The fawn's tail was broad and white underneath and, when she ran, she flagged it as white-tailed deer do. However, the top of her tail was pure black like a Columbian black-tailed deer (Odocoileus hemionus columbianus), who look somewhat like a hybrid of a white-tailed deer and a mule deer, and that is what Pepper's new fawn appeared to be. The rancher named her Doodle Baby.

Black-tailed and mule deer are the same species, with mule deer considered to be a subspecies of the black-tailed deer. Mule deer are the youngest deer species that are still alive, having split from the Columbian black-tailed deer about 10,000 years ago. They are both closely related to the white-tailed deer, which the black-tailed deer is thought to have originally split from over a million years ago. This close relationship makes it possible for them to interbreed.

Apparently, Pepper hadn't become pregnant when she was bred the first time she came in season, so was bred again, over a month late, by one of the male white-tailed deer who lived on the ranch. She usually chased them around the meadow and through the timber, like she was going to stomp them into dust. It was a surprise to all of us that she had a hybrid fawn. It was even more surprising when Pepper did the same in 2005. Again, a month later than normal, she had one hybrid female fawn, which the rancher named Lily. Lily's tail was like a skinny white-tailed deer tail with a strange crook in it. Otherwise she looked exactly like her sister, Doodle Baby, with big ears like her mother and hair the color and texture of her white-tailed deer father.

When Zeus was a year and a half old, he went exploring after hunting season was over in fall 2004 and never returned. We don't know what happened to him. It is possible he went to hang out with a group of young male mule deer, as yearling bucks often do. Apollo stayed with Pepper until after hunting season in fall 2005. In early winter, he left and didn't come back. He was two and a half, so likely went to find a herd of mule deer bucks with whom to spend the winter. Doodle Baby went exploring in early fall. She didn't return for some time, causing us to fear she had been shot during hunting season, until she suddenly reappeared one mid-winter day. Pepper and Lily remained together on the ranch all fall and winter. With the arrival of spring, we were all waiting expectantly, analogous to opening a special present, to see what kind of surprise Pepper would present us in 2006.

The new year brought us a sad disappointment and two welcome surprises. Of course, one very happy surprise was when a fat, healthy, and pregnant Doodle Baby returned from her extended "walk about" to hang out with her mother, Pepper, and sister, Lily. June brought another pleasant surprise. Pepper had twin pure mule deer fawns, both males. The rancher named them Zeus II and Deuce. Lily quickly became attached to her little brothers and helped with babysitting chores. To the disappointment of all the humans keeping track of Pepper's extended family, Doodle Baby's fawn died or was killed and eaten by predators about a week after it was born. We didn't get to see the fawn, as it disappeared before it was old enough to begin following its mother. We were not privileged know whether the fawn was fathered by a white-tailed deer or a mule deer. What we did learn is that Doodle Baby, even though half white-tailed deer and half mule deer, was able to produce a fawn.

By spring 2007, we were excitedly hoping to be able to see fawns from all three does, as Pepper, Doodle Baby, and Lily were all pregnant. Unfortunately, nature pays no attention to human expectations. Pepper, at four months less than seven years old, didn't make it through the winter. In late January or early February, something happened to cause her to die while crossing the creek that runs through the ranch. We knew she was missing, but the rancher didn't find her until March when the creek was quite high. Her waterlogged body was lodged between two rocks in the creek. Because the rushing water washed all of Pepper's hair away, it left her body looking quite bizarre. Her carcass was intact except for her large ears, which had also been partly worn away by the water. There were no broken bones or bite marks. She just died in the creek or possibly slipped on slick rocks and, being unable to regain her feet on the slippery, moss-covered rocks, she drowned or died of hypothermia. There was no way to know exactly what had happened. The rancher pulled Pepper's body out of the creek and placed it in the woods to avoid further contamination of the water. It remained untouched for over a month, then was found and completely consumed by a hungry bear not long out of hibernation.

We were all heartbroken by Pepper's death, but to cheer us up, Doodle Baby had twin fawns, Magic and Merlin. They looked like white-tailed deer so a white-tailed deer must have been their father, making them only one-fourth mule deer. Those three deer, with Pepper's pure mule deer sons, Deuce and Zeus II, and her younger hybrid daughter Lily, were left to carry on Pepper's legacy of doing the unexpected and surprising us with their exploits.

In spring 2007, Deuce left to find a less violent environment when Doodle Baby began pounding on him with her front feet and chasing him just prior to the birth of her fawns in mid-June. The rancher and his family never saw Deuce again.

Lily had her first fawn or fawns in June that spring. She disappeared at regular intervals, apparently to care for her young for about a week. Then Lily stopped going to feed her fawn and her udder became enlarged. Something had happened to it or them, but no sign of a dead fawn or fawns was ever found. Likely it was caught and eaten by local coyotes.

So, as had happened to Pepper and Doodle Baby, Lily carried on the family's legacy by failing in her first attempt to raise a fawn.

In mid-July, when we had record-breaking heat here in western Montana, both Zeus II and Lily left the ranch area, likely to find a cooler place to live in the high mountain valleys west of the ranch. By the time he and Lily left, Zeus II had grown unusually large antlers for a yearling, with four points on each antler, like a typical adult mule deer buck, plus a brow tine on one side. For male deer, having large antlers is not conducive to a long life here in western Montana. Most hunters in our area want to find and kill those with the largest antlers. This practice results in genetically reducing antler size in the deer population, as primarily males with small antlers are left to breed the does.

For those of us watching the drama of Pepper's extended family in spring 2007, the appearance of Doodle Baby's twin fawns, Magic and Merlin, was both exciting and concerning. While they otherwise looked like white-tailed deer fawns, both had slightly overlarge ears because of being one-fourth mule deer. Doodle Baby's twins were born in the meadow not far from the rancher's house. As usual, the fawns stayed hidden much of the time, but when they stood up to nurse, the rancher and his family could see that one was unable to straighten his front legs. Both legs had either foreshortened ligaments or tendon contracture at the radiocarpal/carpalmetacarpal joints, those on the front leg that bend like our knees.

He could barely stand on his crooked legs long enough to suckle. He did manage to move short distances by walking on the very tip of his front hooves. Quite often the joint just above the hoof suddenly folded so the fawn walked on the top of the foot for a few steps. Then he would tip forward and fall down. We expected the joints to strengthen and eventually straighten, as the fawn attempted to use his legs, but after three weeks, there was no improvement. If anything, they were becoming worse and the fawn appeared excessively stressed when he tried to follow his mother and twin brother.

After a discussion, we agreed the rancher should try giving the two cell salts (Hyland's Calc. Phos. 30X® and Hyland's Bioplasma®) to the malformed fawn. They had helped underdeveloped bones on other grazing animals grow to normal, but we didn't know if they would help contracted tendons. We didn't want to touch the fawn or take him away from his mother. Fortunately, the rancher came up with a solution that produced amazing results. Since Doodle Baby liked grain, he put three tablets each

Doodle Baby and her two fawns: Magic the one on the left with contracted tendons in his front legs; Merlin on the right with normal legs.

Doodle Baby licking Magic after his front legs had recovered.

of bioplasma and calc. phos. 30X in grain, placing it where she could find and eat it morning and afternoon. He saw the twins the day he began giving the cell salts but didn't see either of them the next two days. Doodle Baby went to nurse the fawns, wherever they were hidden, but they didn't follow her back to the buildings. She came to eat her grain sprinkled with cell salts on the third morning, but the fawns still remained hidden.

The third afternoon after the rancher began giving Doodle Baby cell salts, both fawns were with her when she came to eat her grain. The front legs on the fawn who had had contracted tendons since birth were perfectly straight, so the rancher's family immediately named him Magic. He could walk and run just like his twin, whom they named Merlin. While their mother was busy eating, the twins were soon celebrating their new ability to play together by racing at top speed up and down the meadow. In disbelief, the rancher's whole family watched as the fawns ran together across the meadow and up into the timber, zig-zagging through the pine trees. Then the twins came bounding back down the slope and across the meadow as fast as they could go. Magic actually won the race.

We surmised the cell salts' cell-stimulating effects went into Doodle Baby's blood cells, then into her milk, and directly into the fawns when they nursed. Magic's cells then went to work and fixed the problem. Amazingly, after only three days of receiving cell salts in his mother's milk, he was walking and running normally on his straight front legs. The rancher was wise enough to take before and after video; otherwise, no one would ever believe Magic's amazing transformation. True to form, Pepper's grand-fawns were carrying on her family's legacy of completely astounding the people who observed them and cared about them.

Doodle Baby and her twins left the ranch on August 28, possibly to join the other deer in the high country where it is cooler in summer. Or she may have gone to the other area, unknown to her human friends, where she frequently lived for extended periods. The day before she left, a large, adult male black bear was visiting the apple trees and berry bushes along the creek on the ranch. Doodle Baby may have considered the bear a threat to her fawns, causing her to move them to an area safer for them.

Maybe because Pepper was no longer on the ranch, her extended family didn't come back to winter there as they had in the past. We had hoped for a never-ending story, with Pepper's fawns, grand-fawns, and great grand-fawns continuing to amaze us for a long, long time.

Unfortunately for us observers, the rancher never saw any of Pepper's family members again, but we learned many things from them before they left.

> With graceful leaps, deer
> bound through meadows and trees in
> a joyful ballet.

ANTLERS

Antlers are a wondrous growth,
With the beauty of precious stone.
Composed of minerals and calcium,
They actually are living bone.

The heads of moose, caribou, elk,
And deer grow antlers large and small.
They are sought and bought by many
To hang on their trophy wall.

No two of them are quite alike
In shape or curve of beam,
But antlers when viewed from afar
Are smaller than they seem.

Surely one of nature's wonders
Every year they are reborn,
Each one unique and beautiful,
So please don't call them horn.

Skin-like velvet containing blood vessels on the antlers of a male white-tailed deer provides nutrients to enable the fast growth of the antlers. Photo by Eugene Beckes.

CHAPTER 26
WALKING HAND IN HAND

One of the most interesting young animals I have cared for is a baby raccoon (*Procyon lotor*) who has not yet opened its eyes to see its mother and siblings. When they are hungry, they demand to be fed in a loud cry that sounds much like a screaming human baby. Baby raccoons readily drink their formula from a human baby bottle, holding the bottle between their delicate little hands, like a miniature baby in a fur coat. I have raised a lot of young raccoons but only received two prior to their eyes opening.

Our first very young baby raccoon came to us a long time ago, a few years after we moved to our home beside Willoughby Creek in the Bitterroot Valley. I called him Rackety Coon because he outdid himself with his loud crying whenever he thought it was time to eat. When he first came to us, he slept most of the time in his box with soft blankets for his bed. About every three hours, his empty tummy prompted him to let me know he was hungry. As he grew larger and his eyes opened, he became a squirmy little bundle of curiosity. He wanted to feel everything possible with the long thin fingers on his tiny human-like hands.

Rackety always wanted to hold my finger in his hand whenever he drank from the bottle while I held it for him. As he grew older, he held my finger and walked upright on his hind legs, like a tiny toddler. After raising more young raccoons, I discovered this was unusual behavior. Rackety was the only one who liked to walk upright on his hind legs, similar to people. Maybe he thought that was the right way to walk because it was the way I walked; young animals learn a lot by mimicking their mother. Since his eyes hadn't yet opened when he came to us, the first animals he saw were humans who walked upright.

After Rackety was weaned, I let him run loose in our yard. He first explored throughout the yard, and then began examining the riparian area along Willoughby Creek. He loved playing in the water of the creek, as all raccoons do. I made a box for him to sleep in on a shelf on the back deck so he could come and go as he pleased. If he was exploring in the yard when I went outside, he ran up to me, stood up, and took my hand in his. Then, remaining on his hind legs, he walked with me hand in hand to wherever I was going.

Rackety Coon learning to climb in tree branches.

When winter came, Rackety was reluctant to come out of his box if it was cold. It was covered with two blankets to keep it warm and cozy inside, with thick soft hay for Rackety to sleep on. I put his pan of food on the shelf directly in front of the round entrance hole, allowing him to reach his hand out under the edge of the blanket and take a piece of dog food without coming out into the cold. Except an occasional foray for a drink of water or to relieve himself, he spent all the really cold days of winter snug in his box. On warmer days, he went down to the creek, climbed trees for the fun of it, or followed me around while I fed the wild birds and other critters.

When spring came, Rackety began traveling half a mile south across our hay field to the neighbor's creek bottom where there were fallen cottonwood trees, many with hollow centers making perfect hiding places for a raccoon. I discovered that once Rackety became an adult, the resident male raccoon who lived on our land took exception to having another male in his territory. Rackety came the half mile to our house from across the field each morning to eat the food I provided for him, then went back across our field to the South Fork of Willoughby Creek, where he was safe from the older male.

A crippled six-year-old white-tailed doe named Janey Doe, whom we had raised from a small fawn, also slept during the day in the thick bushes along the South Fork of Willoughby, the same area as Rackety's daytime hiding place. Our kind neighbors, who owned the land where Rackety and Janey Doe hid during the day, had left the creek bottom on their land natural, with the bushes and fallen trees that are usually along dryland creeks. All previous owners of that land had also preferred the creek bottom to remain natural, leaving several old, decaying, fallen trees with large hollowed out centers. Those were perfect homes and hiding places for small mammals such as raccoons, squirrels, chipmunks, and others.

Unfortunately, our neighbors decided to sell their place that spring and by mid-summer, they had moved away. The people who bought the house and land were from Nevada. Apparently, they didn't like trees with branches, fallen trees, or even bushes. The man sawed down all the bushes with his chain saw. He even sawed off all the lower branches as high as he could reach on the cottonwood trees and pines along the creek. Then he piled all the brush and branches on the hollow logs used by the animals and burned everything, leaving no place for Rackety Coon and Janey Doe to safely hide. Rackety moved a short distance west across the fence to fallen trees that remained on another neighbor's land next door. Unfortunately, a new family with large dogs and two teenage boys had moved into that place the year before.

I never knew what happened to Janey Doe. She just suddenly disappeared a month prior to hunting season. I looked on all the nearby roadsides, in case she was hit by a car but found nothing. None of the neighbors reported a dead deer on their property.

Rackety Coon stopped coming home for his food soon after our neighbor burned the piles of brush and logs. I greatly missed our walks together. I would never have known what happened to him, but that fall, I happened to see the teenage boys waiting for the school bus. I asked them if they had seen a raccoon that summer. They bragged about how their two dogs had caught one in their field and killed it, thus explaining why Rackety stopped coming home to get his food and walk with me. I told the boys the raccoon was my friend, but I don't think they believed me.

Years later, in spring 2006, I received three tiny raccoon babies with their eyes still closed. All were female, so I thought they would be fairly safe when I released them here (females are usually accepted by a resident male). All three did well for the first week. The smallest kit had been eating well without any apparent illness but had not visibly grown any bigger. She was only about half as big as the largest kit when she and her slightly larger sister suddenly died with no warning symptoms.

Necropsies showed the two kits had almost no thymus, a very important organ essential for the immune system of baby mammals to function correctly. The largest kit continued to eat well and grow. I named her Susie Coon. She, like Rackety, was one of the sweetest little babies I have ever raised. She liked to hold my finger in her hand the same way Rackety had. Her temperament was a lot like Rackety's, except she just chittered softly when she was hungry, rather than crying loud enough to wake the dead. Also, unlike Rackety, Suzie didn't walk on her hind legs. She loved to be petted and brushed while she drank from her bottle. When she was old enough to eat from a bowl, she continued to appreciate being brushed or stroked while she ate.

Once Suzie was big enough to climb and explore, I let her play in the back yard, where there is a long hedge of low growing juniper bushes, nearby large pine trees, and other bushes. In the afternoon, she climbed up into the top of the three to four-foot tall junipers to nap, curled up on a bed of juniper branches. She always came when I called her, expecting a treat or a brushing. When she was still fairly small, I put her in a pen at night for her safety. I didn't trust the resident coons and was afraid roaming dogs might hurt or kill her.

In late summer, Suzie met a resident raccoon family consisting of a female and three young raccoons the same size as she was. The youngsters let her eat and play with them. They began spending a lot of time together playing in the juniper hedge. It's like a jungle under the hedge, with many tunnels running through and under the juniper branches. One of the young raccoons began napping in the same juniper as Suzie, just a couple feet from her. Hoping the adult mother of Suzie's playmates would protect Suzie along with her own youngsters, I began letting Suzie remain free both day and night.

Raccoons do most of their exploring and searching for food at night. The kits play much of the time, when they aren't learning the basics of survival from their mother. Each morning after her permanent release, I found Suzie curled up in the top of her favorite juniper, sleeping soundly. I placed her bowl of food on the ground under the bush and called her name. She slowly raised her head, yawned, stretched, and looked at me like she was saying, "Is it time to get up already?" Then she slowly climbed down to her food bowl and ate all of her duck egg omelet, fish, canned cat food, dog food, or some combination of those. After cleaning her bowl, she ran down the tunnel through the middle of the juniper hedge to drink from the water pan we kept full on the east end of the hedge. Then she ran back to the west end of the hedge and climbed up to her soft sleeping platform of juniper branches near the top of one of the bushes. She was soon fast asleep and slept until late afternoon. If I happened to be working outside, Suzie often came to find me when she woke up. She always came when I called her to play tag with me or to get brushed. Suzie did raccoon things at night with her adopted family and slept or played during the day for the rest of the fall and winter.

The next spring, Bob and I decided the west end of the juniper hedge was too close to the back of the garage. Growing directly under the eaves as it did, it would be a serious fire hazard if we ever had a wildfire in our area. Wildfires had become much too common in our county after seven years of drought. Bob cut down four or five bushes on the west end, eliminating about 20 feet of hedge including the bush where Suzie had made her bed. We thought she would move to another bush somewhere in the remaining juniper hedge and she must have, but I couldn't find where she was sleeping.

Suzy Coon coming out of one of the tunnels under the juniper hedge when she was nearly a year old.

When I put her food down and called her, she peeked out from under one of the juniper bushes, then came running up to me to greet me with her rump up in the air and her nose down, like a puppy inviting play. After she finished her breakfast, we went for a walk or played tag, before she disappeared back into the bushes.

It appeared all was going well until the first week in March; Suzie didn't come for her food for two days. When she suddenly appeared out of the juniper bushes on the morning of the third day, her condition was horrifying. Suzie's right hind foot was pointed to the rear and she was dragging her leg. I called her to me so I could examine her leg. It was crushed just above the hock joint and the joint itself was dislocated. There was a huge gash in her foot. It appeared some kind of animal had caught both her foot and her leg in their teeth, crushing the bone and twisting the leg completely around. I couldn't imagine how badly it must have hurt.

I put her in a large kennel, so she could not go anywhere while I decided what to do. Suzie went totally crazy trying to get out of the kennel. That is where I would have had to keep her while her leg healed, if there were any way to keep it splinted long enough. The damage was so great I knew her foot and leg would never have normal use, even if it could heal. Raccoons are not good with splints or bandages of any kind; they can take them off much faster than I can put them on. More importantly, raccoons have to have functional hind legs to be able to climb trees to escape dogs and other dangers. Suzie didn't want to be a captive raccoon for the rest of her life. She was making that very plain, even though she was visibly in shock. I took her out of the kennel, carried her to a nice spot in the sun and euthanized her. She died in my arms. I buried her on our back hillside, where other animals and birds I failed to save are buried.

The moral of this story about my two raccoon friends is that no matter how big or how small the destroyed habitat, its destruction can seriously and adversely affect the animals who depend on that particular habitat. Removing a few bushes in a hedge and burning all the brush and downed logs in just a few hundred feet of creek bottom had a significant negative impact on all the animals using those habitats. It is difficult to imagine how much wildlife is displaced and caused to die by clearing and burning tens of thousands of acres of rain forest, clear-cutting large areas of timberland, or plowing millions of acres of grasslands and sage. This is, unfortunately for the affected animals, something few people consider before they do it.

**A long ranger, masked
raccoons came by themselves to
colonize the west.**

SECTION FIVE: CLEVER CORVIDS

**A jay's astounding
mental abilities are
always on display.**

CHAPTER 27
THE COME BACK CROW

Many years ago, before we moved to our place in the Bitterroot Valley, we lived in a house we built half a mile east of East Missoula, Montana. We had 10 acres in a valley just south of a mountain named Mount Jumbo, not far from the Clark Fork River. After we finished our home in 1980, I began rehabilitating birds who were orphaned or injured. One spring, someone brought us a hatchling American Crow (*Corvus brachyrhynchos*) who had fallen or been blown out of the nest. I never knew his gender but always thought of him as a male.

He was a bright little trickster and noisy. We named him Kaw, so when he was old enough to fly, we could call, "Kaw, Kaw, Kaw!" and he would fly to us for his pinky mice and puppy food tidbits. Like all pre-fledglings, Kaw just sat around for the first week, occasionally calling, "Caw, caw, caw!" loud enough to let me know he was hungry even if I was working outside. He often preened his fast-growing feathers or flapped his wings to strengthen his flight muscles. When all his feathers had grown in, Kaw began hopping around and getting into mischief.

Once he started trying to fly, I let Kaw loose in the yard so he could practice while I worked outside. That way, I could keep a close watch on him, to hopefully prevent him from getting into trouble. He followed us around like a little black puppy, watching whatever we did with great interest. When we were not going to be around to watch and protect him, I put Kaw in a flight room. Once he could fly well, I left him out all day so he could learn to be a crow. That was when his mischievous nature became increasingly apparent.

Kaw liked small, bright-colored objects, like the metal brass-colored fasteners holding the initials MDFWP on both tips of the collar on Bob's uniform shirt. The little metal clasps were under the collar tips. Kaw often flew up onto Bob's shoulder and, faster than you can say "bad bird," he reached under the collar tip, pulled the clasp off and flew up to the roof of the house to stash it in one of his hiding places under the shake shingles. There are probably still some of Kaw's stolen treasures under those shingles, unless the people to whom we sold the house when we moved to the Bitterroot Valley replaced them. In that case, a roofer likely found Kaw's treasure troves.

Kaw especially liked to go into the garage when Bob was working there, occasionally nabbing one of the nails, a screw, or shiny metal nut to hide in his growing caches. One day, I forgot to tie the side door of the garage open so the wind would not slam it shut. As usual, when Bob was in the garage, Kaw flew in to watch him, patiently waiting for the opportunity to fly down and steal something shiny. Unfortunately, Kaw decided to use the top of the garage door for a perch; a gust of wind suddenly blew it shut, trapping his toes between the door and the doorframe. Luckily, there was a fairly large crack, or all six of his front toes would have been cut off. It skinned the middle toe on his right foot and obviously pinched his toes but did no permanent harm, not even breaking any bones. First, I heard the door slam, then immediately, Kaw's loud screams. I didn't know there was a crack between the door and the doorframe as wide as his toes, so when I rushed out to release him, I feared the worst.

Bob was inside the garage, so he rushed over to Kaw, hanging by his toes on the garage side of the door, and grasped him around the body to keep Kaw from breaking his toes while struggling to get free. I was on the other side of the door, so I slowly opened it releasing Kaw's toes. Other than the small abrasion, he was uninjured. I was never sure which of us was the most frightened. Bob and I were afraid Kaw was seriously injured and Kaw was just plain scared. We all learned our lesson. Kaw never sat on top of the garage door again and we always checked to make certain the door was tied so it couldn't be blown closed by a sudden wind gust.

Kaw continued to follow us around when we were working in the yard. When we went into the house, he had to amuse himself by teasing the resident magpies. Another of his favorite pastimes was to sit on the backs of our horses and attempt to pull hair from their mane or tail. He also played with baling twine from the hay bales, feathers he found that had been lost by other resident birds, or anything shiny that caught his attention. Kaw didn't miss much and, as we provided nearly all of his food, he had a great deal of free time to play and get into mischief.

Kaw as a young adult, just before leaving with the other crows in fall from our place a half-mile east of East Missoula, Montana, with Brickyard Hill in the background.

Eventually, he became more independent regarding finding food for himself, catching and eating grasshoppers and other insects. Even so, he seemed to always be hungry, quickly coming when I called him to eat the dog food, pinky mice, and pieces of deer meat I took to him.

In early fall, a flock of 30 to 50 crows stopped at our place. They appeared to be a group passing through on their migration south. I had placed a quarter (one full leg) from an accident-killed deer on a platform for Kaw and the resident magpies to eat whenever they wanted. The migrating crows found the meat and decided to stay awhile. I kept putting more deer meat on the platform as fast as they ate it, so they stayed for over a week. Kaw flew around with them, socializing for the first time with members of his own species. When the crow flock left to continue their southward migration, Kaw went with them.

I didn't expect to see Kaw again, so when the crows appeared the following spring to eat deer meat off the platform, both Bob and I were thrilled to find Kaw was with them. It was easy to know which crow was Kaw. He was the one who came flying over to us to get pinky mice from me when I called, "Kaw, Kaw, Kaw!" just as he always had as a youngster. Again, the crows stayed about a week. One morning, after they had eaten their fill of deer meat, they all flew off together, going northwest toward Missoula. Though Kaw was perfectly willing to come to us for his special treats, he went with the flock when they left. I assume he (or she, whichever Kaw actually was) had a mate in the flock or would soon take a mate, since it was early spring and the mating season for crows would soon begin.

I hoped the flock would come by for a visit in the fall, so I made sure a piece of road killed deer was on the platform for them, especially in September. Bob picked up several carcasses a week as part of his job as a game warden, so there was a constant supply of fresh deer meat. The resident magpies appreciated the food they received and the crows didn't disappoint us. One day toward the end of September, a big flock descended onto the platform and the corral poles nearby. Kaw was still with them, appearing happy as always to see us and receive his special pinky mouse treats from me.

The crow flock stopped each spring and fall for three more years and Kaw was with them each time. Then one spring, no crows came to visit and we never saw them again. I assume something must have happened to Kaw, so he didn't guide them back, or maybe something happened to the entire flock on their migration. At that time, some states through which crows migrate or go to spend the winter allowed thousands of crows to be killed each year by poisoning them, which I consider a despicable thing to do.

Bob and I were extremely pleased each time Kaw and his crow friends and family came back to visit us. I hope he and his mate (or she and her mate) fledged many little crows and I hope their great, great, great grand-crows are playing and having fun somewhere, as only a crow can.

**Intelligence of
crows proven by making hooks
to use to snag food.**

A Steller's Jay like Blue and his family looking mischievous as usual in a photo by Eugene Beckes.

CHAPTER 28
A TRUE BLUE FAMILY

When Bob and I went to the Montana Department of Fish, Wildlife and Parks office in Missoula one autumn morning, the receptionist immediately handed me a box. Lying on the bottom was what looked like a mound of brilliant blue feathers. I reached in and lifted the almost lifeless dark head and looked into the pathetically dull eyes of a very sick adult Steller's Jay (*Cyanocitta stelleri*). That the jay was still able to look back at me gave me hope it wasn't too late to save it.

As a wildlife rehabilitator in western Montana, I often receive such "presents" in boxes of various sizes and shapes. A note on the box said the jay was found on Blue Mountain, a forested area on the southwest edge of Missoula. By that time, we had moved to the Bitterroot Valley and lived five miles south of Stevensville, approximately 39 miles from where the jay lived.

Blue seemed an appropriate name for the little jay as it was from Blue Mountain and deep blue in color. I couldn't tell right away whether it was male or female. Determining sex is difficult with Steller's Jays without being extremely intrusive. The name Blue may not have been imaginative, but the bird quickly learned to respond to it. With regard to Blue's gender, I later deduced from the bird's actions that he was a male.

I obtained some water from the MDFWP office restroom and coaxed the jay to swallow a few drops. Then we took him directly home, where I could give him electrolytes and put him in a warming box. Fortunately, there were no broken bones or other injuries. Blue was suffering from some type of illness, but I had no idea what it might be. He was quite emaciated, indicating he hadn't been able to eat anything for at least three days.

Blue was not strong enough to pick up and swallow pieces of solid food, so I fed him by placing a tube into his crop. A syringe containing electrolytes, a mixture of cooked egg yolk, and special food made for baby birds with plenty of vitamins and protein, was emptied through the tube into his crop. This is a fast and easy way to get nourishment into a bird without causing increased stress. I also gave Blue an antibiotic made for birds, in case he had a bacterial infection. During the first night, I had to get up several times to tube feed him with the electrolyte and food mixture. There was no apparent change in his condition all night. He slept lying on his stomach on the soft cloth on the bottom of the box I prepared for him. He remained there, sleeping with his head under one wing between feedings. The only encouraging sign, other than he was still alive each time I went to feed him, was his droppings indicated his digestive system was working properly.

The next morning, he raised his head and, even more encouragingly, looked up at me with those bright, mischievous eyes all jays have unless they are extremely ill or dead. He was still digesting food just fine, always a good sign with sick animals but made no attempt to stand. His symptoms suggested poisoning by an organophosphate pesticide. It took two more days of around-the-clock tube feeding before Blue was able to stand or walk. When I went to his box to feed him on the afternoon of the third day, he was standing there looking up, likely plotting the best way to escape from that box. I felt confident for the first time since he was handed to me that he was not going to die.

Once Blue was able to walk and hop up on a perch, I put him in a big box with branches poked through the sides to make perches at different levels. He would have liked to fly out but wasn't yet strong enough. He did his part to get well by eating all the soaked dog food, grasshoppers, pinkie mice, and other delicacies I gave him. On the fourth day after coming home with me, Blue took a bath in his water pan. Then he preened for a long time to smooth his ruffled feathers back into their proper positions.

On the fifth day, he was able to fly out of his box, so he immediately graduated to a big flight room where he could rebuild and strengthen his flight muscles. Once there, he flew around the room investigating everything. He bathed at least twice a day, with a great deal of wing flapping, splashing, and preening, until his beautiful blue feathers were shiny and smooth. On the eleventh day, he was ready to be released.

Our land has a riparian area with trees and brush along Willoughby Creek, surrounded by open, irrigated pastureland, hay fields, and dryland sagebrush habitat. Steller's Jays usually live in more forested areas, not dryland habitat. We hadn't seen them on our land or visiting our bird feeders, so I hadn't had the opportunity to observe one for longer than a few minutes when I was up in the forests on the west side of the Bitterroot Valley. It is four or five miles to the east or west of our land to forested habitat where Steller's Jays are commonly found. I didn't expect Blue to stay at our place for long but hoped he would stay long enough for me to observe his behavior in the wild for a few days at least.

Before releasing Blue, I placed a feeding platform in a hawthorn bush down by the creek. I put his favorite foods on the platform before standing him on a branch nearby. He flew to a higher branch and looked around. He was obviously not in familiar territory, so after checking things out, he flew into a tall ponderosa pine for an even better view. Soon he was flying around the riparian area with great curiosity, checking out everything he saw there. The next morning, he was in a tree not far from the feeding platform when I went out to feed him. I called "Hey Blue!" as I put his food on the platform and, as soon as I moved a short distance away, he flew down to eat. He quickly learned to come to the platform from wherever he was in our riparian area when I called to let him know I had brought food for him. He chattered excitedly while flying to the platform, which always let me know he had heard me. I often left dog food and deer meat on the platform for any bird who liked it. Our resident magpies quickly ate any food on the platform, so I couldn't leave Blue's special food, like pinky mice, on the platform unless he was there to eat it. I had to stand nearby and wait until he finished. The magpies wouldn't come to eat when I was close to the platform, but Blue didn't seem to mind my presence at all.

Blue and I soon developed a feeding schedule. Each day, I took food down several times, beginning early in the morning. Each time, all I had to do is call, "Hey Blue!" and he flew to me. His chattering call sometimes came from quite a long distance away. After he ate, he followed me as I scattered grain under various tangles of brush for the game birds and songbirds who frequent our land. On the 14th morning after his release, Blue didn't come when I called. I called repeatedly while putting food in the feeding areas, but there was no answering chatter and no sign of Blue. The only sound was a chickadee calling from the bushes near the feeding platform. After putting out the songbirds' food I searched under all the favorite feeding perches of the Goshawks, Cooper's Hawks, and smaller Sharp-shinned Hawks who occasionally swooped down from the pine trees in their attempts to catch unwary or ill songbirds and Mourning Doves. Much to my relief, there were no scattered blue feathers to be seen. I went out several times that day to call him and again the next day, but he neither answered nor came for food. I thought it was likely he had gone back to his former territory on Blue Mountain, where his mate might still be waiting for him.

Often when birds I release disappear from our area, I never see them again. However, enough come back the next spring to indicate that a fair number of my released youngsters survive and return to have young of their own. Blue was an adult, with a home and likely a mate, so I didn't expect to ever see him again. Even so, I called, "Hey Blue!" each morning when I went out to distribute the songbird food, but there was no answering chatter.

A little more than two weeks passed with no sign of Blue. I had given up calling for him when I went outside to work or hike in the creek area, but I often took my binoculars to observe the behavior of other birds who lived here then. Their activities are interesting and their interactions with each other are often amusing. I didn't expect to ever see Blue again but one morning, just under three weeks after I last saw him, I went out to fill the feeders with sunflower seed. As I was going from one feeding area to another, I heard the unmistakable chattering call of a Steller's Jay from up the creek east of the bird feeding areas. I yelled, "Hey Blue!" and to my utter amazement, not one, but four Steller's Jays came flying directly toward me. Blue, chattering an excited greeting, was several yards in the lead.

I hurriedly collected a dish of Blue's favorite foods and dumped it into his food tray on the platform, while Blue and the other three jays watched from nearby trees. The three new jays followed Blue to the tray and the four of them ate until the food was gone. I gave them food several times that day. The three new jays seemed right at home and didn't appear at all concerned by my presence. I suppose Blue had told them what a kind and generous benefactor he had found, or at least that I was a safe and reliable food dispenser.

For the rest of the fall and all through the winter, Blue, his mate, and the other two jays came when I called, followed me on my food distribution route through the creek bottom, and playfully chased each other up and down the creek. Since they didn't have to find food for themselves, they had plenty of time to play and they all enjoyed it. At night or when it rained or snowed, they used perches in the tall, thick-branched ponderosa pine for shelter. It was delightfully entertaining to have four playful jays following me around. They chattered constantly. One acted like she was Blue's mate, staying at his side and remaining near him wherever he went.

The other two jays also acted like a pair, but they could have been siblings. They were likely Mr. and Mrs. Blue's youngsters they raised the spring before. Blue seemed to be the leader, or at least he was almost always in the lead when they flew to me when I called them. Sometimes, Blue and his mate came from one direction and the other pair came winging in from somewhere in the opposite direction, indicating the two pairs did split up to look for food or that they roosted in different areas at night. Blue was always highly vocal when he flew in for food and he and his mate let me approach much nearer to them when they were eating, as close as two or three feet, so I could easily tell the pairs apart at feeding time. When they were all together playing, chasing each other around in the treetops or looking for food in the bushes, it was impossible to keep track of who was whom.

One day in March, after the weather warmed and the greens of spring were beginning to show, the four jays left, likely heading back to their home territory on Blue Mountain to raise a new family. They never returned.

It was intriguing that Blue had been found lying ill on the ground 39 miles north of our land. That must have been where he and the other three jays lived. When he left our place the first time, he had to fly 39 miles north to get to Blue Mountain. When he arrived there, he was able to find his mate and the other two jays. He then had to somehow persuade them to follow him all the way back to our land to spend the winter. It took him over two weeks to make the round trip. Blue obviously expected he and his family would be fed during the winter, as he had been after I released him. All four of the jays came flying toward me as if expecting food when I called Blue soon after they arrived. That definitely appeared to be cause and effect reasoning on Blue's part and, impressively, he was able to communicate this information to his family.

To persuade the other jays to follow him to a completely new habitat would have taken an advanced form of communication between the jays. Even though I tried very hard, I seldom could understand what the four jays were talking about when they chattered back and forth. From their actions, it was clear they knew what they were saying. I could sometimes tell when they were discussing food or predators like a visiting Sharp-shinned Hawk. What they said about me, I never knew, but I hope it was something nice.

A late warbler lands
in the willow, bright yellow
against falling snow.

Clarkie sitting in a dead pine tree.

CHAPTER 29
CLARKIE, TV STAR

Eight years after we moved to the Bitterroot Valley, in late February 1988, a pair of Clark's Nutcrackers (*Nucifraga columbiana*) built a nest of short branches and grasses, lined with feathers, in a ponderosa pine in the town park in Victor, Montana. In mid-March, Clarkie, her brother Lewie, and sister Sassy broke out of their grey-green shells into a world of cold and snow. With only the female's body between them and the frigid cold of late winter snowstorms, most would consider the likelihood of their survival marginal at best. However, with their mother's ever-present warm body sheltering them and their father industriously bringing pine seeds, bark beetles, mice, and other tasty tidbits to his hungry family, the three babies thrived. Father nutcracker took turns babysitting to keep the young ones warm while their mother flew to the nearby creek to drink or eat what her mate brought to her.

By the first of April, feathers were appearing on the bodies of the young nutcrackers, having come out of the sheaths that protect the feathers while they grow. With warmer weather, ground-dwelling insects began emerging from their winter hiding places and became a welcome addition to the nutcrackers' diet. Insects and an occasional mouse provided vital protein and calcium for the young nutcrackers to grow healthy feathers and bones. At this age, with the young birds sporting their new, warm feathers, both parents were free to forage for food for their ravenous brood.

In another week, the youngsters were not quite at the "branching" stage, when fledglings venture out of the nest to hop about through the tree branches. Branching develops their coordination and strengthens their wing and leg muscles, in preparation for flying and landing. The young birds' wing and tail feathers were still partly encased in the long sheaths that contain the feathers while they are growing. Their flight feathers would soon have been fully-grown, but disaster struck the small family, which is why I came to know them.

On April 12, a rainstorm with high winds came through the Bitterroot Valley. The wind, strong enough to blow down many trees, especially in the Victor area, blew the nest containing the three young nutcrackers completely out of the tree branches. In the tumble to the ground, Clarkie's right leg was broken. Lewie and Sassie were uninjured, but all three were wet and chilled. Worst of all, they were on the ground where they had no protection from predators. When the sun came up, they were even more vulnerable. By mid-morning there was a feral cat on the hunt, stalking directly toward the little nutcrackers huddled together in the short grass.

Fortunately, the parent nutcrackers, diving at and scolding the cat, drew the attention of a young girl and her friends, who had come to the park to look at all of the fallen branches and trees. The concerned children chased the cat away just in time to save the three fledglings. They picked up the little birds and carried them to the girl's home. Her mother called me for directions before bringing the cold, frightened babies just before noon. I told the girl she was a hero for rescuing the nutcrackers and thanked the mother for bringing them to me for care. I explained to them how important nutcrackers are to the propagation of pine trees, and thus to the survival of bears, squirrels, and other animals. When they grew up and were released, the three little nutcrackers would each plant enough seeds to produce a large forest in their lifetime.

After checking the birds for injuries, I fed them several quickly-thawed baby mice, tucked them into a warm box lined with an old sweater, and placed the box on a heating pad. They were in the pre-fledging stage. At that age Clark's Nutcracker youngsters are adorably cute. While they were resting and getting warm, I made a splint for Clarkie's leg. Fortunately, it was broken in the middle of the lower leg, without feathers and easily splinted.

I cut a splint from the bottom of a large eagle wing feather shaft, the strongest and lightest leg splinting material I have come across. When making a splint for this type of fracture, I cut the shaft in half, line the inside of each half with a strip of soft gauze, and place the two halves on each side of the broken bone, surrounding the leg to keep the bone perfectly straight. I tape the shaft tube together so that a tab I leave on each side of the top and bottom of the shaft extends over the joint above and the joint below the break, holding the leg and foot straight.

After being taped, the bird can walk on the leg while it heals, and the break is totally immobilized. The hollow feather shafts from molted wing feathers of hawks and eagles are perfect splints for birds with a broken leg. All that is needed is a bit of trimming and shaping. Medium-sized feather shafts work perfectly for the legs of wading birds and even smaller feather shafts, such as those of hawk wing feathers, are the perfect size for splinting songbird legs. It's quite remarkable that the best splint for a bird's broken lower leg is the hollow shaft from a larger bird's wing or tail feather.

After four or five days of eating all they could hold every 45 minutes, Lewie and Sassy were ready to go exploring and were becoming a bit too rowdy for Clarkie. Being a somewhat clumsy fledgling, in addition to having her leg splinted, Clarkie couldn't hop around nearly as well as her uninjured siblings. I put the two rowdy ones in a flight room filled with tree branches at various heights for them to practice hopping and flying, leaving Clarkie with me for company. I had to spend a good deal of time with her to encourage her to use her nearly-healed leg and working to help her learn to open and close the foot properly. After nine days, her leg was completely healed and I removed the splint. She was soon hopping around in the flight room branches with Lewie and Sassy, but the extra time I spent with Clarkie resulted in her being tamer and more tolerant of humans than her siblings. That tolerance continued for several years.

After a few more days in the flight room, the three adventurous youngsters were ready for release. Young birds need to learn about their new territory and practice their flying skills, so I release them as soon as they can fly well. Their real parents would have flown around with the youngsters all summer to show them how to take seeds out of pine cones, catch insects and mice, pull grubs out from under tree bark, and all the other things Clark's Nutcrackers need to learn to survive. I could not do that, since I am completely lacking flying abilities.

It takes much longer for young birds to learn all those things by trial and error or by watching each other. If I leave food out for them, other birds help themselves, leaving nothing for the youngsters. To prevent this problem, I say their name (or a certain word if there are several young birds) each time I feed them, which teaches them to come to me when I say their special word. That ensures they receive adequate nutrition, while they practice finding their own food. For the Clark's Nutcrackers, I just said "clarkies" every time I fed them. They soon learned to fly quickly from wherever they were in our riparian area trees to the feeding platform when they heard me call. In between feedings, they flew around, playing and learning hunting and foraging skills.

The three young nutcrackers had been released for about nine days when one evening, only Clarkie and Sassy came for the last meal of the day. The three birds always flew in to fill up their crops just before going to roost for the night. Lewie didn't show up for breakfast in the morning, so I suspected the worst. When one of my newly released youngsters went missing, it was usually because the inexperienced bird had become lunch for an accipiter. I began searching all of the thick bushes on our land where accipiters like to hide while they eat, looking for a circle of grey feathers. Under a pine tree in the creek bottom, I found Clark's Nutcracker feathers in the typical large circle characteristic of accipiters when they pluck their prey. Either a passing Cooper's Hawk or the Sharp-shinned Hawk who lived in our neighborhood had caught Lewie sometime the day before.

Fortunately, Clarkie and Sassy somehow avoided the hawk and all the other predators who could have had them for dinner. Sassy had always been the most aggressive of the three youngsters. After several more weeks, she came for her handouts less and less often, eventually becoming totally independent. Clarkie could also find her own food, having learned by flying around with Sassy and the resident wild nutcracker young of the year. The resident youngsters had learned from their parents, so were proficient at prying pine seeds from cones and catching insects. Because she wasn't afraid of me, Clarkie continued to come in for handouts for several months. She often visited our back porch to eat from the hanging suet feeder and continued that for as long as she lived. Consequently, I saw her often during her first winter, enabling me to track what she was doing. In January, she began keeping company with a handsome male nutcracker. He accompanied her to the trees behind our house and waited there while Clarkie came in for treats and suet. Her mate wouldn't come to the suet feeder himself until their three youngsters were flying the following spring.

The next year, 1990, they nested and again produced three healthy young hatchlings. When those fledglings were just out of the nest and beginning to branch, Steve Kroschel, photographer for the Wild America television program, contacted me. Someone had told him I was a wildlife rehabilitator, so he thought I might know where to find a Clark's Nutcracker nest. He needed to shoot film footage of parent nutcrackers feeding their young for a Wild America program on Clark's Nutcrackers and White-bark Pine trees. The program was to include a discussion of the life history of Clark's Nutcrackers, the White-bark Pine's dependence on the nutcrackers for seed dispersal, and the grizzly bear's dependence on White-bark Pine nuts to enable female bears to successfully produce healthy cubs.

246

I told Steve about Clarkie's family and suggested that, because she was tolerant of human presence, it should be easy to get footage of Clarkie and her mate taking food to their fledglings. He came to photograph them on a bright, sunny day. The new grey, white, and black feathers of the fledgling nutcrackers were beautiful against the green pine needles and rich blue sky. Clarkie and her mate paid no attention to Steve as he filmed them for nearly an hour after I showed him their nest tree.

The producers didn't use much of Steve's footage of Clarkie and her family in the final program, but what was used was interesting and showed seldom-seen nutcracker behavior. Clarkie came in with a mouthful of insects, putting her bill into each fledgling's open mouth. As soon as they were fed, Clarkie flew off to get more insects and the three fledglings, looking extremely cute, promptly fell asleep. There was also footage of the two adults foraging for pine seeds they had hidden the fall before. Steve was pleased with the nutcracker family's performance. Our other contribution to the Wild America show was a pine bark beetle Bob found for Steve to film. After much prompting, it crawled slowly along the piece of pine bark we used for a background. Bob was pleased that scene was also used in the show. Because it was a close-up of the beetle on the bark, no one could tell it was filmed on the coffee table in our living room.

Clarkie lived in the pine forests on and around our land for six more years, doing what Clark's Nutcrackers do best: removing pine seeds from their cones and hiding them in underground caches in soft dirt. The places she hid the pine seeds, usually five or six at a time, are excellent habitat for ponderosa pine seedlings to grow. Nutcrackers remember most of the places where they hide seeds, but for various reasons, they don't recover all of them, leaving some to sprout into tiny pine seedlings each spring. Consequently, each year, Clark's Nutcrackers plant millions of pines of a variety of species. Each nutcracker collects and hides at least 30,000 to 60,000 pine seeds every year. Many nutcrackers live 10 or more years, so actually plant the equivalent of an entire large forest during their life. The hidden caches of pine seeds the nutcrackers recover are used for food during the winter and early in the nesting season. That allows them to begin nesting in late winter, so the young fledge in April, at about the time many insects are hatching from hidden eggs or emerging from hibernation.

Clarkie and her mate had two or three young each year until spring 1995, when the pair didn't produce a family. Clarkie didn't come for suet after early spring that year so I can only guess what may have happened to her and her young. Possibly a raccoon or Great Horned Owl raided the nest. Clark's Nutcrackers still live and nest on our land and likely some are Clarkie's progeny. Steve sent us a tape of the Wild America program starring Clarkie and her family. Whenever I want to travel down memory lane with Clarkie, I put in the tape and watch her and her family's excellent performance.

Clarkie and her mate raised many youngsters. Considering the thousands of pine seeds planted by Clarkie and all of the young she produced, she must have several forests as her legacy by now. Because they plant so many pine trees and because of their incredible ability to remember where they hide their caches, I consider all Clark's Nutcrackers to be truly amazing birds. Clarkie was my special friend, a mother of many Clark's Nutcrackers, the Johnny Appleseed of ponderosa pine trees in our area, and the star of a television show. That is a lot for one little bird to do in one lifetime.

**Lives of White-bark Pines,
red squirrels, and bears depend
on Clark's Nutcrackers.**

CHAPTER 30
HELLO, QUOTH THE RAVEN

After Jasper (American Kestrel) and then Chicklette (Grey Partridge) were finished using our basement room, the next resident was an adult Common Raven (*Corvus corax*). It was brought to me for rehabilitation because someone in Missoula had illegally kept it in a cage for about 10 years after finding it as a fledgling and raising it. Because the raven had been kept so long in a small area, it couldn't fly. Except for being unable to fly, likely because of wing muscle deterioration, I could find nothing wrong with the otherwise healthy bird.

I found it interesting that the raven could say some English words. The one said most often was "hello," which is how he received the name I gave him. I assume he had a name since he was kept as a pet for so long but the game warden who brought him to me didn't tell me what it was. I never knew Hello's gender but assumed he was a male because of his size.

Hello was soon able to fly up onto the higher perches in the room but didn't begin flying from a perch on one side of the room to those on the other for over two months. He was quite tame and would hop onto my hand and remain there, so I could carry him around without jesses. He arrived in late winter; as soon as warm, early spring weather allowed I began turning him loose in our yard for several hours each day. He had quickly learned to come to me in the room when I called him by the name I had given him, so he did the same when he was free in the yard.

When called, Hello flew to my hand so I could carry him back to his room for the night. If we were going to go somewhere, I did the same, keeping him safe while we were gone. Even with freedom to practice, he still didn't fly up into the trees in our yard until mid-summer. I was afraid someone's dog or a fox or coyote might come through our property and find Hello on the ground. Once he began flying up onto tree branches, he fly/hopped from branch to branch to get higher in the tree. Unfortunately for Hello, I couldn't fly up into the tree to feed him and he was quite reluctant to fly down once he acquired a high branch from which to watch the other birds and everything that went on around him. Eventually, he got hungry enough to come down. When I heard him saying hello or cawing in his loud voice from the front porch, I went out and fed him. His bowl of water was always on the porch, so he could get a drink anytime.

Eventually Hello began flying better and flew farther, sometimes from tree to tree in the creek bottom. At first, he had trouble getting back so, following his calls, I went near where he was and called to him. By that time, he had learned he would get fed if he flew down to me, rather than waiting for me to fly up to him. One day in late summer, I could hear his calls, but they sounded quite far away. I finally determined they were coming from large pine trees across our hay field to the southeast, about a half-mile from our house. I walked over to the trees and there he was in the top of one. As soon as I got close enough, he said, "Hello, hello" and then, "Come here." After a bit of coaxing he flew down beside me and then up onto my arm. I gave him a small mouse and took him home for more food and a drink of water.

I was becoming a bit worried that Hello might fly off our land and not be able to find his way back. He was beginning to fly quite far in one flight but then didn't seem to know how to fly back. In September, he did just that. He flew up over the hill behind our house onto Sunset Bench to the north of our land. Sunset Bench is quite large, going several miles east to the foothills of the Sapphire Mountains and north for several miles from the south edge just above our land. It has many houses, ranches, and acres of farmland on it. I had no idea where Hello might have gone, since he had flown too far away for me to hear him call.

All I could do was hope he would find his way back when he became hungry enough. He was still absent after two days. The morning of the third day we had to go to Missoula, almost 40 miles north of us, to get groceries. When we returned in the afternoon, there was Hello playing on the lawn. I was happy to see him and even happier because I thought he had found his way home. As it turned out, he had not found his way home by himself.

That evening, a woman I knew, who lived in the middle of Sunset Bench, called me on the phone and told me she had brought my talking raven back that afternoon. Hello apparently had spent the two days in her yard. She had given him some dog food and table scraps. Because we weren't home, she left him in the yard and hoped that was all right. She said she assumed Hello belonged here because he said "Hello" and "come here" in English, stating that most ravens don't talk English. I told her the raven was in the yard when we arrived home and how grateful I was that

250

she had brought him here. I also told her I had not taught him the English words he said.

Hello didn't fly far away again before winter arrived. During the winter, I kept him in the flight room, only putting him outside on sunny days when there wasn't a lot of snow on the ground. By early spring, he was quite good at flying around and finding his way back, although he never went far when he was outside during the winter. Maybe he didn't want to get lost and hungry when it was cold out.

One day in May, when he was out flying around, he failed to come back. Hoping one of the local school children might see him or more likely hear him, I asked teachers in the Stevensville schools to announce to their children to watch for a raven who said "hello" and gave them the number to call if they saw him. Children pay attention when birds do something unusual, like speak English, and the teachers and most of the school children knew who I was because I had taken live, unreleasable birds to most of the classes.

After several days I received a call from a sixth-grade girl who told me she and her brother had seen a raven in a pine tree while walking home from school that afternoon. She said they heard the raven say "hello" several times. The area where they saw Hello was about five miles east of our home. I immediately drove to the place the girl described. There was only one pine tree out on a hillside, but no raven was there. I called there for quite a while, then went both east and west of that spot to call for Hello, but I never found him.

I never received any more reports of a raven saying "hello" and he didn't come home. It was the beginning of nesting season for ravens. I always hoped he found a female raven to mate with and had a happy life in the wild. After living in a small cage for 10 years, he certainly deserved it.

**Young ravens play with
their siblings and friends; learn skills
that help them survive.**

Ravens are the largest of the Corvid Family. They can be mischievous but often look quite regal. Photo by Eugene Beckes.

CHAPTER 31
AN EXTRA SPECIAL MAGPIE

Many people dislike Black-billed Magpies (*Pica hudsonia*), but I find them to be not only one of the most intelligent but also one of the most attractive of Montana's birds. Being both beautiful and intelligent, the Black-billed Magpie should have been considered for Montana's State Bird. Montana is likely blessed with more of them than any other state. Unfortunately, a number of people do not consider them a blessing.

Magpies are a strikingly beautiful bird. When light hits their black feathers, they shine with an iridescent blue-green. Such iridescent or "interference" colors on feathers are explained scientifically as the "effect of a thinly laminated structure consisting of a layer of special cells which overlie the dark brownish basal pigment cells in the barbules of the feathers." Those special cells interfere with light rays striking the feathers from different angles, scattering the rays and causing the observer to see brilliant blue-greens, greens, purples, or reds. Hummingbirds have many feathers with the special cell layer. Many species of duck also have iridescent feathers in a patch on the wing called the "speculum."

Injured or orphaned magpies are often brought to me for care. Both the magpies I raise and the resident ones who fledge here and live here year around are constantly busy. Like other corvids, they are usually doing something of interest to anyone intrigued with bird behavior. This is a true story of a magpie who exhibited many characteristics commonly referred to as "human traits," including a high level of intelligence. The hero of this story is a young Black-billed Magpie I named Einstein because of his obvious intelligence. It is impossible for me to determine whether juvenile magpies are male or female, so I usually give somewhat generic names to all magpies brought to me for care. However, judging by the behaviors Einstein exhibited, I concluded he was most likely a male.

Einstein was exceptional from the beginning of our relationship, because he brought himself for care. He was newly fledged from one of the many magpie nests on our property. Soon after he learned to fly, he became ill. When I first saw Einstein, he was sitting on the roof of our front porch, looking bedraggled and all fluffed up, sure signs he was not feeling well. He had been eating quite a few sour cherries from our cherry trees. It is possible that eating a steady diet of sour cherries wasn't providing adequate protein or had adversely affected his digestive system.

In retrospect, I guess I could have named him Cherry Pie. His parents had taken cherries from our trees to feed their babies while they were still in the nest. After the young magpies learned to fly, they went to the tree and ate cherries until they were full. After a brief rest, they flew around the yard talking magpie language to each other and chasing the robins, who also enjoyed feasting on sour cherries.

Hoping more nutritious food was what Einstein needed, I began to throw small mice and pieces of moistened dog food up on the roof for him. He ate the food I provided but after several days appeared to have become weaker. Early one morning I found him sitting on the porch steps, looking even more bedraggled and too weak to fly. I picked him up, deloused him, gave him some antibiotics, and put him in a large box where he would be warm and comfortable. The box had a branch pushed through the sides for a perch and food and water dishes in one corner. I gave him all the mice and dog food he would eat plus vitamins every day. In two or three days, he looked much better and was eating well. Assuming he had internal parasites, which most birds do, I dewormed him with Ivermectin®. After that he began gaining weight and strength even faster, indicating that intestinal parasites were at least part of his health problem. A bath and preening returned his black feathers to their rainbow sheen and his white feathers to their immaculately bright white. Soon after his bath he proved he was feeling much better by poking holes in the sides of the large cardboard box, which had served as his recovery room.

While Einstein was recuperating, two more starving fledgling magpies were brought to me for care and rehabilitation. Although they were siblings, one was somewhat larger, healthier, and more completely feathered than the other. I called the larger one, Maggie Pie and the smaller one, Little Pie. Interestingly, it turned out that Maggie Pie, Maggie for short, was likely a female.

When Einstein began taking his recovery box apart, I concluded he was trying to tell me he was well enough to be placed in an outdoor flight pen. By that time, the little magpies were healthy enough to join him, since all they had needed for recovery were a few good meals and deworming. I hoped watching Einstein pick up food and eat it would teach the little ones to do the same, rather than waiting for me to feed them. Unfortunately, they continued to make loud, insistent food calls at regular intervals all day. I still had to put the food in their mouths, since they hadn't yet learned how to close their beaks on the food and eat it by themselves. Picking up food in their bills as fledglings is an achievement that takes practice for young altricial birds. Altricial hatchlings are unable to move around on their own for some time after hatching. They are usually nearly naked at hatching and take three weeks or more, depending on the species, to grow to full-sized fledglings. Birds like those of game bird or waterfowl species who can walk and run soon after hatching are called precocious hatchlings. They can find and pick up insects or other food when only a day or two old.

After two or three days in the flight pen, Einstein and Maggie were becoming quite rambunctious. Einstein, especially, indicated he had had enough of captivity by flying against the side of the pen, looking for a way out. That seemed to excite Maggie, so she also flew against the side of the pen. I didn't want either of them to damage their feathers so I released Einstein. He quickly learned to come for food when I called him. I placed his food and water on top of the pen and he flew right to it without any coaxing.

With just Little Pie for company, Maggie quickly calmed down. I waited two more days before releasing her. She could fly well and came to me to be fed, so I took her out of the pen and placed her in the tree where Einstein was perched. Maggie and Einstein seemed ecstatic at being reunited and celebrated by playing follow the leader through the pine trees in the immediate area with Einstein as leader flying ahead of Maggie.

Predictably, about two hours later, Maggie was hungry and let me know it by food calling at extreme decibel levels. She and Einstein flew to the top of the cottonwood tree closest to the pen as soon as I called to them. Maggie perched there looking down. She continued to give her magpie food call insistently but absolutely refused to fly down close enough for me to put the food in her open mouth. She appeared to assume I would fly up to the top of the tree to feed her, or possibly her taste of freedom had rekindled her natural fear of humans. Either way, it was apparent that Maggie was going to have to be very hungry before she would come down low enough for me to feed her. Einstein, as he always did, immediately flew to the top of the pen and began to eat the moistened dog food in their food pan.

I repeatedly gave a magpie call to try to persuade Maggie to fly to a lower branch so I could feed her. Einstein, who was busily eating, suddenly stopped, looked up at Maggie for a few seconds and picked up a chunk of dog food. I thought he was going to hide it for a future snack, as magpies often do. You can imagine my surprise and delight when he flew up to Maggie and put the dog food into her gaping mouth. She quickly swallowed the food and began food calling for more, so Einstein flew down, picked up another piece, and fed that to Maggie. This was repeated until she finally stopped food calling. Einstein then flew to the food dish and swallowed a few more pieces of dog food. Then they flew off together to perch high in a nearby pine tree to take a nap and digest their food.

Every feeding time for over a week, Einstein ate a few bites, then fed Maggie. After that he ate until he was full. When they were both satisfied, off they went to amuse themselves in the large trees along Willoughby Creek. Finally, Maggie learned to fly down to the food dish and pick up pieces of raw deer meat and dog food by herself.

According to an ornithologist who has studied Black-billed Magpie behavior, "males are highly philopathic," which means the alpha male in a nest of magpies stays in the area where he fledges. This is why we assumed Einstein was a male. He was definitely the alpha male of the fledglings I released. Einstein had fledged from a nest on our land. Maggie and Little Pie were both from another area. They were not related to Einstein and the other local magpies. The ornithologist thought Maggie was a female, since she elicited a feeding response from Einstein by her food begging. That might have been common behavior for adult magpies during breeding season, but both Einstein and Maggie were fledglings.

I released Little Pie several days after I released Maggie. Little Pie flew down to a branch right beside me when I called him or her, so I was able to give Little Pie food whenever I heard a magpie food calling. Little Pie learned, after only two days of following and observing the other two magpies, to pick up and eat the dog food or deer meat I left for them in their food dish. Immediately after release, Little Pie joined the other two magpies in their games of chase, tag, and tease the robins. The three magpies remained friends, staying together all fall and winter. I could no longer tell them apart, but they all showed up for handouts whenever they saw me working outside.

Very early the next spring, two of the magpies built the usual covered basket-like nest and fledged a new generation of six beautiful young with the assistance of deer meat I provided for them. Since Einstein was most likely a male and Maggie Pie a female, the evidence was strongly in favor of them being the pair who nested. The two were inseparable even before

Little Pie rejoined them. While nesting and raising young, they allowed me to come closer than other magpies living on our land and expected food to appear whenever they saw me. I was unable to keep track of the third magpie after nesting season began. The pair lived happily ever after on our land, raising new fledglings each year for several years, just like a real live fairy tale.

I have been unable to find any documented occurrence of juvenile magpies feeding other juvenile magpies, so I don't know how special this behavior might have been. I do know Einstein was intelligent enough to come for care when he was ill and compassionate enough to feed his young magpie friend. He was a very special magpie, at least to Maggie and me.

Fresh tracks in new snow
leading through frost covered trees
to winter solstice.

A Black-billed Magpie looking gorgeous and intelligent. Photo by
Eugene Beckes.

CHAPTER 32
THE MAGPIE FROM HELL

Scraps was an ordinary Black-billed Magpie when she hatched out of an egg in a domed magpie nest near the Clark Fork River in spring 1993. She was still just an ordinary pre-fledgling magpie when her brothers and sisters finished growing their feathers and began hopping one at a time out of their hot, crowded nest onto the surrounding branches of the Hawthorne bushes that sheltered it. Scraps was the "runt of the litter." She was the last to hatch and so was younger and smaller than the other fledglings. With her survival in question, there was nothing about her to indicate that, in the next two years, she would be known in two western Montana counties as the "Magpie from Hell."

About five days after the young magpies left the nest, they all began flying short distances. All except Scraps, who, try as she might, could not begin to keep up with her siblings. Her mother and father brought food back to her at first. As the other youngsters flew farther and farther away, testing and strengthening their new flight muscles, the parent birds were so busy keeping up with the demands of feeding and protecting the older fledglings that Scraps was forgotten or abandoned. Hunger drove her to try following the sound of her family's calls in the distance but she only ended up on the ground under a bush.

Scraps wasn't able to hop up into the branches of the bush so she spent the night in the cold grass on the ground, where she was found the next morning by a jogger named Frank. She was hypothermic, dehydrated, and suffering from malnutrition. Luckily the jogger was a nice man who knew all about birds, since he had several pet birds including parrots. When Frank picked up Scraps and put her under his sweatshirt to warm her, he not only saved her life, he started her on her journey to becoming the infamous "Magpie from Hell."

Frank took Scraps to his home on the western edge of Missoula. As soon as she was warmed, she began food begging as only a loud, insistent young magpie can. He gave her water with a medicine dropper, then some moist dog food pieces. Warm and full of food, Scraps soon settled down for a nap.

Young Black-billed Magpies are tough and resilient. Scraps quickly became a healthy fledgling who learned to fly around Frank's house when he let her out of the cage in which she was usually kept. She copied all manner of screeches, squawks, and other sounds made by parrots and often associated with the background noises of a jungle movie. Frank's parrots said a lot of English words and phrases, many of which Scraps learned to say. She developed quite a large vocabulary for a magpie, including "Hello", "Scraps," "I want some scraps," "I'm hungry," "I want some strawberries," "Frank" or "Hi Frank," and she most appropriately quite often said in a grouchy tone, "Get out of here!" and "Stop doing that!" Scraps must have been a mischievous little magpie right from the beginning. "Get out of here" and "Stop doing that" were her loudest and most often repeated phrases. Someone must have said them many times to her in a loud, annoyed tone of voice. People who came in contact with her didn't have to know her very long to find out why.

Her favorite tricks were to hover in front of an unsuspecting person and peck their hands viciously, dive at their heads, land on the ground behind them, run up to their legs and peck their ankles or, last but certainly not least, land on their shoulder and peck the back of their neck or ear. Her pecks were sometimes hard enough to draw blood. Those not so endearing pranks were what earned Scraps the seemingly universal title of the "Magpie from Hell," independently bestowed on her over the course of her first year of life by a fairly large number of people around Missoula in Missoula County and Stevensville in Ravalli County. Most of the individuals who came in contact with Scraps were completely unaware of her interactions with the other people who had the sometimes unpleasant fate of making her acquaintance.

In July, Frank turned Scraps loose in his yard. She hung around his house, begging for food when she was hungry and sneaking up on visitors to peck them. She quickly became a somewhat dangerous nuisance. One day Scraps attacked the woman who delivered his mail. Reluctantly, Frank decided it was time to break all ties. He caught Scraps, put her in a box, drove to Council Grove Park, and left her there in a cottonwood tree.

The next day, a man named Matt went to the park to fish. After catching several fish, he packed up to go home. As Matt started to drive away, he heard something land on the roof of his car. He stopped and got out to see what had made the thump sound. There standing on the car was Scraps. They stared at each other for a short time, then Scraps astounded

Matt by saying in a loud clear voice, "Stop doing that!" Scraps liked men, likely because she was initially rescued, fed, and cared for by a man.

She allowed Matt, who fortunately for Scraps happened to be a wildlife rehabilitator, to pick her up. He put her under his coat and drove to his daughter-in-law's home to show Scraps to his wife Linda, also a wildlife rehabilitator. Linda and her daughter Susan didn't believe Matt when he told them Scraps talked in English as well as in magpie language. Linda picked her up and, while Scraps was perched on her hand, she began talking, saying mostly strange, guttural, unintelligible words strung together with some easily recognizable English words. The words that could be clearly understood were, "I want some strawberries," "Frank," "Stop doing that," and "scraps." Linda and Susan had to admit Matt was not hallucinating. They named the magpie Scraps because that was one of the words she said.

Linda and Matt took Scraps with them to their home near Missoula. She was obviously a young bird, acting as if she were hungry by opening her mouth in a food begging posture between strings of words and jungle sounds. At their place in the country, Scraps was allowed to fly around outside or come into the house, which she liked to do. Scraps talked quite a lot, mixing words like "strawberries" "scraps" and "stop doing that" with normal magpie vocalizations and parrot-like squawks. Linda and Matt enjoyed her antics. Scraps was a well-behaved addition to their family for a while, accepting their food and hospitality without exhibiting any of her aggressive behavior.

Then one day a woman with red hair came to visit, along with several other people. For some reason, Scraps showed an intense dislike for the woman, possibly because of her red hair, and instantly began to manifest her "Magpie from Hell" behaviors. Scraps literally terrorized the woman by diving at her and pecking at the back of her neck. The woman had a mole there, which Scraps was determined to remove. Although small, when Scraps attacked in deadly seriousness, she was like a monster from a horror movie to someone not used to being around birds, especially attack birds with relatively large, sharp bills.

After the visitors left, Scraps retained some of the aggressive side of her personality and began to occasionally dive at Linda and Matt. Her playful, gentle side emerged when Linda called her to give her food, which Scraps accepted eagerly with many guttural, strange-sounding vocalizations and a great deal of tail flipping and hopping into the air. She had always been fed by people so was not adept at finding food for herself. Consequently, she flew to Linda from quite a distance when called.

Scraps had a strange affinity for vehicles. One of her favorite antics was to fly beside a slow-moving car or pickup and land on the mirror on the side of the car. She hung on while the car went faster, leaning forward into the wind. She appeared to thoroughly enjoy the wind rushing by her as the vehicle picked up speed. One day, this eccentric behavior led her to leave Linda and Matt for new adventures and new acquaintances. It wasn't until nearly a year later they found out what had happened to their somewhat malicious but interesting and entertaining guest.

In late summer, Scraps followed a visitor's car for a long distance. After losing her race with the car, she flew to the east around the bottom of the mountain, the opposite direction from Linda and Matt's place, finding her way to another couple's yard. There, Scraps was again on her best behavior for the first few days, talking in English, making strange-sounding noises, and begging for food. The people thought Scraps was a strange bird but cute and interesting, until something again triggered her aggressive side. She began flying at them and pecking their hands. Or she sneaked up on them, rushing out on foot to vigorously peck at their ankles. Not wanting to harm the English-speaking but mean little bird, the people called the Department of Fish, Wildlife and Parks, who told them to call me. I suggested the people call Byron Weber, the wildlife rehabilitator who at that time specialized in caring for crows, magpies, and ravens in Missoula. They were able to catch Scraps and soon arrived at Byron's home with her. Thus, Scraps again had a new home and was one step closer to becoming my responsibility.

Since Scraps was healthy and could fly, Byron allowed her to fly free in his yard. Scraps liked Byron but took an immediate, strong dislike to Jane, Byron's wife. Her "Magpie from Hell" personality returned with a vengeance. She was like a real-life Jekyll and Hyde. After only a few days of putting up with Scraps, Byron called me, sounding a bit frantic. He wanted to know if I would take a very strange young magpie who talked English and attacked his wife whenever she stepped out the door.

I had several other juvenile magpies in rehabilitation. I thought if I put Scraps in the flight room with them, she would learn from them how to act like a magpie and stop attacking people. Imprinted juvenile owls, falcons, and hawks had always exhibited normal behavioral characteristics after spending time with others of their own species. Some Great Horned Owls who are handled a great deal and allowed to walk around in homes like puppies do some non-owlish things after they learn to fly. If they were put with wild Great Horned Owls, they soon became much wilder and quickly learned to behave like Great Horned Owls when released. I hoped an intelligent bird like a Black-billed Magpie could be retrained in the same manner.

I told Byron to leave her with a friend who was coming from Missoula, where he lived, to Stevensville, a small town near where I live. I met my friend in Stevensville to get Scraps. She handed me a box containing a slightly scrawny, confused-looking magpie. That is how I met the endearing little "Magpie from Hell." When we got home, I checked Scraps for lice, deloused, and dewormed her. She seemed healthy, so I put her in the flight room with the other six young Black-billed Magpies who were building up their flight muscles and learning to pick up food and eat by themselves.

I left their mouse pieces and moistened dog food in dishes but went to the flight room several times a day to feed any who food-begged, indicating they were hungry. For some young birds, learning to pick up food in their bills and eat it without it being placed in their mouth takes practice. Parent birds feed fledglings while they gain experience in finding, catching, or picking up their own food. Once one bird in a group begins picking up food, the others quickly learn by watching it. Scraps already knew how to get her own food and eat it, so would be helpful in teaching the younger birds.

Scraps appeared to be an ordinary, though smallish, female magpie. Her looks didn't reveal anything unusual. At that time, I knew nothing of her history prior to what the couple who had called me said before taking Scraps to Byron at my suggestion. Even Byron's description of her attacks on his wife Jane didn't give me an indication of the bizarre behavior of which Scraps was capable. When I received her from Byron, I didn't know about Scrap's adventures with Linda and Matt. After I had personally heard what Scraps said in English words and phrases and the parrot sounds she made, I was able to piece together some of her past history. Then, several weeks after I received her, I happened to mention Scraps to Linda while talking to her on the phone. I told her I had gotten a strange-acting magpie from Missoula who said "Frank," "strawberries," "scraps," "Get out of here," and other English words and sentences, as well as sounds usually made by parrots. When we began comparing what we each knew of Scrap's adventures, it became obvious that she was the same young magpie Linda and Matt had as a guest earlier in the spring.

Three days after I put Scraps in the flight room, she flew at me with the obvious intent of pecking my hands. I clapped my hands making a loud pop sound and said "No" in a very stern voice. That definitely made an impression on her, as she never made any attempt to attack me again. Also, she never tried to attack me when I wasn't looking or when my hands were occupied, as she had done with many other people. Unfortunately, she also no longer allowed me to pick her up or even get near her, making it difficult for me to catch her when the need arose.

When the seven young magpies were ready for release, I turned them all loose in the barnyard area so I could put food out for them. Since Scraps had acted like a completely normal wild magpie after our brief aggressive encounter, I released her with the others. She remained with the magpie group and appeared to enjoy flying around with them. They explored our land, the surrounding neighbor's yards, and the creek bottom. When I called, "Hey Pie. Come here Pie" in a loud voice, all seven came to the food platform to eat what I left for them.

Everything seemed fine with the young magpies, including Scraps, for nearly two weeks. One day, I found our neighbor's children, Ricky and Annie, playing with Scraps. She let them touch her and walked on the ground, following them like a small, black and white puppy. Concerned that she might attack their legs, I asked them if she had done anything unusual like pecking them. They said she just followed them around and sometimes she said some English words. They indicated they thought she was a funny bird because she said words they could understand, followed them, and rode on the mirror on the passenger side of their car when their parents took them somewhere. I warned them not to let her get near their eyes; they agreed to be careful. That was all I could do since Scraps wouldn't let me near her, quickly flying away whenever I approached her.

A few days later, I received a phone call from another neighbor boy, eight-year old Zack, who lived three quarters of a mile west of us. He said there was a tame magpie sitting on the window ledge pecking on the windowpane of his bedroom. Zack loved birds and occasionally went on bird counts with me, until his family moved away. He didn't want the funny little magpie to get hurt. Since Scraps flew down to him and landed on his shoulder whenever he went outside, I asked him to try to catch her and put her in a box so I could bring her home. He agreed, so I hurried to Zack's house with a transport box. When I arrived, Scraps wasn't exactly captured, but she was inside their house, flying around Zack's bedroom. Zack had opened the window while she was sitting on the ledge and

Scraps came right in. Zack quickly closed the window, trapping her in the room where I had no trouble catching her. After letting Zack and his little brother pet her, I put her in the transport box and brought her home. Zack assured me he would call if Scraps returned to their house. I put out plenty of food in case she was hungry after her escapade and released her back in the barnyard with her magpie friends.

I drove a four-wheeler to the barn area, which is a quarter mile from our house, to feed and water all the animals, milk the goats, and clean bird rooms. Scraps could hear the four-wheeler for a long distance and came flying to it whenever she heard me arrive at the barn. I left food in the basket on the four-wheeler for Scraps to eat while I was working. She flew down and helped herself, also landing on the basket when I was driving down the road, as long as I kept both hands on the handlebars.

About a week after retrieving Scraps from Zack's bedroom, I received calls from several neighbors about a talking magpie stopping by for a visit. Even though there were no complaints, the knowledge that she was out "making friends" was a bit disconcerting. I didn't know when or if she would revert, with no warning, to being the "Magpie from Hell," as she had done in her not too distant past.

I am ashamed to admit I couldn't help but feel a bit relieved when Scraps suddenly stopped coming for food when I called the magpies. After several days, she was still nowhere to be found. I hoped her absence meant she was just out exploring with her magpie friends. I considered it more likely that the goshawk who came through our area on hunting excursions may have had Scraps for dinner. I looked but couldn't find a neat circular pile of magpie feathers like accipiters leave after eating birds they catch.

I missed Scraps but, with no inkling of where she went or what might have happened to her, there was nothing I could do except watch for her in case she returned hungry. I found out in July 2017, while talking to a woman named Dani, that Scraps had flown several miles west, across the Bitterroot River, and all the way to the foothills of the Bitterroot Mountains. Then she turned north and apparently began flying back toward Missoula.

Dani said she and two friends were visiting in their yard on Indian Prairie Loop Road when a smallish Black-billed Magpie flew down and landed 10 to 15 feet away from them. All three heard it say "Hello," so began watching it. It hopped around on the ground saying other things in English and making un-magpie-like noises. Then it said "Hello" again.

265

Indian Prairie Loop Road is approximately six miles northwest of our place. I find it amazing that I am still learning about Scraps' adventures and where she went 24 years later. Apparently, she made a lasting impression on all who met her.

Scraps travelled north and back to the east from Indian Prairie Loop, because when she began getting into trouble again, it was in the town of Stevensville, seven miles north and a little west of us. A little over two months after I last saw Scraps at our place, a woman called from Stevensville, asking if I would take a tame magpie if she brought it to me. I don't remember the woman's name, but from her exasperated description of the magpie, I knew immediately that Scraps was on her way home. The woman said the magpie, which spoke English, had been staying in the area around their house for several weeks. They thought it was a unique bird and went out to give it food several times a day. She said it made un-magpie-like sounds, some like a loud parrot squawking. They could easily understand many English words it said, such as "strawberries," "Get out of here," and "Don't do that," leaving no doubt about the magpie's identity.

Eventually, for no apparent reason, Scraps had begun attacking the people, pecking them on the neck, hands, and ankles. They decided to get rid of the "Magpie from Hell," as she called her, by taking her to their parents' ranch several miles to the northwest of Stevensville. After catching Scraps and putting her in a box, they drove to the ranch and released her. They began the trip home with Scraps riding on their passenger side mirror for the first half-mile, flying off when they picked up speed. They thought they had seen the last of her until they arrived back at their home in Stevensville. Scraps was already there, perched on the front porch waiting for them to feed her. By this time, they were beginning to think they were never going to elude the crazy bird who seemed to be an escapee from an Alfred Hitchcock movie.

Someone suggested the woman call me. She did, hoping I would take the "Magpie from Hell" out of their lives permanently. Oddly, like everyone else Scraps had attacked, they didn't want to hurt or kill her. I told the woman to bring the magpie right over so I could lock her in a flight room. That way, she wouldn't be able to return to their place. I deliberately neglected to mention I knew that magpie very well. I wasn't responsible for Scrap's propensity for attacking people, but I was responsible for releasing her into our neighborhood, from which she flew to their place in Stevensville. It seemed wisest not to volunteer any information concerning my previous association with Scraps.

When she arrived, I deloused her again, in case she had picked up any unwanted, bloodsucking hitchhikers such as lice or feather mites. She was healthy and appeared to have been eating well. I put her into the flight room, where she was alone, since there were no magpies in rehabilitation at the time.

After almost two weeks of imprisonment, Scraps became so lonely that her attitude toward me changed. She began flying down beside me when I went into the flight room. One day she wanted out so badly that, when I went in to feed her, she landed close enough for me to touch her and said softly, "Get out of here." I felt so sorry for her that, against my better judgment, I gently put my hands around her, carried her outside, and set her on a tree branch. She flew to a higher branch in the huge old elm tree and began making every parrot vocalization and jungle noise you could possibly imagine coming out of a bird. I guess that was her way of celebrating and telling the world how happy she was to be free again. She didn't go far away after that, but she still found ways to get into mischief.

Unfortunately for the neighbors who lived about 200 yards away from our barn, only a short flight for a magpie, Scraps decided to spend most of her days in their yard. The neighbors, Rob, Sue, and their three teenage children, thought Scraps was a nice and extremely interesting bird. I often saw her sitting on the roof over their front door or in the big ponderosa pine in their front yard, where she had a good view of the front door. When I went by on my four-wheeler to feed the other animals and birds, Scraps could easily see me and came flying over to eat her food from the basket on the four-wheeler. Rob and Sue's son Robby liked Scraps and also fed her all through the winter.

The warm weather in February stimulated Scraps to look for a mate. Unfortunately, her choice was not one of the many handsome male magpies who lived on our land and helped me by cleaning up what was left of the accident-killed deer I fed the carnivorous animals and birds of prey in my care. The unwitting object of Scrap's affection was none other than Rob himself. Persuading Scraps to act like a normal magpie was obviously not going to be easy. She was nearly a year old and some of her worst transgressions were yet to come.

Until Scraps chose Rob to pursue as her mate, she hadn't attacked anyone since the people from Stevensville the previous fall. She followed Rob as he worked around his yard but never attacked him. Just the opposite, her behavior toward him was extremely amorous. Rob's wife Sue, however, began being perceived by Scraps as a rival and serious competitor for Rob's attention. Scraps became more and more aggressive toward her. She also occasionally dived at his two daughters, trying to chase them away from their father.

I was becoming concerned that Scraps might seriously injure Sue or the girls, especially if she pecked at their eyes. In mid-March, I asked Rob to catch Scraps for me. She hadn't let me close enough to catch her since I had taken pity on her and released her in late fall. She would come as close as she could to Rob, sitting down beside him with her tail straight up in the air and her head tipped way back, with her eyes kind of rolled up in the sockets. She sat that way shaking her wings and shivering all over so that her feathers rattled. Rob said I didn't need to lock her up, but he did want to know why that crazy bird kept landing beside him and why she had suddenly begun acting so strange. I didn't think her strange behaviors were all that sudden, but Rob wasn't aware of her past adventures of the summer before. He said she had been fine all winter but had recently begun to "act weird."

I told him if he didn't know why she was acting that way, he might not want to know. Rob said he very much wanted to know, so I told him. "She wants you to mate with her. She is presenting herself to you." Rob looked shocked, turned very red, and said, "Get out of here," which at the time was slang for "You are not serious," or "You have got to be kidding." I laughed and said, "That's funny because that is exactly what Scraps says all the time." I assured him Scraps really did want him to mate with her. I pointed out all her obvious actions, which clearly showed that was exactly what she wanted. I explained that, because she had been rescued and cared for as a fledgling by a man named Frank, she liked men and had chosen him as her mate. Rob became embarrassed again and turned even redder than before, so I changed the subject.

A week and a half later, Bob and I left for a two-week vacation. Scraps remained free, and still caused trouble for Sue whenever she went outside. Before we left, I told Rob to catch Scraps if she caused them too much trouble and showed him where to put her in the flight room. I gave him a key and left a large pan of water in the room in case he needed to lock her up. He agreed to feed her if jailing her again became necessary but didn't want to confine her. I think it was because he liked having her flirt with him. As I feared, leaving her loose turned out to be a gigantic mistake.

268

Another of our neighbors was Zack's mother, Diane, a good friend who kindly agreed to feed our goats while we were away. Whenever Diane came to give grain and hay to the goats, Scraps immediately flew to the barnyard. Apparently, she considered herself the guardian of the area, because she attacked Diane viciously as soon as she got out of her vehicle. When Diane brought any of her children, including Zack, Scraps landed on their back and pecked them on the neck. Scraps usually waited until Diane had her hands full of hay to swoop down and land on the hay. Then Scraps walked on the top of the hay to Diane's hands and began pecking them with the full force of her sharp pointed beak. If Diane put the hay down to protect herself, Scraps flew up to the top of the barn and sat there watching for her next opportunity. As soon as Diane's hands were occupied, Scraps again went into attack mode. She either pecked Diane's hands or sneaked up behind her and attempted to peck her on the ankles. Diane finally tried bringing an adult friend with her to distract Scraps while Diane did the feeding. That worked fairly well, but by the time we returned, Diane's hands still had several blue spots and even some spots where the skin had been broken by Scrap's bill. Fortunately, Diane wore long, full skirts, which protected her legs, so they escaped the little bird's dagger-like beak.

Diane was extremely relieved when we arrived home, because she would no longer have to go anywhere near that "horrible bird." Diane never swore and I had never heard her say the word hell before she emphatically stated on my arrival home that the magpie who lived in our barnyard was a "Magpie from Hell." I had not told Diane about Scraps' history. Everyone who called Scraps the "Magpie from Hell" did so independently and apparently quite justifiably.

Scraps had also terrorized Rob's wife Sue all the time we were gone. The day before we arrived home, Sue was outside painting the white trim on her house. Scraps sat on the roof above, and without warning, dived down at Sue, once nearly pecking her in the eye. Dodging an attacking bird is difficult when standing on a ladder and obviously extremely dangerous. Sue finally discouraged the attacks by hitting Scraps on the back and tail with the paintbrush. That scared Scraps and left a white paint streak on the black feathers, which didn't come off for a long time.

The day following our return from vacation, I was at the barn doing the feeding. I also had to clean rooms, a chore that hadn't been done while we were away on our trip. Rob drove by in his car with Scraps following, yelling at him in very loud squawks. I waved him to a stop and asked if

269

Scraps had caused any trouble for them while we were gone. He had just finished telling me about Sue being pecked a fraction of an inch from her eye, when Scraps, sporting the white racing stripe down her tail, landed beside him. I asked him to catch her for me. Scraps obligingly let Rob pick her up. I took her from Rob and thanked him. Poor Scraps was again condemned to solitary confinement in the flight room.

I called Sue as soon as I got back to our house and apologized for Scraps' horrible behavior. I assured her I wouldn't release her again unless I could cure her of attacking people. I had just about given up hope of ever accomplishing that but didn't like the alternative. I can't keep healthy birds locked up for life. If Scraps didn't learn to be a normal magpie, she would have to be euthanized. I was not ready to even consider that option for a healthy bird.

It turned out that Sue was painting their house because they were planning to sell it and move to Florence, a town 20 miles north of us. Fortunately for Scraps, their property sold quickly. By the end of April, Rob, the object of her affection, was no longer around. I released Scraps the day after they moved. She immediately flew over to their empty house and yard and found it deserted.

With Rob gone, Scraps' behavior changed completely. She began flying around with a handsome male magpie. Even though it was somewhat late in the season, they built their nest in a juniper tree beside our lane not far from the barn area. I continued to put out food for them and for their five youngsters who fledged in June. Scraps and her mate graciously accepted my handouts, which usually consisted of pieces from accident-killed deer carcasses. When the two magpies were not feeding and caring for their youngsters, they pulled off meat from the deer legs I left for them and hid it for future use.

When magpies have a good supply of meat, such as a deer carcass, they eat all they want, then cache as much as they can in numerous hiding places. They can carry quite a bit of meat in their sublingual pouch, a space under their tongue, which evolved for carrying food to hide it. They place it under leaves or hide it by covering it with grass blades. Other Corvids also have sublingual pouches. Clark's Nutcrackers use theirs to carry thousands of pine seeds, a few at a time, to where they cache them, providing seeds to eat all winter. Often, if a magpie sees another bird watching when it is hiding its meat, it will pick the meat up and take it to a new hiding place out of sight of the other bird or birds.

After Scraps' young fledged the end of June, the new family remained together, coming to me for handouts all fall and winter. By the next spring, the young magpies had scattered to find mates and nesting territories of their own. Scraps and her mate nested and raised several more families in the years following, beginning their nest building earlier, in March rather than April. Scraps' transformation into a normal female Black-billed Magpie was fully accomplished. She never again attacked anyone. Except for coming for the food I left for her and her family, she never went near people again. The "Magpie from Hell" was gone forever, but Scraps, the good mother, lived a fairly long life for a wild magpie.

Many people in Montana kill magpies, though it is against state and federal law. They even kill magpies just for eating dog or cat food the people themselves put outside their homes, right where magpies can see it. Why Scraps had gotten away with terrorizing people in two counties, most of whom had independently called her the "Magpie from Hell," is a mystery. It can be assumed the fact that Scraps clearly spoke distinguishable English words made her seem special, deterring people from seeking revenge for her transgressions. It also shows that, in spite of all those who illegally kill wildlife (usually for no logical reason), there are still many people who care deeply about wild animals and their survival.

Thankfully, Scraps was not killed for being her mischievous self. I enjoyed the company of Scraps, her mate, and their youngsters for all the years they lived here. Piecing together her travels and hearing about her escapades from the many people she met, including those she attacked, has been intriguing. Scraps was an interesting and intelligent bird. Even though she was definitely a challenge to rehabilitate, she was worth all the work it took. For the rest of her life she was more like a little angel than a "Magpie from Hell."

A beast in the eyes
of others, is a prince in
the eyes of his mate.

BLACK AND WHITE

The magpie is an intelligent bird.
The skunk has a smelly potion.
Between them, they bring upon themselves
A mountain of human emotion.

The feelings of humans about these two
Are just like night and day.
People either love them or hate them.
There are no shades of gray.

They have something else in common,
Besides being black and white,
All they have to do is be themselves
To make some people uptight.

CHAPTER 33
MAGPIE FAMILY REUNION

In spring 1990, a pair of resident Black-billed Magpies built their large, roofed nest in one of the bushes on the south side of our irrigated hay field. We moved the irrigation pipes each morning and night, so I walked past the nest twice a day. Through the tightly woven sticks, we could catch glimpses of the female sitting on her eggs. The male was usually either out foraging for them both or standing guard in a nearby tree. After the eggs hatched, with five hungry mouths to feed, the father magpie was always busy finding food for his family.

The young magpies grew fast and, by early summer, the fledglings were sitting up and flapping their wings to strengthen their flight muscles. Each day, after moving the irrigation pipes, I intentionally walked past the nest to watch the magpie family from a distance. The parents were used to us going by each day and, since they didn't become alarmed, the youngsters paid no attention to me.

One morning in late June, I found the nest damaged, with no birds remaining in it. From tracks in the wet dirt at the base of the bush and the mess made of the nest, it was apparent a raccoon had raided it during the night. I assumed it had eaten all of the young birds but, just in case one escaped or was injured, I walked up the row of trees and bushes lining the edge of the field, searching for any who might be alive. I found the mother magpie and one of her young sitting on branches high up in a large cottonwood tree about 50 yards east of the nest bush. The mother's left wing was drooping badly. I assumed the raccoon had injured her during the raid. The fledgling, who could hop from branch to branch, seemed uninjured.

There was no way to get to either bird to help them. While I was watching them, the father brought food to the youngster. That gave me an idea. I could put food and water at the base of the cottonwood tree to help the father provide for his injured mate and his remaining youngster. I hoped the female's wing would heal so she would eventually be able to fly. She couldn't remain in the cottonwood trees forever. There was nothing else I could do for her unless she came down. At least, with its

273

father providing food, the fledgling would soon be able to fly around with him.

After watching the three magpies for a while, I continued my search for any others who might have escaped alive. I hoped since one fledgling had survived, maybe others had, too. There had been five young in the nest. I went to the west past the nest to search a patch of tall grass and weeds, where I found another fledgling hiding, obviously somewhat younger than the one who was with their parents. I picked it up, intending to take it to the tree where the other magpies were, knowing the father would take food to it until it learned to fly. Unfortunately, that plan quickly became impossible. As soon as I picked it up, its dangling right foot indicated a broken leg. A quick examination showed a break in mid tarso-metatarsus. In terms more easily understood, that is in the middle of the bone between the foot and the joint just below the drumstick (the part of the leg with scales). It is an easy bone to splint with an excellent prognosis of complete recovery and release for that type of break. I carefully held the little magpie so its leg would not be damaged any more, while I took another quick look in the grass and brush along the fence. I didn't find any more fledglings, so hurriedly walked the quarter mile to our house. I wanted to splint the broken leg as quickly as possible.

When a bird the size of a magpie has a break in the long bone just above its foot, the best splint is the hollow lower portion of an eagle's primary wing feather. Just as when I splinted Clarkie's broken leg, I chose a piece of the base of an eagle wing feather shaft from those in the drawer where I keep splinting material. Snipping off the rounded tip of the shaft created a long hollow cylinder. After trimming the shaft to be slightly longer than the tarso-metatarsus on the fledgling magpie, I cut the cylinder in half and lined the inside of both halves with gauze secured by tape. That made a lightweight, padded splint that fit perfectly on each side of the long leg bone. The feather shaft, being stiff and strong, can hold the leg bone securely in place.

If the eagle feather shaft is long enough, a tab can be trimmed to fit on each side of the foot and on each side of the top joint so, when taped, both joints are held in place. If not, a lightweight Styrofoam or wire splint on the outside of the leg immobilizing both the joint above and below the break is necessary to hold the foot straight forward in the proper position while the bone is healing. There cannot be any movement at the break, or the bone won't heal properly.

After the leg was splinted, I gave the little magpie water and food and propped it up in a nest of fresh, clean hay. I decided to name it Lucky, for obvious reasons. Lucky promptly fell asleep, so I went back to check one more time for other grounded fledglings and to take food and water to the other three magpies. I put a pan of water and a pan of small sized dog food under the cottonwood tree. The fledgling and its injured mother had remained in the top of the large tree, with the father a few trees east of them on the edge of the field.

I could observe the tree where the two magpies were all the time I was searching for more grounded fledglings. The female magpie called to her mate right after I left the food and water. The male flew over, saw the dog food, and flew down to it. He ate several pieces, then filled his mouth and flew up to feed his mate and his youngster, just as I had hoped he would. Unfortunately, after searching the grass for a considerable distance on all sides of the damaged nest, I didn't find any more young magpies. If any were hidden in the grass somewhere, the father magpie should have taken food to them. He only fed the two magpies in the tree all the time I was searching. The raccoon must have eaten the other three fledglings.

For the next two weeks, while I cared for Lucky, the father magpie took excellent care of his fledgling and mate. I helped him by putting out dog food and deer meat every day and keeping their water bowl full. After about a week, his fledgling was flying everywhere with him. The female was flying only short distances from tree to tree, but her injured wing appeared to be healing. The male was still feeding both of them. I had hopes of a full recovery for both Lucky and his mother.

A broken bone on a young bird at that time (before I was given the homeopathic cell salt Hyland's® Calc. Phos. 6X by my neighbor, Jean Atthowe) usually took from 10 to 12 days. If a young bird is given calc. phos. 30X while its bone is healing, healing only takes five to six days. Lucky could walk and hop, using his leg in a normal manner in 12 days. With his main splint removed, he was ready to be placed in a flight room to practice flying and picking up his food. Just to be safe, I left a short piece of the light eagle feather splint around the break area for extra support for his first few days in the flight room.

Lucky could fly short distances, but birds, especially fledglings, always need to strengthen their flight muscles before being released. Fledglings also need to practice landing skills, which Lucky could do in the flight room. I had hopes the magpie family would teach Lucky how to find food in the wild, but just in case supplemental feeding was needed after release,

I quickly taught the intelligent bird to come to me to get food when I called, "Lucky Pie, come here."

By the time Lucky's feathers were fully-grown and he was flying well enough to release, slightly over three weeks had passed since the raccoon's raid on the nest. Lucky's mother had completely recovered, except for a slight droop to the tip of her wing. She had no trouble keeping up with her mate and the uninjured fledgling when the magpie family flew around in our neighborhood. I stopped putting food under the cottonwood tree after the mother began flying with the other two magpies. Accident-killed deer meat was continuously replenished on a piece of plywood placed on top of one of the large kennels near the barns. All of our resident magpies were welcome to eat whenever they wanted. The small family of three remained near the kennels, eating deer meat from the kennel top, flying around in the trees along the creek, and hunting for other food, such as insects and worms, in the pasture near the barn and kennels. They were usually somewhere in the area near the kennels most of the day. I could tell the magpie threesome from other magpie families, because of the mother's droopy wing tip.

Meanwhile, Lucky had become proficient at flying and landing in the flight room, always coming to me when I called. On a sunny day in July, when I could see the other three magpies looking for insects in the pasture not far from the barnyard, I put Lucky on top of the kennel where the deer meat was. After looking around for a few seconds, Lucky flew up to the top of our old log barn, and began calling. In less than 30 seconds, the magpie family flew over to land on the barn roof beside Lucky. They were all talking to each other in magpie language. Lucky's mother, father, and sibling acted like they were very happy to find him. They were like a human family welcoming a long lost child. I could imagine the parent magpies were saying, "Where have you been? We thought you were dead." After a few minutes of talking with each other on top of the barn, they all flew over to the trees near the creek, where I could hear them still chatting together.

Lucky came to me for treats when I called "Lucky Pie, come here." but he didn't actually need supplemental feeding. His family kept him well fed, quickly teaching him how to find food and avoid predators. The four remained together until the next spring, when mother magpie with droopy left wing and her mate, the good father magpie, made a new nest in which to raise another family.

Lucky found a mate and I assume the other youngster did, but once the family split up, I couldn't distinguish it from other wild ones. Lucky remained much tamer than the other magpies who lived on our land. He often brought his mate with him when he came for dog food treats or deer meat. They built their own nest that spring and raised four young ones. We still have magpies nesting on our land. Some may be descendants of Lucky's family. Whenever a number of magpies get together to visit with each other, it is like a noisy family reunion. Lucky's return to his family was a very special magpie family reunion, for him and for me.

Mountain top snow melt
flushes silt from stream bottoms.
Nature's spring cleaning.

**Butterflies mate, hide
precious eggs, carrying genes
of generations.**

The Sandhill Skipper (*Polites sabuleti*) is a small butterfly that had never been found in Ravalli County until we found it on our land in 1999. It has since been found in at least three other sites. Many butterflies who were once common on our property have not been seen for over 10 years and are difficult to find anywhere in Ravalli County. Our Sandhill Skipper population also appears to be in decline, but a few can still be found in spring and fall as they have two broods.

SECTION SIX: FASCINATING BIRD BEHAVIOR

Many wings, one mind,
synchronized Horned Larks dancing
through an aqua sky.

CHAPTER 34
THE HELPFUL PINE SISKIN

One summer, I received an adult female Pine Siskin (*Carduelis pinus*) for care. Unfortunately, Piney, as I named her, was unreleasable because one wing had been badly damaged by a cat's bite. Piney liked to eat white proso millet, niger seed, and game bird starter. She had a dish of each in her box, as well as one of shelled sunflower seeds, which she seldom ate, and a dish of small gravel.

While Piney was in my care, I received three hatchling House Finches (*Carpodacus mexicanus*) from a nest that blew out of a tree in a windstorm. When they became fledglings and began to fly, I placed them in the large flight box with Piney. Young House Finches, also seed-eaters, learn to eat by themselves more quickly if placed with an experienced adult they can watch and emulate. Not having an adult finch at the time, I hoped watching Piney pick up food and eat it would help the fledgling finches learn. As soon as they saw Piney, all of the finches immediately began food begging. To my surprise, she hopped down to the dish of shelled sunflower seeds, the favorite food of young House Finches. She picked up a seed and carefully placed it in one of the open mouths. She repeated this over and over until all three finches had full crops and stopped food begging. Amazingly, she fed the little finches only shelled sunflower seeds, even though she ate millet and niger seeds. Those seeds would have been difficult for the fledglings to digest since they had not had time to ingest enough stones for their gizzard to grind the harder seeds. The gizzard is a muscular organ in some birds' digestive systems, containing small stones the birds pick up and swallow; gizzard muscle contractions use the gravel to mechanically grind the food they ingest into a mush-like consistency that can be more easily digested. Besides food and water, I supply birds with a gizzard a dish of sand or small pebbles.

Piney was an adult female bird, so the act of food begging by the young House Finches triggered her response to feed them. Ornithologists have shown in studies using captive birds that those of one species will feed young of another species when they food beg. However, it remains a mystery to me how Piney immediately knew the young finches liked or needed to be fed the more easily digested sunflower seeds rather than the niger and millet seeds she preferred. I could find no studies addressing that aspect of cross species feeding behavior.

Even though she was much smaller than they were, Piney fed the young finches each time they food begged. It took many trips carrying shelled sunflower seeds from the food dish to the mouth of each fledgling to fill their crops. By watching Piney, they learned to use their bills to pick up the sunflower seeds. When they were able to eat by themselves and fly well, I put them in a large room where they could build up their flight muscles. With practice, they learned to shell whole sunflower seeds, and to eat other seeds. Adult wild House Finches seem to prefer sunflower seeds to all other seeds and often eat fruit in late summer and fall, especially apples remaining on trees after the first frosts.

The three fledglings were eventually released in our yard, where they joined the flock of House Finches who frequently visit our bird feeders. By feeding the three fledgling finches, Piney gave me at least two hours a day to do other things. I was extremely grateful to the amazing little Pine Siskin for the help she so willingly provided.

**When chorus of House
Sparrows sing together, mid-
winter sounds like spring.**

CHAPTER 35
IT TAKES FIVE TO RAISE FIVE

Sharon seldom used the front door of her home near Stevensville, Montana. A wreath made of natural materials hung on the outside of the door, left over from the previous year's holiday season. One day in April 1995, she walked by the front of the house and noticed two House Finches (*Carpodacus mexicanus*) sitting on the wreath. They seemed to be pecking at it, so Sharon decided to take it down. As she approached the wreath, the finches flew a short distance away to a bush by the porch. When she was close enough, she discovered a delicate, cup-like nest tucked into the branches of the wreath. Removing it and thus disrupting the finches' nesting was not an option for Sharon. Instead, she began watching the finch family from her window. She discovered that, rather than pecking at the wreath, they were actually weaving finishing touches of grass into their sturdy nest.

As soon as the nest was finished, the female laid five eggs. She sat on them for two weeks, faithfully keeping the eggs warm until they hatched, producing five tiny, naked babies. All went well with the House Finch family for six days. The little hatchlings were growing fast with both attentive parents bringing them frequent mouthfuls of food. Around noon on April 28, when a few pinfeathers were beginning to peek out of their otherwise bare pink skin, Sharon noticed a disturbance between the usually peaceful adult finches. The male was sitting on one side of the nest facing the female on the other side. They were scolding loudly and flapping their wings in an aggressive manner. It appeared they were fighting, but they flew away together. A short time later, the male returned with food for the hatchlings. The mother didn't come back and Sharon never saw her again.

House Finches are thought to be monogamous, at least during the nesting season while raising their young. It appeared those two didn't get the memo about that, since the female left and appeared to have abandoned her hatchlings. Interestingly, another common belief was that female finches choose their mate because he has the reddest color on his head and breast. A new finding using genetics produced evidence the females also choose a mate who is as genetically different from her as possible, apparently to avoid inbreeding. No one has determined how the finches know they are genetically different and that may remain a mystery, since they don't talk human languages and can't tell us.

The male continued to bring food to the hatchlings until dark. However, male House Finches apparently do not brood the young, so the hatchlings were left by themselves with no protection from the cold during the night. Nights in Montana in late April and early May are quite cool. Sharon checked on them frequently during the early evening to determine whether the mother had come back to keep her family of five warm. When no adult bird had appeared by 11 p.m., Sharon covered the hatchlings with clothes lint retrieved from her dryer, hoping it would keep them warm.

In the morning, upon observing the male come to the nest with food, Sharon removed the lint, exposing the hatchlings. Even with their makeshift blanket, at 46 degrees during the night, they had become too cold to food-beg. If they were unable to open their mouths, the male would be unable to feed them. Also, hatchling birds cannot digest properly if they are chilled. Seeing there was a serious problem, Sharon called me for advice. I told her they would have to be warmed before they would open their mouths for food. Sharon placed a tall goose necked lamp on the porch so the bulb would provide heat to the nestlings. As soon as they were warmed, they all began making their food begging call. The devoted father responded and faithfully brought food to them all day. At dusk, he left to go wherever he spent his nights, leaving the babies alone again.

Following another of my suggestions, Sharon unhooked the wreath from the outside of the door and carried it with nest and baby finches into her warm house, where she hung the wreath on a nail on the wall. Early in the morning, after seeing the male finch had arrived with food, Sharon hung the wreath back on the door. Warm and hungry, the little finches began food begging even before Sharon could carry them outside.

Seeming relieved to find his young ones had reappeared, the male finch fed all the hatchlings, after which he flew away. He was absent for a much longer time than was usual between feedings. At mid-morning, he returned with a female House Finch, not the one who had laid and incubated the eggs. The new female had completely different head markings than the male's original mate. Having watched the first hen finch through the window all the time she brooded the eggs, Sharon was very familiar with her. The new female helped the male finch with his feeding duties and the two of them kept the five little finches well fed for the rest of the day. When evening came, both the male and new female left the babies alone. The naked young finches still had no adult bird to keep them warm. Apparently, the newly recruited female was willing to help feed the babies but wasn't motivated to brood them.

Until the young finches were fully feathered, Sharon continued to take the wreath inside at night after the adults ceased their food deliveries. Each morning, she returned it, with the nest and its five hungry occupants, to the door as soon as the adult finches arrived to resume caring for them. After the young were fully feathered, they began to exercise on the edge of the nest to strengthen their wing muscles for flying. At that point, we decided it would be best to leave the pre-fledglings outside at night so they wouldn't jump out of the nest inside the house, perhaps getting lost under or behind furniture. Protected by their new feathers, they withstood the cool May nights without any problem but were more than ready to eat when the male finch and his new mate arrived with their breakfast.

Three days before the young birds left the nest, the two adults recruited another House Finch to help with the feeding. Apparently, even a pair of finches working together was unable to provide enough food for five constantly hungry, full-grown fledglings. The new helper was a one-year-old male with pale orange coloring on the head, chest, and back, rather than having bright red feathers in those areas like the older male. All three adults brought food throughout the daylight hours to keep the youngsters fed. When a House Sparrow landed on the edge of the nest, all three dived at the sparrow to drive it away from the fledglings. How the father finch was able to enlist the help of the other two birds to raise his family of five remains a mystery. Possibly they were his progeny from the year before. Immature birds of several other species have been observed to help feed young siblings. Young bluebirds from a first hatch often help their parents feed a second brood.

Thinking that the fledgling finches might need a nearby place to land on their first flight out of the nest, Sharon placed her old Christmas tree on the porch half way between the door where the nest hung and a thick bush growing by the edge of the porch. As planned, the fledglings flew from the nest to the Christmas tree, using it as a stepping-stone to the leafy bush, where they could hide until they were ready to make a longer flight. Soon, all the young finches were following the three adults around the yard. They continued to feed and care for the fledglings until all five had learned to find their own food. The eight birds made up their own little flock as they flew around the yard searching for seeds and insects.

Sharon found the unfolding House Finch soap opera fascinating. She kept a close watch on them each day from finding the nest until the finch family flew off to join other finches in the neighborhood. She kept me apprised of their progress and the activities of the adults. It was interesting that it required the efforts of one human and four adult birds to successfully raise five young finches. I have raised and released many fledglings but have never had the opportunity to observe how adult House Finches raise their young. It is unclear whether the seemingly unusual behaviors of the adult finches observed by Sharon were common for House Finches. Regardless, their amazing story was almost like a soap opera in plot but far more interesting and entertaining.

**From birds, people learned
to fly, but they alone must
resolve how to soar.**

CHAPTER 36
DIPPING DIPPERS

One summer afternoon, a woman and her daughter brought me two little dark grey fledglings. Cuddled together in the center of a cluster of moss and lichen placed in a cardboard box, the pair was the epitome of cuteness. I had to watch them for a few minutes before being able to determine what kind of bird they were. I hadn't previously cared for American Dipper (*Cinclus mexicanus*) fledglings, so didn't immediately recognize them. At first, they just sat there looking up at me with their large, dark brown eyes. Then one suddenly stood up and began dipping up and down as if trying to tell me what it was. That was all it took. Dark grey birds that dip have to be American Dippers, previously called Water Ouzels. American Dipper hatchlings begin making their characteristic dipping motion as soon as they are strong enough to stand on their relatively long legs. Adult American Dippers are the only North American songbird who regularly searches for insects underwater in flowing streams.

I asked my visitors where the birds were found. The girl said some teenage boys and other people were swimming near a bridge over the Bitterroot River. When the boys spotted the moss and lichen nest up on the side of a steep bank near the bridge, they threw rocks at it and knocked it down. The girl saw what they had done and rescued the two little birds before the boys could kill them. The boys should have been reported to the authorities because killing protected birds or damaging their nests is against Federal and State law. Also, parents should either teach their children to be respectful of wildlife, or never let the destructive vandals out of their sight. With so many more people now sharing the planet with wildlife, everyone needs to protect young birds. It is important to remember that we need wild birds in order for us to survive. Protecting birds, their families, and their habitat should be as imperative as protecting ourselves.

I told the mother and daughter heroes what kind of birds they had rescued. I also told the mother how much I appreciated their bringing the birds to me. I had never raised an American Dipper and knew I was destined to learn a great deal from the two little birds. One of nature's secrets I had always wanted to learn was what prompted dippers to dip. I had suspected it was a way to quickly pump blood through their bodies, especially their feet and legs, to help keep them warm when foraging in cold streams. Adult dippers I had observed hunting insects in our mountain streams seemed to dip much more when they came out of the water on cold winter days than on warm summer days.

The dipping action is like a deep knee bend, causing the whole body to move up and down. Bird websites on the Internet say three hypotheses have been suggested for why dippers exhibit this behavior. One is that the repetitive dipping up and down against the background of the rushing water helps conceal the bird from predators. Actually, movement attracts predators, so this hypothesis does not seem logical. In addition, possibly because dippers are quite small and have thick feathers (compared to many other birds), few predators seem interested in eating them. It may take more energy for a hawk to pluck the dense feathers prior to eating a dipper than it would receive from digesting the bird's small body.

Eugene Beckes often takes fantastic photos of American Dippers hunting for water insects in streams and rivers. Twice while watching for dippers to photograph, Beckes observed one of the smaller accipiters, either a Cooper's or a Sharp-shinned Hawk, flying low over the water, working its way upstream. Beckes thought it might be hunting dippers but said he had no dippers in his view either time and never saw an accipiter go after a dipper. All other small birds freeze in place when they know accipiters are around because those hawks hunt by sight and are attracted by movement. It seems highly unlikely a dipper would use their dipping behavior to hide from an accipiter. A dipper would be more likely to dive under the water to hide from a hawk.

Another suggestion is that dipping helps the bird see the water insects it hunts between rocks under fast-flowing water, but from my observations of dippers, this is also not likely. They don't appear to dip while under water or even when partially submerged.

The third postulation, that dipping and the rhythmic blinking of their bright white, feathered eyelids help dipper pairs communicate and keep track of each other, may have merit. It has been observed that they exhibit robust dipping during courtship and as aggressive behavior when confronting other birds. Robust dipping would suggest to a potential mate or a rival that the bird is healthy and strong. However, this hypothesis does not explain why single dippers use the dipping movements when they come out of the water to stand on rocks or branches, after finding, killing, and eating their catch. While it is highly likely the dazzling white eyelids are for communication between pairs and their young, the dipping behavior is obviously not done solely for that purpose.

The two hatchlings soon strongly suggested another reason for dipping. The second little dipper joined its nest mate in doing quite rigorous dipping in the center of the cup of wet moss and lichen. I suspected the cold nest material, which had become wet when falling into the water, was chilling the youngsters. A wet nest can cause young birds to become hypothermic. I placed them in a box on a makeshift nest of clean, dry rags covered with soft tissues. After setting the box on a heating pad, I gave each of them some baby bird food and several mealworms. They much preferred the mealworms. As soon as they were warm and had full crops, they quit dipping, sat down, and promptly fell asleep. A short while after the woman and her daughter left, I whistled to see if the dippers were hungry again. Their eyes opened instantly and they both began food begging, but since they were warm and comfortable in their cloth nest, they didn't stand up or dip. I fed them each several mealworms and, with crops full, they quickly went back to sleep.

After five days, the two little dippers were able to run around on their sturdy, relatively long legs. I put them in a big flight box with a pan of water containing mealworms. They quickly learned to wade into the water to pick up and eat the mealworms without my assistance. Three days after they began going into the water to catch their own mealworms, I moved them to a flight room with a bigger wading pan. I put rocks in the pan so they could step down off the rocks into the water to pick up the mealworms on the bottom of the pan. I hoped that would help them learn to find water insects hidden in rocks in running streams, even though the water in the pan wasn't moving.

Early in the morning, when the temperature in the flight room was fairly cool, the little birds dipped almost continuously unless they were in the water. When they were in the water to pick up and eat mealworms, they didn't dip. As soon as they came out onto the rocks, they began to dip again. In the afternoon, when it was warm in the room, both dippers stood on the rocks, ran into and out of the water to pick up and eat mealworms, and ran around the room without dipping at all. It definitely appeared they were not impelled to dip unless their bodies became too cold. Of course, such observations of two fledglings does not constitute proof of why all American Dippers exhibit this behavior, but it did support my hypothesis that it may be at least partly to help warm themselves.

Each afternoon, while it was sunny and warm, I put the two fledgling dippers into a carrying box and took them to play and look for aquatic insects in Willoughby Creek. I hoped they would learn how to walk on the rocks and hunt for insects in fast flowing water. At first, I scattered mealworms for them to find and pick up from between rocks on the edge of the creek where it was quite shallow. The dippers clearly liked exploring rocks in the running water. As always, going into the cool water resulted in an increase in their dipping behavior as soon as they came out to stand in the sun on rocks at the creek's edge.

Fledgling American Dippers interacting on a branch above the stream. Photo by Eugene Beckes.

One beautiful sunny day, two famous wildlife photographers, Erwin and Peggy Bauer, came to visit. While they were here, I took the dippers to the creek to practice hunting insects in the rocks. The Bauers thought the two little birds were adorable and highly entertaining to watch. They each took several rolls of film of the dippers, while the birds practiced finding water insects on and between rocks in the creek, occasionally coming out onto the rocks to stand in the sun and dip.

The Education and Information Officer, Bill Thomas, from the Montana Department of Fish, Wildlife and Parks came on another day to videotape the dippers. Apparently, there were not many opportunities to photograph fledgling dippers learning to hunt water insects and he needed video of exactly that for a television segment he was making on dippers. He took some excellent action footage of them searching for insects among rocks on the bottom of the stream, standing on the rocks, and posing close together while dipping up and down in unison. What dippers lack in color, being a rather plain charcoal grey, they certainly make up in energy and charisma.

Eventually, the two young dippers were fully-grown, could fly well, and were proficient at finding food in the rocks of the creek. I took them to a mountain stream on a friend's land on the west side of the Bitterroot Valley and released them. The last I saw of them, they were searching rocks under the water, looking for and catching water insects. They came out occasionally onto the larger rocks above the water to stand in the sun and dip for a while before again going back into the fast moving water to hunt for food.

They appeared to be having fun, as they always had when they played and foraged in Willoughby Creek. Snowmelt water in the mountain stream was quite cold and, as I had observed while they were growing up, the cooler the water, the more they dipped. I hoped they would live for many years, find mates, and raise their own young to carry on the interesting and entertaining behaviors of their species.

Diving and dipping
Ouzels dance to songs of the
white-water chorus.

An adult American Dipper with a caddis fly nymph. Photo by Eugene Beckes.

Fledgling American Dipper foraging in the stream. Photo by Eugene Beckes.

CHAPTER 37
BACKYARD BIRD TALK

Birds communicate with each other in ways similar to human communication. Some bird species, especially the Corvid Family (also called the Jay Family) including Raven, Crow, Magpie, Clark's Nutcracker, Steller's Jay, and other species of corvid are thought to call each individual in their group by name.

Birds of different songbird species and other birds regularly communicate with each other, often concerning predators in their immediate area or an abundant food source. Songbirds all seem to use the same "word" for a dangerous predator. When one bird, such as a Black-capped Chickadee or a House Finch, spots a snake it says a universal bird word for snake, that sounds like "ssszzzitt." All the birds in our yard, including European Starlings, if they are around, will form a group (called a mob) around the snake. All individual birds of the various species make a similar sound or "word" for snake, but some species have a slight but distinct accent.

One day when I was working in the garden, I heard several birds saying "ssszzzitt." A pair of Mountain Bluebirds who had four hatchlings in a bluebird house Bob had placed on a post in the orchard near the garden, was the most agitated and vocal. When I heard the commotion, I immediately recognized the birds were watching a snake. I ran to the garage, grabbed the welding gloves and a five-gallon bucket, and dashed out to the bluebird house. All the birds in the mob were looking down at one spot, so finding the large gopher snake wasn't difficult. It was nearly four feet long, quite big around, and absolutely gorgeous.

I love snakes and greatly admire them for their abilities, one of which is climbing up wooden posts. I didn't want the hatchling bluebirds eaten, which is why I had taken the pail with me. I put on the welding gloves because a large gopher snake, though non-venomous and without fangs, can break human skin with its many small teeth. After carefully capturing the snake, I placed it gently in the bucket, took it to a different area of our 100 acres, and released it where there were plenty of meadow voles it could catch. Voles are a favorite food of gopher snakes. As voles are much more plentiful than Mountain Bluebirds, I reasoned it would be better for the snake to have vole for lunch, rather than four baby bluebirds.

The snake didn't find its way back to the birdhouse and the four Mountain Bluebirds grew up and fledged. The bluebird family flew around in the area of our yard and garden catching insects for several days before leaving, likely to begin their southward migration.

Snakes are not the only predator about which all the smaller bird species communicate. One day, while observing bird behavior at our feeders to the east of our house, Bob noticed that suddenly all the birds froze in place, wherever they were. Even the House Finches and Juncos who were feeding on the ground flattened themselves against the ground and remained motionless. He watched to see what kind of predator might be causing that behavior. In about 30 seconds, a Merlin came flying from the west, over our house and then over the feeding area. Not one bird moved. The Merlin kept going to the east and landed in a tree. It was obvious the feeding birds were warned that the Merlin was coming. Also, it must have been communicated to the feeding birds that the predator was a Merlin, a small, fast-flying falcon who snatches songbirds out of the air if they panic and fly.

Far more Sharp-shinned Hawks than Merlins come to our yard to attempt to catch songbirds and doves. We had already observed how small birds always scatter in all directions right before a Sharp-shinned Hawk swoops over the house into the feeding area. In that case, birds all flew into the thickest bushes they could find or deep into the brush pile we had placed near the feeding area to serve as a hiding place for smaller mammals and birds. It was clear that birds to the west of our house were warning the birds at the feeder not only that a predatory bird was on the way to the feeding area but precisely which predatory bird it was.

If the birds remain motionless when a Sharp-shinned Hawk comes through, the sharpie can easily catch them. A Sharp-shinned Hawk or other accipiter,* such as its larger cousins the Cooper's Hawk or Northern Goshawk, will run after birds, sometimes actually following them into thick bushes or brush piles. Unless a small bird is ill or injured, it can usually escape by quickly flying into thick enough cover that the much larger accipiter can't follow. If an accipiter is able to catch a bird, they usually eat it on the ground after plucking the feathers to get to the meat. That leaves a neat little circle of feathers to tell observers an accipiter ate its dinner there.

*(Accipiters are a group of hawks having short, broad wings for fast flight through wooded areas, and long legs to chase their prey on the ground.)

Merlins, being small, fast-flying falcons, pursue birds in flight, so those on the ground or motionless in tree branches do not appear to attract the attention of a Merlin. Usually, a Merlin hits the small flying bird with its feet, dazing it and causing it to fall. The Merlin then does a tight turn and catches the stunned, falling bird in its talons before it can hit the ground. Some Merlins simply snatch flying birds out of the air, killing them with their talons while flying. They carry the dead prey to a hidden spot in thick trees and land on a branch to eat it.

I have not heard what "word" or "words" lookout birds use to warn feeding birds about the specific predator bird who is approaching, except for Black-capped Chickadees. The chickadees are quite vocally loud saying dee, dee, dee many times when they see a predator. I can't tell by what they say whether the predator is a cat, raccoon, Sharp-shinned Hawk, or Merlin, but apparently they and other birds in the area can.

A Merlin (*Falco columbarius*) has large eyes with a dark iris, thus is easily distinguished from the similar sized Sharp-shinned Hawk (*Accipiter striatus*), with a yellow or red iris depending on their age and the food they have been eating.

I have usually been inside the house while witnessing the behaviors of both prey birds and their predators. Someday, I hope to be in the right place to hear the sound the smaller birds make or "say" to warn others a Merlin is swooping through the feeding area. I'd like to see if I can distinguish the difference between their warning for a Merlin and for the more common accipiters.

A study of Black-capped Chickadees reacting to various predators showed they had several unique sounds to communicate the approach of different predators. Also, if the predator was dangerous to the chickadees, their calls were faster, with more "dees" in the series. Electronic recording equipment used by researchers showed chickadees also made many sounds not audible to humans. By analyzing all the different sounds the chickadees made, both audible and inaudible to us, they found chickadees have amazingly sophisticated communication skills.

It may be that I wouldn't be able to hear the birds' "word" for Merlin, Sharp-shinned Hawk, or other predator. I did understand their word for the gopher snake, which was obvious and fairly consistent for all the species of bird present at that event. The reactions to predators by birds in our yard show how bird species who fly around in mixed groups and feed together can and do constantly communicate with each other concerning predators and their food sources.

Like feathered lightning,
a Merlin is gone before
you know it is there.

CHAPTER 38
INVENTIVE BIRDS

Individuals of several bird species who eat suet or sunflower seeds have devised ingenious ways of minimizing the loss of precious food particles as they are eating. Downy and Hairy Woodpeckers will peck one or more shallow holes into wooden posts or trees located near suet or seed feeders. They carry their chosen sunflower seed to the hole and use the hole to hold it while they peck the meat out of the shell and eat it. When they are eating suet, if a piece breaks off that is too large for them to swallow, they carry it to one of their prepared holes. After placing the suet firmly in the hole, they peck at it to break it into smaller pieces that are easily swallowed.

Woodpeckers and nuthatches have short legs and long toes designed to hang onto tree bark, making it difficult in most cases for these species to hold a seed or other food particle in their feet. Even birds who are able to use their feet to hold a seed or piece of suet seem to prefer to use holes if they are available. At our feeders, Black-capped Chickadees and all three species of nuthatch (White-breasted, Red-breasted, and Pygmy) use holes made by Hairy and Downy Woodpeckers. Using holes to hold food while pecking it apart is much more economical for the bird. All of the pieces remain in the hole until they are eaten, with none wasted by falling to the ground. Most members of the woodpecker family, except Northern Flickers, are usually reluctant to feed on the ground. Chickadees and nuthatches will fly down to the ground to pick up a whole sunflower seed, quickly returning to the safety of thick branches with the seed to peck it apart and eat it.

Chickadees are highly adept at holding various types of food with their feet while they peck it apart, but many still prefer to use holes made by woodpeckers. Small birds like nuthatches and chickadees also use such holes or natural cracks in tree bark to hold grubs or large insects while they peck them repeatedly to kill them. They are then able to pick the insect apart to eat it. Chickadees usually remove their insect prey from the crack or hole after pounding it to death, holding the dead insect with their feet while pulling it into small enough pieces to swallow.

For almost a year, my friend Mary observed the following interesting and possibly unique behaviors of a resident Hairy Woodpecker (*Picoides villosus*) family who came to her feeder nearly every day. Early in spring, a female Hairy Woodpecker landed on the tall wooden post on which the sunflower-seed feeder was hanging. She pecked six holes in a straight line down the back of the post. Then she flew the short distance to the feeder on the front of the post, picked up a seed, flew to the back of the post and carefully placed it in the top hole. After putting a seed in each hole, working from the top down, she pecked apart each seed and ate the meat from each one as she worked her way back to the top. She repeated the process until she had eaten all she wanted. Her mate observed her closely while she did this. He was soon using the holes she made to hold his seeds while he ate each one from the shell. By waiting until the female had finished eating, he was able to use the same holes. Also, one of the birds may have been acting as a lookout for predators while the other was eating.

The pair nested nearby; in late summer their four youngsters fledged from a hollowed-out cavity in a large cottonwood tree. As soon as they could fly, the fledgling woodpeckers began following their parents to the feeder. The young birds waited in the pines at the edge of the yard while the two adults took turns placing sunflower seeds in the holes and removing kernels from the shells. Both parents carried the meats from the shelled sunflower seeds to the youngsters to feed them. After several days of carrying shelled seeds to the young birds, the female Hairy Woodpecker filled all the holes, but neither parent went to the post to shell the seeds. Instead, they encouraged the young woodpeckers to go to the holes to shell their own seeds. One of the parents would fly to the bottom hole and begin pecking at the seed. It would then fly a short distance away to watch, leaving the seed in the hole. After seeing their parents make several trips to the holes, with no food brought to them, one of the young birds finally flew down to the hole, finished pecking the seed apart and ate the meat. Within a couple hours, all the young ones were flying to the holes to shell and eat sunflower seeds as fast as their parents could refill the holes.

After a few days, the parents stopped filling the holes for the young birds, so the fledgling woodpeckers began attempting to carry sunflower seeds from the feeder to the holes. They were quite clumsy and appeared to become frustrated when they dropped the seeds. With their parents no longer bringing them shelled sunflower seeds to eat, the youngsters had to go to the feeder, eating the seeds shell and all. This continued for two or three days, while they perfected their seed carrying abilities. About two weeks after fledging, with their coordination greatly improved, the young woodpeckers had developed flying and seed carrying skills nearly equal to that of their parents. They learned how to proficiently fill the holes from the top down and peck the sunflower seed pieces from the crushed shells as they hopped back up the pole. Each member of the woodpecker family took their turn using the holes. The female Hairy Woodpecker had successfully taught this behavior to all the members of her family. This intelligent and enterprising Hairy Woodpecker family continued to share the six holes all fall and winter.

These behaviors are interesting examples of adaptive problem solving, tool manufacturing, and tool use by common bird species. Solving the tricky problem of getting nutritious seeds out of the shells of seeds found in the wild or in bird feeders and into their mouth without losing precious pieces of the food is an interesting behavior young birds learn from their parents or by watching other birds. Birds didn't evolve with feeders full of sunflower seeds, so it appears they have adapted how they process seeds found in the wild to include successfully extracting the meat from sunflower seeds provided by their human admirers.

**Trees hum, birds sing, beaks
drum, squirrels chatter, in a
forest symphony.**

PURSUIT

A sleek Sharp-shinned Hawk
Swoops without warning
Like an arrow shot from a bow.
From her lookout branch she
Dives swift and deadly, straight
At the feeding Juncos below.

Juncos scatter like brown leaves caught
In a dust devil's whirling breeze.
Targeting one appearing slow,
In swift pursuit of the fleeing
Bird, she dives, with ready talons
To deliver a fatal blow.

Just as the deadly talons close,
The desperate Junco folds its wings
And drops straight down, to hide
In spiked branches of wild rose,
A single feather floats slowly
Down, flicked from the Junco's side.

CHAPTER 39
THE LAZARUS HUMMINGBIRD

After a whirlwind romance with a dazzling male during the first week of June, a female Rufous Hummingbird (*Selasphorus rufus*) laid two tiny, white eggs in a diminutive cup-shaped nest insulated with grey-green mosses and yellow-green lichens. The nest was built of woven bits of plant material, well camouflaged by lichens, and hidden near the middle of a horizontal branch of a large spruce tree, which gave protection from wind and rain.

The choice of this nest location by the female hummingbird was not an accident. The tree was growing on the edge of Suzanna McDougal's herb garden filled with flowers that bloomed continuously throughout spring and summer. The male hummingbird had jealously guarded this choice territory from other males, but after mating with the female, he moved on, leaving the nectar of many flowers for the female to feed on while raising their young. Female hummingbirds do all the work connected with raising young hummingbirds, including brooding the eggs and collecting nectar and insects to feed the hatchlings.

Two days separated the laying of the two eggs by Mother Rufous. They were elliptical in shape and although they looked tiny, they were quite large in relation to the mother bird's size, weighing from 10 to 20% of her weight. In comparison, larger birds' eggs weigh from two to four percent of their weight.

As soon as the second egg was laid, the incubation period began. This was a busy time for Mother Rufous. She had to feed on nectar many times a day to maintain her body temperature at 104 degrees. Her warm breast then kept the eggs at 90 degrees so the tiny birds could develop inside. A mother hummingbird can leave the nest for longer periods on warm days but not at all or for only a very short time when the weather is cool or if rain is falling. That is why it is so important for a good source of nectar to be close by, like Suzanna's flowers.

In spite of many days of cold and rainy weather during incubation, one egg hatched on June 19. This exciting event was happily noted by Suzanna, who had been checking the nest nearly every day by climbing a ladder she had set under the tree. Suzanna had found the location of the nest by watching Mother Rufous to see where she went after visiting flowers in the herb garden. Since Suzanna had checked the nest holding two unhatched eggs on July 18, she knew the day the baby hatched but not the precise hour. Waiting until Mother Rufous was off gathering nectar on the big day, Suzanna climbed the ladder and looked into the nest. She saw an unhatched egg and a tiny, naked baby bird, who appeared brown and lifeless. She considered removing the "dead" baby from the nest, thinking its cold body might interfere with the hatching of the remaining egg. Fortunately, she decided to call me first and ask what she should do. I advised her to leave the baby in the nest, as it was likely just torpid. At that time, I didn't know books on hummingbird behavior say newly hatched or older hatchling hummingbirds do not go torpid, not that it would have changed my advice. I learned long ago that birds don't follow rules made up for them by people.

Suzanna checked the nest again on June 21, 48 hours after first seeing the newly hatched baby looking brown and lifeless. The second egg had still not hatched and never did hatch, eventually disappearing from the nest. However, Suzanna was delighted to see that, with a resurrection that rivaled Lazarus, the seemingly dead hatchling hummingbird had come back to life. Its color was healthy pink and it was sitting with its beak up, looking alert and ready to be fed. Mother Rufous returned and fed the ravenous hatchling immediately after Suzanna climbed down the ladder and moved away from the tree.

For the next two weeks, Suzanna checked on the hatchling at least every other day and often sat in her garden watching Mother Rufous feed the little one. The hatchling was always up and alert when Suzanna observed it during this period of warm days. On July 3, the sky was cloudy and the temperature was cool, from 45 to 50 degrees. Because it was so cool, Suzanna made it a point to climb the ladder and check on the young bird while the mother was out nectar gathering. It had pinfeathers showing in the feather patches, but again it was brown and looked lifeless. This time she knew Little Lazarus was just torpid, not dead. The next day the weather was warm, consistent with a beautiful sunny 4th of July. Little Lazarus was a healthy pink between the patches of emerging feathers, alert and watching her with bright eyes when Suzanna checked on him in late morning.

By July 6, Little Lazarus's feathers had mostly emerged. When I finally had time to go to Hamilton to see the hummingbirds on July 8, he was fully feathered in beautiful juvenile Rufous Hummingbird plumage.

I watched as the mother collected nectar from several flowers. She went by a very circuitous route to a branch behind the nest from where I was watching. After checking in all directions, she quickly flew to the young bird, who was standing as tall as possible with beak gaping, put her bill into Little Lazarus's wide-open mouth, and transferred the nectar. Soon after eating, Little Lazarus backed his rear end over to the edge of the nest and shot a stream of yellowish white feces an amazing distance straight out from the base of his raised tail. Then he settled in the nest and went instantly to sleep.

Suzanna was watching when Little Lazarus left the nest on July 11, 23 days after hatching. The fledgling hummingbird flew around the herb garden where his mother was doing her usual nectar gathering. He flew to her to be fed and followed her around for as long as Suzanna watched. Two days later on the morning of July 13, the temperature was unusually cool for July. Suzanna found Little Lazarus hanging upside down from a limb on a bush under the nest tree. The bird looked quite dead, but again like Lazarus, he revived soon after Suzanna cupped him in her hands to warm him. She placed him in the nest where he could be further warmed by the sun. Little Lazarus was soon wide-awake and hungry. After Mother Rufous provided much needed energy in the form of a cropful of warm nectar, Little Lazarus was again busily zooming around the garden with his mother while she collected more nectar from the bright-colored flowers.

During his short life, Little Lazarus was observed in torpor by Suzanna when newly hatched, again as an older hatchling and finally right after he had fledged. The Internet says the following concerning nesting females and hatchling hummingbirds: "To maintain the temperature of her eggs or young, an incubating or nesting female hummingbird does not lower body temperature and become torpid. The nestlings do not enter into torpidity either." Obviously, Rufous Hummingbird youngsters don't adhere to misinformation on the Internet.

Mother Rufous continued to feed Little Lazarus until the young bird learned which flowers contained nectar, what predators to avoid, and other knowledge important to hummingbird survival. Then the two left the garden for their marathon flight to South America, where hummingbirds spend the winter months. It is an amazing journey for such tiny birds. Hopefully, they were able to survive their long trip to South America and back to western Montana. One of them may have returned to Suzanna's bountiful flower garden the next spring.

**Rufous Hummingbird,
dazzling jewel embedded
in pearly blossoms.**

An **Osprey** (*Pandion haliaetus*) photographed by Eugene Beckes standing on the crossbars of a high line pole. Osprey often build their nests on the crossbars, which endangers them and can cause problems for the electrical company. In our area, some osprey nests have web cameras that are watched by many during nesting season. Studies have shown mercury levels in the blood of the average osprey chick hatched along the Clark Fork River is about 100 times higher than what is dangerous for humans, but the osprey seem to be somewhat immune to mercury's effects. A preventable danger to osprey chicks is becoming entangled in discarded baling twine which, with proper disposal, would not be available for use in nests.

CHAPTER 40
HOW CROSSBILLS CROSS THEIR BILLS

I have raised several hatchling Red Crossbills (*Loxia curvirostra*), so have had the opportunity to observe them closely as they matured. As hatchlings, their bills are similar to others of the Fringillidae (Finch) Family, being quite wide and cone-shaped. The bills of hatchling crossbills, both Red Crossbills and White-winged Crossbills (*Loxia leucoptera*) have to be fairly large and uncrossed to enable parents to place food into the gaping baby mouths with the tips of their crossed bills.

As fledglings, the bills of young crossbills are still straight and cone-shaped, looking much like those of a House Finch fledgling, though slightly larger in size. The top and bottom bills are thick at the base, each forming half of a cone in shape. Both bills are nearly even in length, with the upper slightly longer than the lower, as is normal for most bird species. The bills of fledgling crossbills remain cone-shaped for more than a week after fledging from the nest. During that time, the young birds follow their parents as the adults find food for the fledglings and themselves. By watching their parents, crossbill fledglings learn what to eat and how to find the seeds and insects commonly eaten by that species.

Youngsters quickly learn to extract seeds from various evergreen cones by observing how their parents do it. When the young birds are ready to pry seeds from cones of ponderosa pine or other conifers, the tips of both the top and bottom bills suddenly begin to grow very fast. It is not only the rhamphotheca (the horny bill covering) that begins growing and bending; the bones within the upper bill also elongate and bend. Immature bones of young birds can change shape depending on stress placed on them before the cartilage has completely hardened into bone.

One question I was asked is, "Are the bones and rhamphotheca genetically programmed to cross?" It appears from the behavior of healthy fledgling crossbills that the answer is no, the bones and rhamphotheca are not genetically programmed to cross. However, it definitely appears the bones and rhamphotheca of the upper and lower bills *are* genetically programmed to begin a rapid-growth period after the birds have fledged and are ready to begin extracting seeds from pinecones.

Another question was "Are the crossed bills the result of fledgling crossbills being genetically programmed to help complete the process by twisting their bills at the appropriate time?" This appears consistent with what rehabbers have observed in the fledglings they raised, so the answer to that question is likely yes. However, whether this behavior is completely genetic or if the birds know they need to twist their bill when the bill tips are in the fast growth period is unknown.

It was also asked, "What determines whether a young crossbill twists its upper bill to the left or to the right?" As far as I can find, this question has not been answered. Some birds are "right handed" and some "left handed," but on birds I have tested for handedness (actually footedness) only about one out of 10 or 12 were left footed, with most using their right foot to pick up or hold things. This was consistent with what I found in dogs, horses, raccoons, and other mammals I tested, and is close to what is found in humans.

It has also been suggested that lefties (crossbills with upper bill curving to the left) may utilize seeds from different species of evergreen trees or different sized cones than righties do. Both lefties and righties have been observed feeding from ponderosa pine cones, as well as from those produced by other evergreen trees that grow here in western Montana. Another hypothesis for having some birds with upper bill tips twisted to the left and some to the right was to make it possible for birds in a flock to utilize all the seeds in the cones. Because some birds work around the cone clockwise and some counter-clockwise, eventually all the seeds in each cone are consumed.

It has been established by studies on Red Crossbill populations that the upper bill is twisted to the left on about 50% of the individuals. In some populations there were somewhat more left-billed birds than right-billed. White-winged Crossbill studies found about 70% were left-billed to 30% right-billed, so up to three times more left-billed than right-billed. I couldn't find any information regarding why there appears to be only a slight difference between the ratios of left-billed to right-billed Red Crossbills but such a significant difference in all studied White-winged Crossbill populations. However, since those ratios are not at all consistent with what I found with handedness/footedness, it is unlikely that which way the upper bill is twisted by a young crossbill is related to that behavior.

The side to which the bird twists the upper bill tip, as well as the actual twisting behavior appears to be dictated by their genes. Obviously, the sudden rapid growth of the bone and rhamphotheca of the bills after the birds fledge is definitely genetic. For me, those issues were never in question. What was, and apparently still is, disputed by some, especially ornithologists, is whether the bills just automatically and suddenly become crossed at some point after hatching. Or, does each individual bird engage in behaviors crucial to the process of making the tips of the upper bills cross either to the left or to the right of the lower bill?

One fledgling crossbill raised alone begins twisting its bills on protrusions it finds on branches used as perches as soon as the tips begin the fast growth period, indicating that particular behavior is more likely genetic than learned. In addition, the bird's genes may dictate whether it twists the upper bill to the right or to the left, though this can't be scientifically proven by observation. It is possible the bird decides which way to twist its bill. Unfortunately, the young crossbills didn't learn to speak English like Arnie and Nicki and I couldn't read their minds. The important consideration is that all healthy fledgling crossbills other rehabbers and I observed during the fast growth period of the bill tips, twisted their bills on protrusions to make them cross. Based on our observations and my photo documentation, **there definitely is necessary behavior by the bird itself involved in the bill crossing process.**

Crossbills and European Starlings are two of the most common bird species who open their bills to pry things such as cone scales, pieces of bark, or leaf litter apart to get food. Crossbills place their bill tips between two scales on a cone and twist slightly while they open their mouth, prying the scales apart to expose the seed, which the bird then extracts with its dexterous tongue. The crossed bills make it possible for these interesting birds to utilize a food source that is usually readily available to them. If there are not enough seed-filled cones in one area, they migrate to a new location. When they find an area with an abundant seed crop, crossbills remain there, build nests, and raise young. Availability of food is more of a determinant for the nesting season for crossbills than the actual season of the year.

When crossbills who are brought to rehabbers to raise are fledglings, they are kept in flight rooms until ready for release. There they can practice flying, landing, and pine seed removal skills. All the wildlife rehabilitators I have worked with observed that at the time when the tip of a post-fledgling crossbill's upper and lower bills begin to grow more rapidly, the birds found a protruding knot, the butt of a small broken branch, or some other protrusion to grasp and use to twist the upper bill either to the right or to the left. While the tips of the bills have their temporary accelerated growth, young crossbills constantly twist the top bill to one side and the bottom bill to the other. They bite on whatever protuberance they can find and twist several times per minute except when eating or sleeping. Once the bird begins to pry the top bill sideways, it always twists it the same way. After three or four days, the bill tips are fully-grown and in their permanently crossed position, where they remain for the rest of the bird's life. Although the birds are quite common, the fascinating phenomenon of how fledgling Red Crossbills or White-winged Crossbills actually participate in making their bills cross does not appear to be well documented. This behavior appeared to be fundamentally unknown until I reported it on bird websites several years ago.

I was once asked by an ornithologist what would happen if a young crossbill was not able to twist its bills while the tips were growing. I told him I assumed the tip of the lower bill would grow up into the bottom of the upper bill, forcing the bills in a permanently open position. In spring 2009, when I received a fledgling Red Crossbill with a broken leg, that hypothesis was tested and proven to be true. It arrived right at the beginning of its period of fast bill growth. I splinted the leg and propped the bird upright with rags. In the middle of a nest of soft fabric and unable to stand, the bird couldn't twist its bills while the tips grew. The question of what would happen was soon answered. The tip of the fast-growing lower bill began pushing up against the underside of the front of the upper bill, forcing the bird's mouth to remain open.

By taping the bird's bills in a crossed position between feedings, I was able to make them permanently cross. Fortunately, taping the bills so they were crossed during its period of fast bill tip growth worked and enabled it to close its mouth and remove seeds from cones in a normal manner after its leg had healed. If the bills had not been made to cross, they would have been forced open even farther as the tips continued to grow longer. The long lower bill tip would have forced the mouth open permanently, causing the bird's mouth to dry, and leaving it unable to eat and drink.

The crossbill's broken leg healed in only six days with the help of calc. phos. 30X, by which time the bill tips had finished growing. It was soon able to extract and eat seeds from pinecones, and was subsequently released. I sent its photos to several crossbill researchers and other ornithologists to show what happens if a fledgling crossbill is unable to twist its bills during the fast growth of the bill tips. Those who responded

This fledgling crossbill had a broken leg so couldn't twist its bills to make them cross. Consequently, the fast growing tip of the lower bill began pushing up on the bottom of the anterior of the upper bill, forcing the bird's mouth to remain open.

stated one bird is not proof that crossbill fledglings have to twist their bills to make them cross.

I had to wait several more years until April 13, 2017, to get photos of a crossbill fledgling actually twisting its bills against protuberances on branches. I received two pre-fledgling Red Crossbills from Victor, Montana, after the people who brought the birds to me chopped down their nest tree. Sadly, the left wing-tip on one of the birds was badly damaged in the fall, so it was never able to grow primary feathers on that wing. I tried for two months to get the feathers to grow but eventually had to euthanize it because was unreleasable.

It is unfortunate that people don't realize there are seven months during which trees can be safely trimmed or cut down. Tree cutting and trimming between September and the beginning of March will not often result in orphaned and injured birds. Most birds don't nest during those months except for Great Horned Owls and their nests are usually large enough to see. Trees cut down or trimmed between mid-March and the end of

August often have song bird nests built in the branches or occupied nest cavities in the trunk or large branches. Cutting of branches or the entire tree should be avoided during spring and summer months. It is against federal and state law to damage an occupied nest containing protected birds. All birds who nest in trees, except for invasive European Starlings and Eurasian Collared Doves, are protected.

While I was caring for the hatchling Red Crossbills in spring 2017, I took frequent photos to continuously document the bill growth from the top, bottom, left, and right sides of the faces and bills of both birds. I began the series when they arrived as pre-fledglings on April 26, and took more on May 1, May 8, and May 11. On May 8 (the day after their bill tips began the fast growth period), after many attempts, I was able to take a clear photo of the uninjured fledgling reaching for a knot on the branch on which it was sitting. The bird didn't hold on to the knot, a broken branch, or other protuberance for very long while twisting. It took many blotched tries before getting a clear photo of the bird while its bills were actually gripping a short, broken branch, just prior to twisting. Fortunately, with a digital camera, I don't have to pay for film processing.

After both birds had twisted their bill tips for three days, the bills were completely crossed and they stopped the twisting behavior. The fledgling with the injured wing would not bite on a protuberance while I was watching it or clicking the camera. It just sat there looking at me when I tried to photograph it. If I looked through a hole in the box, so it didn't know I was watching, I could see it bite on a knot or short branch and twist its bill tips over and over, just like its less secretive sibling did while I was photographing it.

The uninjured fledgling twisted its upper bill to the right and the wing-damaged fledgling twisted to the left. Since they were siblings with the same genetic background, it would seem the direction of twisting might have been individual preference. However, there was no way for me to test their genetics, so it remains unknown whether the individual itself decides which direction to twist the upper bill or if the direction preference is genetically programmed.

The reason I took so many photos of the underside of the bill and views from the top and both sides was because one crossbill researcher to whom I had reported the results of my observations before I received the 2017 crossbill pre-fledglings told me the following. "Indeed, years ago the late Harrison Tordoff, who bred crossbills and studied them extensively in captivity, told me he could predict which way the mandibles would cross simply by squeezing gently the sides of the bill of uncrossed nestlings." I am not saying Dr. Tordoff was mistaken, but I examined both birds carefully when I photographed them and each time I fed them. I even gently squeezed the sides of the bills, but apparently I didn't do it correctly because they remained in a straight-forward position. I could find no way to predict which way the birds would twist their upper bills. Most importantly, the photos showed nothing but straight bills until after the two birds began their twisting behavior. The day after they began twisting their bills, I could definitely tell which would be a righty and which a lefty and the photos clearly showed this.

These photos showing a view of the right side and a view of the bottom of the injured fledgling's bills, both of which are straight forward, were taken on April 26, 2017. Its uninjured sibling's bills looked the same.

This view of the bottom, with both bills remaining straight forward, was taken five days later on May 1.

On May 7, both birds began twisting on bumps or broken branches. This shows the uninjured bird reaching for a knob on the branch.

Several other crossbill researchers have raised Red Crossbills in captivity. I can't imagine why none of them observed the birds grasping at protrusions and twisting their bill tips. There appears to be a distinct discrepancy between what the researchers observed and what I photographed. It was a total surprise to me that ornithologists would not believe, and in some cases even consider, what rehabbers had seen healthy fledgling crossbills do to make their bills cross when the bill tips began the fast growth period.

After many tries, I finally succeeded in getting a clear picture taken on May 8, of the uninjured fledgling grasping a broken branch immediately before twisting its upper bill to the right.

Even after I sent the most recent series of photos I took of the 2017 fledglings to several ornithologists, they didn't seem convinced the birds actually participated in making their bills cross by twisting them during the fast growth period. One told me I would have to do a large study with many fledgling crossbills, including a control group, for anyone to be convinced. I asked how he suggested I control healthy fledglings. He never answered that question.

After the two birds had been twisting their bills all day on May 7, I took a series of photos on May 8. I could then tell the injured bird was twisting its upper bill to the left.

The injured bird on May 11, three days after the upper bill had been successfully twisted to the left enough times to remained crossed.

A side view of the left side of the bills of the uninjured bird on May 11, after the bills had successfully been twisted to cross with the upper bill going to the right, the opposite of its sibling.

I considered the bird who had a broken leg a "control" because, during the six days required for the leg to heal, it was unable to stand and twist its bills on anything. By the time its leg was healed, the fast growth period for its bill tips was over and its bill was crossed because I taped it crossed. I am not going to wrap up completely healthy birds and tube feed them many times a day to see what happens to their bills when I already know what would happen. Also, I couldn't possibly take care of the number the researchers suggested I would have to include in such a study. There is no place I could get so many crossbill fledglings for one thing. I certainly wouldn't take them from their parents. And definitely the most important factor is that "controlling" healthy crossbill fledglings in the way suggested would be horribly inhumane. All the birds who were "controlled" so they couldn't twist their bills would have to be euthanized at the end of the so-called study because they wouldn't be able to close their mouth or eat and drink. Rehabbers don't do things like that. At least those with whom I work would never consider such cruel actions. It is definitely not worth torturing young birds simply to prove something so obvious.

There is reportedly a decrease in the Red Crossbill population of about three to four percent per year, based on Breeding Bird Surveys. This is thought to be because the crossbills' natural food supply is disappearing in late winter and through spring, causing a decline in the populations. Crossbill researcher Craig Benkman's hypothesis for the lack of evergreen seeds is that increasing winter and spring temperatures are causing the few remaining seeds in the cones to be shed, thus unavailable for crossbills to extract. Another possibility is the massive loss of billions of pine trees in western forests (due to beetle kill and huge forest fires in recent years) resulting in far fewer cones being produced.

Because they can't find natural foods, there appears to be a simultaneous increase in the number of crossbills going to feeders, according to reports from feeder watchers. However, we have not seen many crossbills at our feeders for several years. Eating sunflower seeds sprayed with herbicides and insecticides may be actually be detrimental to the birds' survival and ability to successfully produce viable young, contributing to the population declines.

Crossbills are fascinating and entertaining to watch. They look like small red parrots when scattered throughout the treetops, often hanging sideways and upside down while busily extracting conifer seeds. They are an important part of the forest ecosystem, so population declines should be of great concern. Here in our area of western Montana, Red Crossbills appear to prefer ponderosa pine and can occasionally be observed at feeders. The other species of crossbill, White-winged Crossbills, are more difficult to find but can sometimes be seen eating seeds in large blue spruce trees.

If anyone observes fledgling crossbills twisting their bills on protruding branches and knots on trees, they should report their observations and also try to take photos of the behavior. Eventually, these amazing birds may convince ornithologists and everyone else that while the birds' genes likely dictate when and how they do it, they actually do make their own bills cross.

**Hanging upside down,
parrot-like Red Crossbills pry
seeds from stubborn cones.**

SECTION SEVEN
INTERESTING OBSERVATIONS

**Osprey work hard to
catch large fish that are stolen
by a Bald Eagle.**

CHAPTER 41
A TURKEY VULTURE'S TEACHING CAREER

In May 1993, a man and his wife brought me another extremely interesting bird, a Turkey Vulture (*Cathartes aura*) they found by the road with an old wing injury. The vulture was fat and healthy, even though it couldn't fly. It had been eating ground squirrels killed by vehicles on the busy Stevensville Crossing highway between Stevensville and Highway 93. A highway was not a healthy place for a flightless bird to spend time dining on road kill. The broken bone in the bird's right wing may have been the result of being hit by a vehicle. It had healed improperly, so the vulture would never be able to fly.

Turkey Vultures have always fascinated me. They are sometimes called turkey buzzard or simply buzzard and have been protected for many years under the Migratory Bird Treaty Act of 1918. The name vulture comes from the Latin word vulturus (which means tearer) because of the way they tear meat from dead carcasses.

Not wanting to pass up the opportunity to closely observe a Turkey Vulture, I began including him in the educational presentations I gave at schools and clubs instead of euthanizing him (the only other legal option for an unreleasable bird). My intention was to help people learn about birds, why they are important to us, and the various issues causing population declines in some of Montana's birds.

I thought a Turkey Vulture could definitely be of assistance in educating people regarding how important carrion-eating birds are for keeping the land clean and free from diseases. Birds like Turkey Vultures, Black-billed Magpies, Common Ravens, and Bald and Golden Eagles quickly eat all the soft tissue from animals who die from accidents or contagious diseases. This cleanup crew also prevents the slow, smelly

315

decay of carcasses, which can be annoying to people. Most important, by rapidly disposing of animals who die of a disease, they prevent it from spreading to other animals.

Michael Roggenbuck, a researcher of microbiology at the University of Copenhagen, and his colleagues tested bacteria on vultures' faces and in their intestines. Roggenbuck stated, "Our results show there has been strong adaptation in vultures when it comes to dealing with the toxic bacteria they digest. On one hand, vultures have developed an extremely tough digestive system, which simply acts to destroy the majority of the dangerous bacteria they ingest. On the other hand, vultures also appear to have developed a tolerance toward some of the deadly bacteria – species that would kill other animals actively seem to flourish in the vulture lower intestine." These adaptations, especially strong acids in the digestive system, are what make it possible for vultures to dispose of dead carcasses without getting sick or spreading the infectious bacteria.

Children always laughed when I told them his name was Black Beauty. Turkey Vultures can tell if they are male or female, but I can't. For the 25 years he lived here, I always referred to Black Beauty as he but was never sure of his gender. Vultures fascinate most people, especially children, because the birds have so many interesting characteristics and behaviors.

When I first began giving presentations with Black Beauty, bird authorities said Turkey Vultures were a member of the Falconiforme family, so were related to falcons. That didn't make much sense to me because they have feet more like a turkey, with no talons. Then the experts said genetic studies indicated vultures were closely related to storks, which made much more sense anatomically. So, while I was giving educational presentations, I told people bird authorities said vultures were related to storks. Then in 2014, authorities put the New World vultures (Turkey and Black Vulture) in their own order, Cathartiformes, a group fairly closely related to Accipitriformes, comprised of the Osprey, secretary bird, and accipiters such as Sharp-shinned Hawk, Coopers Hawk and Goshawk, based on whole genome analysis. By the time I found that enlightening study in 2015, Black Beauty was no longer available for presentations.

One of the most interesting anatomical features, besides the turkey-like feet, is the large see-through nasal hole above the upper bill, scientifically referred to as perforated nostrils. It enables them inhale a great deal of air at a time to search for tiny molecules of ethyl mercaptan, a gas released from decomposing bodies of dead animals. The olfactory lobe, the portion of the brain responsible for processing smells, is much larger in a turkey vulture's brain than that of most other animals. The molecules of ethyl mercaptan float in the air wherever the air currents carry them. While turkey vultures soar over the landscape, they can smell and identify even a tiny number of molecules from a decaying carcass. The vulture will then circle until it determines which direction to go to find the dead animal, flying directly to it using the scent like trail markers on a path.

A group of Turkey Vultures often came to eat leftovers from accident-killed animals I butchered to feed birds of prey and other animals in my care. The first Turkey Vulture to arrive seems to circle low several times to assess the amount of food available on the dead carcass. If it sees enough to feed multiple vultures, it glides up very high and soars around and around in tight circles directly over the carcass. Within 15 or 20 minutes, from eight to 15 vultures come flying in from all directions. Several of the vultures perch in nearby trees, while others fly down to the carcass to pry off chunks of meat from the bones with their sharp, ivory colored bills. I assume the birds perched in trees are acting as sentries watching for predators. If an animal, such as a fox, coyote, badger, wolf, dog, or other predator, approaches while vultures are on the ground, the birds will regurgitate part of the meat they have eaten to distract the

Black Beauty's nostrils were so large you could see through them. This helps a vulture detect odors from a dead carcass from a long distance away. He also grew black hair-like feathers on his head and face.

predator while they make their getaway. Throwing up part of their food also makes them lighter, so they can run faster and take off more easily. During nesting season, they carry food back to their nest in their crop and regurgitate the meat for their chicks to eat.

After all the vultures took their turn feeding, they flew up to perch on branches of the large pine trees along the edge of the field, where they remained until they digested the meat in their large crops. The next morning, all of them flew to the tops of posts on the west side of our property, where they sat in a line with wings outstretched and their backs to the rising sun. They looked like a row of angels silhouetted against the glowing pink sunrise. I don't get to see that behavior now because the neighbor subdivided the land on the other side of the fence and a large house was built quite close to the posts. Turkey Vultures are quite wary of people, houses, and pets, so they now apparently sun themselves from the tops of the pine trees, where they are less conspicuous.

One suggestion for the Turkey Vultures' sunning behavior is they are using the sun to sanitize any feathers that may have become contaminated by bacteria while eating on a dead animal. Because I gave Black Beauty small chunks of meat or dead mice, rats, or hamsters, his feathers never became dirty while eating. He opened his wings with his back to the sun every morning, and at first, I assumed it helped him warm up faster. However, he basked in the sun with his wings outstretched for long periods after being out of the direct sun for several days even when the temperature was warm. That suggested that Turkey Vultures may engage in this behavior to absorb vitamin D, which helps process the dietary calcium.

I usually left Black Beauty outside in his large pen unless the temperature at night was going to be below 20 degrees. To keep him from becoming too cold, I put him in a room much warmer than the outside temperature. If the temperature remained low both day and night, I sometimes had to keep him inside for several days. When I put him back in his large outdoor pen, he spent long periods with his wings raised to catch the sun, even if it was quite warm. Black Beauty's sunning behavior supported the hypothesis that vultures primarily do this to obtain adequate vitamin D.

One spring about two years after Black Beauty came to me, I had to take a two-week trip. The local wildlife refuge put out dead accident-killed deer carcasses at that time to feed eagles, vultures, ravens, and magpies. I took Black Beauty out to where the carcasses were so he would have plenty of meat to eat while I was away. There was also a stream close enough for him to walk for water. I left him there not knowing whether I would ever see him again. I hoped he would remain near the carcasses and I would be able to recapture him when I returned.

A Turkey Vulture stands on a branch of a tree while sunning itself. Photo by Eugene Beckes.

Upon returning home from the trip, we went to the refuge to look for Black Beauty but, after much searching, we couldn't find him. Another two weeks went by before I received a call one morning about a Turkey Vulture. Two people said they had picked up a vulture who couldn't fly from beside the highway, where it was eating a vehicle-killed ground squirrel. The place they found it was about two miles straight south of where I had left Black Beauty on the refuge and almost exactly where he was originally found. He must have liked that area by the road between Highway 93 and Stevensville. Turkey Vultures are known to be great long-distance navigators from the air, but apparently they can also find their way around quite well when they can only walk on the ground.

I asked the people to bring the vulture to me, warning them to cover his head so he wouldn't bite anyone. I suspected it was Black Beauty and he was pretty "fast on the draw" with that sharp beak of his. When the people arrived, it was easy to identify the vulture as Black Beauty because of his damaged right wing. I was happy to see him, but the feeling didn't appear to be reciprocated. As usual, he was not at all pleased with being handled.

The people said when they caught the vulture and were carrying him to their car, a man stopped and asked why they had caught it and what they were going to do with it. When they told him they were bringing it to me, he said, "Good, sorry I bothered you," got back in his car, and drove off. It made me happy that at least three people showed concern about the welfare of a Turkey Vulture.

I returned Black Beauty to his large covered kennel with several skinned mice and the hind leg of an accident-killed deer to eat. After that excursion, he remained in captivity for the rest of his long life. One summer, I received a juvenile Turkey Vulture with a bruised wing, so Black Beauty had the company of another vulture while its wing recovered. I released it here before the vultures began to migrate south for the winter, giving it the opportunity to go with them. It came back several times to visit Black Beauty and to eat the deer leg I placed on a piece of plywood on top of his chain-link kennel.

At that time, I always put a deer carcass out in our field for migrating Turkey Vultures to eat as they passed through the Bitterroot Valley on their flight south. After eating for two or three days, they all flew up and circled around in a funnel formation until they hit a fast-flowing air stream. With their wings outstretched, they rode the air current to the southwest without flapping or expending any energy.

Turkey Vultures raised by humans from the time they are hatched are tame and follow their caretakers like puppies. Because Black Beauty grew up in the wild, he wasn't at all tame. I always warn people about keeping the bills of a Turkey Vulture away from their faces or any other vulnerable skin. I learned the hard way when I was showing my unreleasable education birds, including Black Beauty, to the Lions' Club in Hamilton. While holding Black Beauty's wing open to show his feathers to the people, I unintentionally raised his head as high as my face. He quickly reached over and pecked a three-cornered piece of skin off my upper lip. I had to finish the talk with my lip bleeding quite profusely. I was so embarrassed the rest of my face was likely as red as the blood spouting from my lip. Fortunately, the Lions' Club members thought the whole incident was quite humorous. I am a fast healer so, after a few days, there was nothing left but a small scar and my bruised ego. I did learn to never again let Black Beauty's bill get close to my face. This indicated maybe they should have given Turkey Vultures the Latin name for "terror" rather than "tearer," although Black Beauty did his best to live up to both spellings.

An interesting thing Black Beauty did while in captivity was grow fairly thick, black hair-like feathers on his head and face, making them look black in winter, rather than having the bare, red skin showing. Because he didn't have to stick his head into dead animals, most of the fine feathers remained on his head all year, although they were somewhat thinner during summer. The hair-like feathers grew quite thick in late fall. The increased feather growth likely occurred because he was kept for so many years in Montana in the winter, when the temperature is below freezing much of the time. Most Turkey Vultures migrate south to spend the winter in a much warmer climate. Young Turkey Vultures have black hairy feathers on their head and face, but adults normally have only a few scattered feathers in those areas. Because they stick their heads into dead carcasses to pull out meat and other soft tissue, adult vultures do not retain enough of the hairy feathers to make their faces above and around their eyes appear black like Black Beauty's did.

Black Beauty died on January 29, 2016, when he was 25 or more years old. When his wing was injured in 1993, he was at least 2 years old, but there was no way to tell his actual age when I first received him for care. The oldest Turkey Vulture noted in my Audubon Bird Encyclopedia lived in captivity to be almost 21 years old. Black Beauty exceeded that by at least four years.

He was an outstanding ambassador for Turkey Vultures and an entertaining teacher. After Black Beauty died, I gave his body to Larry Weeks in Missoula to make a study skin. Larry uses the study skins of multiple bird species for educational talks he gives to people of all ages, especially school classes. He didn't have a Turkey Vulture study skin, so was happy to have Black Beauty to make one. Larry and his audiences are amazed at how long Black Beauty lived. Black Beauty, with Larry's help, is still educating people about the unique and interesting characteristics of Turkey Vultures, carrying on his teaching career even after death.

**Wings raised in salute
to morning sun, vultures make
lovely silhouettes.**

In the 1980's, this hybrid from Cinnamon Teal (Anas cyanoptera) and Blue-winged Teal (Anas discors) parents came for care because of a broken wing. His neck and chest feathers were cinnamon in color, but his back and head were brown, with a somewhat diffuse light area on each side of his face directly behind the bill, indicating he had Blue-winged Teal parentage. Because he wasn't releasable, I used him in educational presentations, until he died. His body was given to the University of Montana for a study skin, so he continues to educate.

CHAPTER 42
A BIRD IN THE HAND

One look at the exquisite charcoal gray and yellow warbler lying unconscious on the bottom of a cardboard box just handed to me by my neighbor was all I needed to know I had never seen a bird like it before. As a wildlife rehabilitator, I had seen most of the small birds who lived in or frequented our area of western Montana. Since it was late summer, many warblers had been passing through the Bitterroot Valley on their migration south. The mostly 15-mile-wide valley runs north and south, so is used as a migration route for birds going south from Canada and northern Montana.

I thanked my neighbor for calling me. The little bird had flown into their window, obviously hitting quite hard. Except for the slight movement of the body as the bird breathed, it was hard to tell it was still alive. As I hurried the half-mile back to my house, I could see the warbler was beginning to blink its eyes, a sign it was regaining consciousness. The first thing I did upon arriving home was pull out my bird identification books and quickly look up warblers. I wanted to identify the bird before it woke up, while I could still handle it without stressing it. I checked for injuries, making mental notes of its distinguishing characteristics. With the unconscious bird in my hand, I compared it to all the warblers in *Peterson's Guide to Western Birds* and *Audubon Society Field Guide to North American Birds*. Bright yellow feathers on both the top and bottom of the rump, a white throat above a bright yellow chest, the dark charcoal grey color of the head, back, and tail all indicated a Virginia's Warbler (*Oreothlypis virginiae*). A small patch of red feathers almost hidden in the grey feathers on top of the bird's head and the charming white ring around the dark eye, left no doubt he was an adult male Virginia's Warbler.

I made note of all these things on the bird's entry sheet as I filled it out. By then the small warbler was awakening and becoming more aware of his surroundings, as indicated by his open, now unblinking eyes following my every move. Not wanting to stress him unnecessarily, I placed him in a recovery box containing a dish of small mealworms and a tiny pan of water, so he could drink but not get wet. He soon fluttered up to perch on a branch I had run through the sides of the box. The beautiful little warbler indicated he still didn't feel well by promptly placing his head under his wing in a sleeping position. I was sure he had a major headache after hitting window glass hard enough to knock himself unconscious for 15 to 20 minutes.

I placed the box in a warm, quiet place where there would be no disturbances. He wanted to sleep, which would help his recovery, and I had many baby birds to feed. They need to be fed about every 20 minutes and it had taken somewhat longer than that to go get the warbler, identify him, and make him comfortable in the recovery box. Because I was so busy, I didn't have time to consider why I hadn't previously seen a Virginia's Warbler.

I checked him several times before my bedtime, each time finding him still sitting in the same spot on the perch with his head under his wing. Early the next morning, the little warbler was flying around the recovery box, though it was a fairly small box. He looked normal and healthy. Since he could fly inside the relatively small box, he had obviously recovered his coordination. As I watched, he killed and tried to eat a mealworm, but the worm was either too big or too tough skinned. He eventually dropped the dead worm on the floor of the box and looked around for something more palatable.

I didn't want a migrating bird to lose the weight needed to continue his migration. I kept him in the box until the sun was up and warm, bringing out many insects in our garden and hedgerows. Then I carried the box out to our berry bushes. There were tiny insects flying or crawling everywhere I looked, perfect for a hungry Virginia's Warbler to get his breakfast. I unceremoniously removed the top of the box. What should have been the first ever documented Virginia's Warbler for Montana flew straight into the thickest of the bushes and disappeared from sight.

Several days later, I was looking for a plant book and came upon my Montana Bird Distribution book. Curious about where Virginia's Warblers are usually found in Montana, I looked up their range and distribution. No report of Virginia's Warblers in Montana had ever been accepted. I had made a huge mistake by releasing the bird without showing him to several top-level birders or an ornithologist. No one other than myself and the two neighbors who found him under their window had seen the bird. My neighbors' bird identification skills were limited to House Sparrows, Blue Birds, and Robins. My concern had been only for the warbler's welfare. I had deliberately kept him quiet and away from people. I was unaware that no other Virginia's Warbler sighting had been accepted for Montana and that my little guy would have been the first. I also didn't know at that time that several people have to see and identify a bird or a photo must be taken for the report to be accepted. Sometimes even photos arc insufficient proof of identification. Actually, at the time I had the warbler, there was no way to prove where a photo was taken. The only camera I had then was a 35 mm slide camera.

At the end of the year, I always report unusual birds I see or receive for care to the Montana Natural Heritage Program. I included the Virginia's Warbler in my report and stated he was in my hand while identification was made and in captivity for nearly 18 hours. After I sent in the report, ornithologists began calling. They asked me to describe the bird over and over, where I saw him, what kind of habitat, lighting, etc., all of which was in the original report. I told them that, while I identified him, the bird was in my hand under a lamp to keep him warm and so I could see all the distinguishing colors. I explained there is no other bird with the characteristics of an adult male Virginia's Warbler, and that I could see very clearly all the distinguishing features of the bird, since he was in my hand in very good light. But I hadn't taken a photo nor shown him to other people, so I couldn't prove I had actually had a Virginia's Warbler in my hand.

I had to plead guilty to turning a Virginia's Warbler loose to be on his way to wherever he was headed without proper documentation. After he became conscious, taking photos or taking him to ornithologists for examination would have stressed him and delayed his release and finding food. I didn't regret releasing him without harassing him or possibly causing him to die of starvation.

I know Virginia's Warblers must occasionally come here and may even nest here in summer. It is unlikely my little guy was the only one to ever be in Montana or migrate through our state. Migratory birds have to travel thousands of miles from where they nest to where they spend the winter. Many small birds, like warblers, spend most of their time in thick treetops or brush, where they are not likely to be noticed. Except for experienced birders, anyone who saw a Virginia's Warbler would not know what it is and so wouldn't report it.

There have been at least two other reports of Virginia's Warblers in Montana, one before the warbler I had in my care and one after. The other two reports were not accepted so, because I set my bird free without proper documentation, there is still no Virginia's Warbler recorded for Montana. That may be our loss but is of no concern at all to warblers. The lesson for avid birders is a bird in the hand apparently doesn't prove anything unless you take a good photo or the bird is dead so you can produce the body for evidence.

Dressed in stately grey,
the dapper goshawk dines on
pheasant under grass.

An immature Northern Goshawk (*Accipiter gentilis*) eating a California Quail (*Callipepla californica*) after quail were introduced to western Montana by hunters. California Quail are increasing in number and have become a staple food for accipiters like Northern Goshawks, Cooper's Hawks, and Sharp-shinned Hawks who winter in Ravalli County.

CHAPTER 43
KINGFISHER BOUNTY

Unfortunately, what the following poem relates is true, except for the origin of the newspaper story. It was reprinted several years ago in the "Headlines from the Past" section of the *Ravalli Republic Newspaper* published in Hamilton, Montana. It reported that Boy Scouts in Ravalli County had been paid 10 cents apiece for all the Crows, Ravens, Magpies, blackbird of any species, and Belted Kingfisher (*Megaceryle alcyon*) they killed that year. Apparently, the birds could be killed in any manner that worked. The number of each species of bird taken in for bounty by the Boy Scouts was reported in the story. This travesty happened over 75 years ago in the 1940's. If what was said in the old news report was correct, it was commonly done each year back then. The unnecessary, inhumane extermination of those native birds likely continued for many years after the news item was written, possibly until 1972, when it finally became illegal to kill native birds. I was aware people still illegally shoot many of the birds on that list. For Corvids and blackbirds, I know the people's motive for killing them in the past and now illegally in the present. However, no one can give me a reason why the beautiful Belted Kingfisher, never abundant and not harmful to anyone, was included on their list of birds to be eradicated. Several years ago, at the time the "Headlines from the Past" article was reprinted, I asked some older people who had been life-long residents of Ravalli County why kingfishers were included on the kill list. No one had any idea.

Several people I questioned inexplicably became quite irritated with me, apparently simply because I had the audacity to ask such a question. That is what inspired my hopefully somewhat humorous poem about the questionable motives of people when they make anthropocentric decisions that seriously affect the lives of individuals, as well as entire populations of animals with whom we share this planet.

Boy Scouts reportedly collected bounty on 79 Belted Kingfishers in just one year, as reported in the "Headlines from the Past" article. That may be more Belted Kingfishers than I have seen in my lifetime. I have received several for care who were injured or that had short upper bills, a developmental defect caused by exposure to environmental toxins.

There definitely have never, since we moved to the Bitterroot Valley, been an over-abundance of Belted Kingfishers here. They are sometimes quite difficult to find on bird counts. Hopefully this sad reflection on the past will give people cause to stop and think before they do something that has such grave and lasting consequences to all generations who follow.

A pretty but somewhat prehistoric-looking female Belted Kingfisher photographed by Eugene Beckes.

KINGFISHER BOUNTY

I found an old newspaper story.
The paper, all yellow and worn,
Was in the wall of a homesteader cabin.
The item that caught my attention
Was printed before I was born.

It declared the kingfisher an outlaw.
A price had been placed on its head.
Young boys were paid a bounty
For each small kingfisher body
That they could deliver dead.

It seems no one can tell me
What the little birds had done
To provoke the ire of the public so
That it sent an army of Boy Scouts
To annihilate them with a gun.

Was its large bill the problem?
It bothers humans a bunch
When an animal has the audacity
To ignore human etiquette;
And have a person for lunch.

But with a search of history,
I am certain we would find
Though the kingfisher's bill
Is long and sharp, on humans
They never have dined.

A kingfisher eats only little fish,
Albeit without our permission,
A crime that could hardly be
Grievous enough to warrant
Sending them to perdition.

A kingfisher's call is fairly harsh
With a certain primitive ring.
But it's difficult to contemplate,
So many of the birds were shot
Just because they couldn't sing.

Sadly though, the birds were killed.
Shot down in every season.
Now, no one can tell me why
So many kingfishers had to die.
There likely was no reason.

Peregrine falcon
drops from sky; strikes duck in a
feather explosion.

Red-winged Blackbirds are a species historically killed in mass numbers for eating grain piled where the birds can get it. Blackbird species collectively eat billions of insects each year, which is helpful to farmers.

CHAPTER 44
POINTED OBSERVATIONS

Porcupine (*Erethizon dorsatum*) population studies conducted by Katie Mally in 2008 indicated their populations have collapsed in the mountains of western Montana, with few porcupines remaining. Dave Romero, Forest Biologist on the Bitterroot National Forest, speculated that "severe fires were the main cause for the decline in the slow-moving porcupine because they could not escape the flames and smoke." While fast moving forest fires are likely a significant factor in causing porcupine mortality in the areas affected by forest fires, there appear to be other important aspects triggering the declines.

A significant and corresponding factor for the relatively recent widespread declines in western Montana porcupine populations may be the inability of adults to produce viable young. The population cannot be sustained without young to replace the adults who die from diseases, parasites, fires, predators, poisons, or humans who shoot them. Porcupines are the second largest North American rodent, with only beaver being larger. Unlike all our other rodents, who commonly have a short gestation time and multiple newborns per pregnancy, porcupines have only one young per year after a seven-month gestation. A porcupette must be well developed and have protective quills at birth. It does not stay in a nest or burrow so begins following its mother soon after it is born. Quills are initially soft but quickly harden into their protective form.

Many individuals of rodent species, as well as other newborn mammals and hatchling birds, have been observed with multiple birth defects which preclude survival to adulthood. These birth defects and health issues that began being observed in many individuals of vertebrate species in 1995 are discussed in detail in my book *Changing Faces: The Consequences of Exposure to Gene and Thyroid Disrupting Toxins.* The birth defects observed in other rodents have not yet been reported in porcupines, likely because almost no one examines them for such issues. I have only had the opportunity to examine one dead juvenile male porcupine. It had no scrotum at four months of age. No or malformed scrotum is now a common birth defect in males of multiple rodent species here in Montana. I couldn't find in the scientific literature whether there is delayed scrotal development in male porcupines, thus whether the male I examined had a birth defect is undetermined at present.

Most importantly, an adult porcupine and a three-month-old porcupette were observed with adverse neurological symptoms similar to those documented in many other individuals of mammal and bird species in our area. The severe neurological symptoms began in 1994-1995, closely corresponding to when the birth defects began being observed.

The species of small mammals who have been seen to tip over when they tried to eat, walk, and run include several individuals of mountain cottontail rabbit (*Sylvilagus nuttallii*) in the Leporidae family, and rodents, including eastern fox squirrel (*Sciurus niger*), northern flying squirrel (*Glaucomys sabrinus*), red squirrel (*Tamiasciurus hudsonicus*), deer mouse (*Peromyscus manipulates*), house mouse (*Mus musculus*), beaver (*Castor canadensis*), and Columbian ground squirrel (*Urocitellus columbianus*). From 1994 to present (2018), neurological effects on rodents and rabbits have resulted in the deaths of many individuals of those species here on our land, even though we use no poisons. I also received many birds of several species and four deer fawns who had severe neurological symptoms. Many people have reported neurological issues in their pets, including dogs, cats, and domestic birds. Collectively, this appears to now be a fairly common and widespread health issue in animals and may be a serious factor affecting the survival of porcupines.

In addition, poisoning by rodenticides used in marijuana-growing operations on public Forest Service land, or used for rodent control on private property, appears to be responsible for the death of porcupines and other wildlife in many states. The slow, torturous death caused by rodenticide poisoning is extremely inhumane. If observed, any animal with obvious neurological symptoms should be reported to the Montana Department of Fish, Wildlife and Parks so the cause can be investigated. Unfortunately, porcupines are not protected, but other wild mammals who are being poisoned by rodenticides are protected, including species considered rare or threatened. It is heartbreaking for our precious wildlife to be killed in such a sadistic and horrible manner.

There are two types of rodenticides. The kind most recently released for use are called second generation rodenticides because they were developed after rodents became somewhat resistant to so-called first-generation poisons like Warfarin. The second-generation rodenticides are literally weapons of mass destruction. When they are used to kill rats and mice in and around buildings, the exposed rodents don't die immediately, often becoming incapacitated and unable to escape predators. Small predators eat the rodents and, when the rodenticides begin affecting them, they too become lethargic, thus easy for larger predators to catch. The levels of rodenticides continuously build up in the organs of top predators, eventually leading to a slow death. Not only are birds such as raptors being killed, many mammalian predators, including several species of fox, coyotes, wolves, mountain lions, bobcats, raccoons, black bears, skunks, badgers, fishers, martin, porcupine, dogs, and house cats have been killed in fairly large numbers by rodenticide ingestion. This seems to be a widespread environmental disaster throughout the United States.

Here in Montana it appears rodenticides are likely doing extensive, mostly unrecognized, damage to wildlife populations, including that of porcupines. It is evident the porcupine population needs at least the basic protection most other Montana wildlife has under state law. Unfortunately, this likely requires Montana Legislators to pass a law to that effect and many people have a strong dislike of porcupines. This bias may have been passed down from their parents or developed because their dog attacked one and came home with quills in its face. These biases by some people should not preclude protection for an important wildlife species to keep it from being extirpated from large areas of Montana. Western Montana is larger than many states and we have already lost numerous important wild animals because they were slaughtered with no protest or protection.

Much larger numbers of non-target, protected-by-law, and sometimes threatened or endangered animals than we realize may be succumbing to poisoning by rodenticides. For example, a mountain lion in Los Angeles, California, called P-41 (the number he was given when he was radio collared for tracking) became famous with Internet followers. P-41 was found dead in October 2017 in the Verdugo Mountains. Testing of his liver showed he had been exposed to six second-generation rodenticides: brodifacoum, bromadiolone, chlorophacinone, difethialone, diphacinone and difenacoum. Rodenticides disrupt blood clotting, resulting in ruptured blood vessels, with internal bleeding and bruising, nose bleeds, and bleeding gums. Rodenticides can also suppress the immune system of an animal, making it more susceptible to parasites and infectious diseases. His millions of followers were greatly saddened by the death of P-41. Hopefully they were affected enough to never use rodenticides themselves.

P-41 wasn't alone in being exposed to rodenticides. In Los Angeles, 14 of 15 mountain lions, including a cub, tested positive for them in tests done by National Park Service researchers. In addition, 12 of 13 mountain lions in the Santa Monica Mountains tested positive for rodenticide exposure and two died. For tested bobcats *(Lynx rufus)* there, 93 of 105 had rodenticide exposure and over 70 died. Half (12) of the 24 tested coyotes (*Canus latrans*) died, with 20 testing positive for rodenticides.

Long before rodenticides killed P-41, they were found to be the cause of the death of Lima, one of the mates of the most famous Red-tailed Hawk in New York City and possibly the world. Pale Male, the long-lived, much-loved hawk, watched by millions of people via an online nest camera, hatched in 1990 and has had 8 mates.

The following serious finding by the Environmental Protection Agency should be extremely concerning for parents: between 1999 and 2003, at least 25,549 children under the age of seven were poisoned by directly ingesting rodenticide pellets they found lying around. Poisoning so many small children in addition to unknown numbers of non-target and sometimes endangered animals seems an excellent reason for taking second-generation rodenticides completely off the market. Many other products have been banned or prohibited for harming far fewer children. The question is why are these sadistic products still allowed to be sold?

Much safer alternatives can and definitely should be used to rid homes or out buildings of unwanted rats and mice. The most humane are snap traps as long as they are checked frequently, and electrocuting traps that kill the victim quickly. These alternatives to poisoning are far safer and much more effective long term. Most importantly, they don't eradicate mammals and birds that prey on the unwanted rodents, they can't cause resistance to build up in targeted rodent populations, and they don't poison small children.

Porcupines are still being regularly seen on the Great Plains side of the mountains and in the flatlands of eastern Montana. Interestingly, porcupine researchers do not consider factors connected to climate change to be a cause of declines in porcupine populations in western Montana. Porcupines are not heat intolerant, they eat a wide range of plants, and researchers have found no infectious diseases in their populations here. Climate change should be a greater factor on the prairie than in the mountains, with less moisture and thus fewer plants for the porcupine to eat. It has been suggested that with more people living in western Montana and accessing the forests, deliberate human predation such as incidental shooting could be a factor in the disappearance of adult porcupines. Both shooting and poisoning could be mitigated with education and by giving the porcupine the obviously necessary protected status it needs in Montana.

As the porcupine population declines, there are of course, fewer to observe. Porcupines are difficult to find in the wild even when there is a fairly large population. This may be why so few have been seen with neurological problems in contrast to the hundreds of other rodents observed with those health issues. For a porcupine, who must climb trees to escape predators and eat tree bark, a primary food source, sudden neurological damage causing it to continuously fall over would interfere with all life functions and significantly shorten its lifespan. Dead porcupines are even harder to locate than live ones. Also, once dead, it is difficult to tell if the porcupine died because of neurological problems or some other issue. Without testing, the cause of the neurological symptoms or whether the porcupine was poisoned prior to death can't be determined.

I first directly observed an adult porcupine with severe neurological damage in 2003. Being unable to control its legs caused it to fall over on its back when it tried to sit up or climb. It couldn't climb trees and occasionally tipped over onto its side when it tried to navigate through downed branches in the riparian area near Willoughby Creek. I followed it from a distance and watched it for over half an hour. It would suddenly tip over onto its side even when walking on level ground, taking several tries to right itself, losing multiple quills in the grass and leaves in the process. It had even more trouble with falling when it had to climb over large branches on the ground. Unfortunately, I didn't have a way to catch a porcupine with me as I was initially watching wild birds with my binoculars. I finally ran to the house to get a shovel and a garbage can large enough to contain it, but by the time I returned to where I last saw it, I couldn't find it again. I don't know what caused that porcupine to have neurological problems because I wasn't able to catch it and have its blood tested.

It wasn't until summer 2015 that a possible cause was found for such symptoms. My friend and fellow rehabber Adele received a call about a three-month-old male porcupine who was found in a yard just west of Victor. He was tipping over onto his side in a similar manner to the adult I had observed. Adele carefully guided him into a dog carrier which she and the homeowner lifted into the back of her car for transport.

Adele named him Quill and took care of him for nearly a month, trying to mitigate his neurological damage. At first Quill could eat and drink from dishes in an outdoor chain link enclosure, with his balance seeming to improve somewhat. He occasionally tipped over on his side when walking and fell on his back when he tried to climb the chain link panel, a feat that should have been easy for him. Quill ate well and his digestion appeared normal. He loved small chunks of carrot, sweet potato, willow, and apple, holding them in his hands as he chewed. As long as he remained on his belly, this worked well. If he tried to stand on his hind legs, a common position for a healthy porcupine, he tipped over backwards.

Quill was the sweetest little guy, making sounds similar to purring when Adele stroked his head. He never raised his quills or flipped his tail, even when Adele handled him, though he was born in the wild and had been following his mother for a while before he became ill. Even a gentle young porcupine needs to be handled with care because of their quills, which point backward unless threatened. Their long guard hair can be stroked from head to tail, but the other direction would be painful, and picking up a porcupine is difficult. Except for their soft belly, which they protect, quills cover most of their body. Porcupines are unable to "throw" their quills, only leaving them in an attacker when touched. They will slap with their tail when threatened. Dogs who have to have quills pulled out of their face only get them by trying to grab a porcupine with malicious intent.

Sadly, Quill's ability to walk inexplicably began to deteriorate. Adele moved him into a kennel in the house where she could watch him better and provide more frequent care. After a few days, his hind legs became completely non-functional and he was unable to pick up his food with his hands. For a while, he ate small pieces of apple or carrot Adele held for him. Then he quit taking even a minimal amount, regardless of Adele's coaxing.

Because Quill's health continued to decline and he was unable to eat and digest food, we made the sad decision to euthanize him. After examining, Quill for birth defects, I sent his body to the Montana Department of Fish, Wildlife and Parks wildlife laboratory. The lab veterinarian reported he tested positive for exposure to a rodenticide.

Quite recently, porcupine populations in some areas of Montana appear to be the unfortunate target of what are called Coyote Derbies, in which teams of shooters attempt for three days to annihilate as many coyotes,

Quill was an extremely cute porcupette. Photo by Adele Lewis.

and apparently any other unprotected wildlife as possible, for money and prizes. Such killing contests seem to be on the rise in some western states. The 2017 Big Sandy Coyote Derby in the ranching area around Big Sandy, Montana, succeeded in reducing the coyote population by 71 individuals. There is nothing sporting about this slaughter of Montana wildlife. Sadly, the participants also shot nine porcupines for apparently no purpose at all. The reason given for the killing of the coyotes in Coyote Derbies in western states in January and early February is to protect calves born in February and March from predation. I am certain no porcupine has ever eaten a calf, so why were porcupines unequivocally murdered? The answer likely is because they were seen by people with guns! If this doesn't emphatically indicate porcupine populations in Montana need basic protection to keep from being extirpated, I don't know what will.

Interestingly, in the 2018 Big Sandy Coyote Derby, 146 participants killed 191 coyotes, 120 more than in 2017. This suggests research indicating wanton killing of coyotes causes their population to increase may be correct because with fewer coyotes in an area, the litter size increases. However, porcupines have only one porcupette per year, so eliminating even a few females has an extensive detrimental effect on population numbers. In 2017, apparently all porcupines who were seen during the Big Sandy Coyote Derby were killed. Even though far more people participated in the coyote assassination in 2018 than in 2017, in

2018 no dead porcupines were brought in by participants, strongly suggesting no porcupines were seen.

White-tailed jackrabbits, leopard frogs, and fresh water mussels were all living here when we moved to western Montana. We could do nothing but watch while they were annihilated from the landscape. Columbia sharp-tailed grouse, grizzly bears, and others were wantonly exterminated from Ravalli County long before we arrived. The strange and unbelievable long-ago effort to kill all Belted Kingfishers in Ravalli County was addressed in Chapter 43, Kingfisher Bounty. Happily, Belted Kingfishers survived the undeserved attempt to eradicate them and still live in our western Montana riparian areas as one of our most interesting and beautiful birds.

Many years ago, I made quite pointed observations to the Montana Department of Fish, Wildlife and Parks concerning the extirpation of white-tailed jackrabbits and the leopard frog but to no avail. Hopefully, Quill and other dead and disappearing porcupines will help make a case for protecting them before porcupines too are gone. It has been stated the Montana Department of Fish, Wildlife and Parks may be becoming concerned about the low porcupine populations in Montana. Porcupines are amazing and interesting animals who are an important part of the ecosystem. They deserve to be given at least basic protection by the State of Montana as soon as possible. Hopefully, it is not too late.

Gentle porcupines
do not intend to cause pain
with defensive quills.

CHAPTER 45
CLOSE ENCOUNTERS OF THE BIRD KIND

There was a movie in theaters years ago called "Close Encounters of the Third Kind" in which humans made contact with aliens from another planet. I haven't seen any aliens from space, but many others and I have seen some highly unusual birds here in Ravalli County. As with the Virginia Warbler, when we reported the strange-colored or unusual birds, we were not believed, because we either didn't have a body or were unable to take a photo.

In October 2007, a friend who is quite knowledgeable about birds and is a close observer of birds in her yard reported having a Magpie coming for handouts who had a yellow bill and yellow facial skin around the eyes. I wasn't surprised, even though Yellow-billed Magpies *(Pica nuttalli)* are normally only found in certain areas of California. She had experienced a close encounter of the bird kind. What she had seen was a Black-billed Magpie with an abnormal yellow bill and yellow facial skin. These birds are not aliens nor are they migrating here from California. Since western Montana residents first began seeing them in 1996, there have been at least a dozen such magpies observed and reported in Ravalli County and one living near the Snake River in Idaho.

Eleven years earlier, in late summer 1996, Mary, my rehabber friend and Spocklette's caregiver, stopped to look at a strange-looking magpie who was perched on a fence post by a country road near her home. She was astonished to see the bird had a bright yellow bill and bright yellow skin around its eyes. She also noted the magpie was somewhat smaller than Black-billed Magpies for whom she had cared. The bird remained on the post for some time, approximately 30 feet away, so Mary was favored with a good long look at it. She called me as soon as she arrived home to tell me about the magpie. As this was the first one reported to me, I had no clue where a magpie with a yellow bill might have originated. Several times, I went to the area where Mary had seen the magpie to look for it, as did Mary. Neither of us ever found it again. I kept the rare bird report form Mary filled out; without a photo and with only one observer, there was no point in turning it in.

Winter 1996-'97 was long and cold, with deep, crusted snow even in the valley bottom. In January 1997, a couple who lived near Lolo were putting out suet and popcorn for magpies in their neighborhood to help them make it through the cold weather. They called me to report one of the magpies coming to eat had a yellow bill, yellow skin around the eyes, and was smaller than the magpies with black bills. I told a friend who likes to photograph birds about the unusual magpie. He was invited to the couple's home to observe it and hopefully take a photo. We definitely needed a good picture if we were to be believed. The magpie was apparently camera shy. It didn't come to eat while my friend was there, except for possibly one time. It flew in and out so fast he didn't get a good look at it, let alone a photo. The bird was reported by the couple to be around for much of the winter, but even though they also tried hard to take a photo, they were not successful. I had them fill out a rare bird report form and filed it with Mary's.

In fall 1998, a man reported to me that he had observed four Yellow-billed Magpies fledge from a magpie nest near his home in early summer. He lived near the Bitterroot River on the road that leads from Highway 93, across the river to the historical town of Stevensville. Having just moved there from Central California, where Yellow-billed Magpies are common, he didn't consider the fledgling magpies with yellow bills to be unusual. When I asked him about the parents, he said both had black bills. Upon hearing that, I questioned him for some time, as to the last time he saw the young magpies with the yellow bills, whether they had yellow around the eyes, were they visibly smaller than their parents, had anyone else seen them, and whether he and his wife would be willing to fill out a rare bird report, which they did. I added it to the file of reports I had collected. The mysterious origin of magpies with yellow bills in Ravalli County had taken on a bizarre aspect; they were being hatched from Black-billed Magpie eggs.

Another magpie with a yellow bill was reportedly seen near the Snake River in Idaho that fall. And the same fall, a Ravalli County bird watcher, who lived near Victor reported he had seen two Yellow-billed Magpies coming to his bird feeders along with resident Black-billed Magpies. Unfortunately, the last time he saw the two with yellow bills was about two months prior to when I talked to him. I asked the usual questions, had him fill out a rare bird report form, and asked him to call me if he saw them again. He never called, so I assume they didn't return. His report went into the growing file of close encounters with magpies of the yellow-billed kind.

For three years after that, magpies with yellow bills were not seen or at least not reported to me. Then in winter 2001, my rehabber friend, Adele and her husband Don began seeing a magpie with a bright yellow bill and yellow facial skin around the eyes. It came to their magpie feeding area with the resident Black-billed Magpies. They lived southwest of Hamilton. Don and Adele kept a camera out and ready for most of the winter, while the magpie was coming around. As with the others, that bird was camera shy, never remaining still long enough for them to take a photo.

On Christmas bird count day, a woman who was helping me count birds, and I went to Don and Adele's home to pick up their count sheet, hoping to see the magpie with the bright yellow bill to put on the count. We both saw the bird, but it was counted as a Black-billed Magpie. Still, I was thrilled to finally see one of the elusive Ravalli County magpies of the yellow-billed kind. It had a beautiful, brilliant yellow bill and bright yellow skin around the eyes, just as everyone had reported. Don, Adele, and I all filled out rare bird report forms for that bird. I added them to the growing stack, which was still lacking a photo to prove that magpies with yellow bills really existed in western Montana. Magpies with yellow bills and yellow faces are genetically the same as the Black-billed Magpies, but they may also be genetically the same as central California's Yellow-billed Magpies. I suspect when DNA tests are done, there may be very little difference between Black-billed Magpies and Yellow-billed Magpies.

A year after Adele and Don's magpie kept things interesting, in late winter 2002, Pat Barrackman, another friend who rehabilitated wildlife at the time, called to tell me she had a magpie with a yellow bill coming to her bird feeders. At that time, Pat lived six miles west of Lolo, Montana on Highway 12. We had discussed the other magpies with yellow bills who had been seen in western Montana over the years. She said she was trying to take a photo, but it would fly in, grab some food, and fly off before she could focus the camera, just as others with yellow bills had done. Ravalli County "yellow-billed" magpies were not at all cooperative photographic subjects. Pat was not successful in taking a photo, even though the bird stayed around for most of the winter. She filled out her rare bird report form and I put it with the rest.

I sent in the pile of reports, but without a photo or a body there was no actual proof that magpies with yellow bills ever occurred in western Montana. I turned in the reports because I hoped if the birding community was aware of the possibility of seeing a magpie with a yellow bill in western Montana, they might actually look more closely at magpies and someone might eventually get a photo.

Between 2002 and 2007, no new sightings were reported to me or my friends. All the "yellow-billed" magpies had disappeared, and new young ones had apparently stopped hatching from Black-billed Magpie eggs, a phenomenon that is now easily explained by epigenetics. Black-billed Magpies are simply Yellow-billed Magpies who adapted to the colder climates they now inhabit by becoming larger in body size to help maintain heat. Also, the yellow bill and yellow skin on the face reflect heat from sunlight in the warm climate Yellow-billed Magpies had inhabited; they changed to black to absorb the sun's heat here where it is colder. Black-billed Magpies likely still have the same genes as Yellow-billed Magpies. The gene or genes for a yellow bill and facial skin are repressed, so the genetic switch for yellow bill and facial skin is no longer programmed to turn on during development. To cause Yellow-billed Magpies to hatch from Black-billed Magpie eggs, it is likely something happened to produce an epigenetic change during development, resulting in the genetic switch for yellow bill, yellow face, and smaller size to switch on in developing Black-billed Magpie embryos. Thus, when they hatch, they look exactly like Yellow-billed Magpies.

When my friend in Missoula called and told me about her encounter with the unusual magpie with a yellow bill coming to her bird feeders during fall 2007, I thought we might have another chance at a photo. She tried very hard but like everyone else who tried, was not successful. Montana "yellow-billed" magpies are still more elusive than aliens when it comes to obtaining proof positive evidence of their existence. That was the last Montana yellow-billed magpie for whom I have received a report. Whatever was causing the disrupted genes in Black-billed Magpie hatchlings appears to have stopped doing it and all magpies are again being hatched with black bills and black facial skin. If anyone again sees a yellow-billed magpie in Montana, Idaho, or any other state except California, where they live, try to get a photo and report your observation. You will be one of the few people who were privileged to have a close encounter of the bird kind.

Mountain top snow melt
flushes silt from stream bottoms.
Nature's spring cleaning.

CHAPTER 46
ANIMAL INTELLIGENCE

The behaviors of birds and mammals who have their stories told in this book were direct observations. All interactions between animals or between humans and other animals are described the way they happened. Often when I have observed and described animals exhibiting intelligence, reasoning, and emotions, I have been accused of "giving" animals human characteristics, most especially in discussions of bear behavior. To me it is not logical to suggest that someone describing a bear doing what bears do is attributing human characteristics to a bear. Many animals, including bears, whose stories are told in this book, have been on Earth much longer than humans. It would be far more logical to say humans are imitating animal behavior.

Attributing human characteristics to animals is commonly referred to as anthropomorphism, a word I researched. What I found was interesting. Anthropomorphism originally meant the representation of a god, or of God, with human attributes. Giving gods human characteristics has been done for centuries; Roman and Greek gods all had them, living much as humans did but with extra powers. This is also widely illustrated by portraying the Christian God as a man with a beard, sometimes sitting on a cloud.

Nineteenth century religious leaders began using the word anthropomorphism to mean giving other animals human attributes. With humans sharing almost identical genetic codes and all other traits with other vertebrates, this altered meaning of anthropomorphism was highly redundant. It is also extremely arrogant, since humans *are* animals. We consume and digest food, drink water, eliminate waste, and reproduce, similar to other animals.

Vertebrates, and many invertebrates, have been shown by researchers to act intelligently, adjust their behavior to changes in their environment, and show observable feelings and emotions. In mammals and birds, emotions are somewhat more obvious than in other vertebrates, although

343

certain individual fish, including sharks who interacted with special humans and reptiles kept for pets, are reportedly interactive and affectionate. All vertebrates and many invertebrates have an observable ability to learn new things, form abstract concepts, behave with intelligent awareness, flexibly and intelligently adapt to a constantly changing environment, and communicate with other animals, including humans. This has been supported by scientific research for over 200 years.

Early in the 19th century, scientists such as George Romanes documented strong evidence that animals adjust to new situations, act intelligently, and communicate with others. Romanes proposed, "The criterion of mind, therefore, is as follows: Does the organism learn to make new adjustments or to modify old ones, in accordance with the results of its own individual experience? If it does so, the fact cannot be due merely to reflex action, for it is impossible that heredity can have provided in advance for innovations upon, or alterations of, its machinery during the lifetime of a particular individual." Romanes documented significant anecdotal evidence to support his observations, as well as conducting studies and making observations himself. One example of his observations was on how ants communicate to their fellow ants that one of their colony is in trouble. The ants' ability to communicate with each other was clearly illustrated when Romanes trapped individual ants one at a time under various objects such as stones or pieces of clay. Each time, the trapped ant was released by a group of ants who came to its rescue. If a trapped ant was found by a single ant, it assessed the situation and quickly scurried off, to return shortly with a group of ants. As if the arriving ants had previous knowledge of the nature of the problem, they immediately, without further assessment, went to work to release their trapped companion and, in each case, eventually succeeded.

Many of Romanes fellow scientists, including Charles Darwin, agreed with the premise that animals act intelligently and communicate with other individuals of their species and of other species. When Darwin published his book *Origin of Species* in 1859, religious leaders and a few scientists of that time preferred not to acknowledge that humans are animals or that we are related to other animals. Those men fabricated the idea that all animals except humans act by instinct alone. From then on, the word anthropomorphism, with its new meaning of giving animals human characteristics, was used like a club to keep all subsequent animal behavior researchers in line with that dogma. The belief that all other animals except humans act by instinct alone was soon accepted by most people as true because it was convenient to believe it. That doctrine was not scientifically proven, was totally unsubstantiated, and was proven to be false by a large quantity of scientific evidence.

According to a poll reported by the media, more than 50% of people in the United States still accepted this falsehood as fact in the late 1990s. No wonder I felt like I was living in the dark ages! However, many members of the scientific community must now have a different perspective, with over 80% of faculty and graduate students polled by Steve Davis in 2006 at Oregon State University reporting, "They believe that animals have minds and can think." Welcome to the 21st century!

Charles Darwin's hypothesis was that "animal minds differ from human minds only in degree, not in kind." In spite of this enlightened view of animal intelligence by Darwin and other scientists of his era, several generations of children were taught in churches and school classes that animals do everything by instinct, that God gave humans dominion over all the other animals, and that people can therefore use the animals in any manner they choose. That was precisely what I was told in both school and church.

Fortunately, as a child growing up on a ranch, I spent a great deal of time working with or observing domestic animals, and much of my spare time observing wild animals. Many people living in urban areas lack that type of exposure to numerous wild and domestic animals. Growing up with animals made it apparent to me at a very young age that they could reason intelligently, made choices, and very definitely had feelings and emotions. Even as a child, I didn't accept the nonsense that animals do everything by instinct, considering what I was told by adults regarding that concept to be a huge lie. It took some time before I determined why adults told that lie.

The main reason so many accepted and told what I considered the "big lie" was because it made it much easier to justify human behavior. It allows us to shoot, club, trap, net, and otherwise kill, maim, or deliberately eliminate other animals by the billions in inhumane ways. Humans have long been highly inventive in devising painful ways to exploit and kill animals, including other humans if they are somehow "different." This rationale also made it easier to raise or keep animals in inhumane factory conditions simply to increase profit, and still is being used to justify enslaving other humans for profit. Many people were of the opinion that admitting animals have feelings and can experience pain might affect those profits. Thus, the falsehood that animals don't feel pain and other emotions as we do, and acted only by instinct, was actively perpetuated and still is. Similarly, in the 1800s and, as has become painfully clear, long after that, many white men believed all women and people of color were unable to think and reason. That wasn't based on any scientific evidence, just belief and discrimination, as was denying other animals' ability to think and reason.

Because of these beliefs, since Darwin's time until the last 20 to 25 years, most animal behavior research was erroneously based on the presumption that animals, especially birds, were simply instinctual robots. To be truly scientific, a researcher would have to assume, since humans are animals and are born with some instinctual behaviors, practical cause and effect intelligence, and the ability to feel emotions, all animals would be similar, differing only in degree as Darwin proposed. Unbiased animal behavior research would acknowledge these many similarities, and be directed toward determining the degree of difference in levels of various kinds of intelligence and in degrees of emotion.

An example is that most humans have a highly developed symbolic-linguistic intelligence, as well as tool-making and tool-using ability. Many animals, especially most birds, have a highly developed navigational intelligence. Many species of bird also have a well-developed musical intelligence. Some mammals and birds have the ability to make and use tools. Many species of parrots, myna birds (including European Starlings), primates, whales, and dolphins have been proven to have a well-developed symbolic-linguistic intelligence. They learn to communicate with humans by learning to speak a human language or by using specially developed symbols or sign language. All of the species tested have shown by their actions, or by saying so, that they have feelings and emotions virtually identical to those experienced by humans.

Many of the non-human research subjects have shown they have the ability to form abstract concepts. Koko, the gorilla, communicated she understood the finality of death. Koko's pet cub, with whom Koko was very affectionate and said she loved, was hit by a car and killed. When told about the accident, Koko cried and mourned the cub's death. When asked what death is, she said in sign language, "Long sleep, not wake up." Many scientists had long believed other animals didn't understand what it means to be dead. Obviously, Koko understood what death is. Also, if animals don't understand what death is, why do they try so hard to avoid being killed?

Alex, an African Grey Parrot, was viewed as being extremely remarkable. Animal researcher Dr. Irene Pepperberg picked him at random from a pet shop. Alex could link objects with words, sounds with letters, name objects, classify them by shape, size, alike and different, count the objects, and perform other intellectual feats once thought to be far beyond a bird's ability. Alex asked for things he wanted by name, named new objects with creative words he made up himself, and most importantly, expressed feelings and emotions using words in English so Irene and other researchers could understand what he felt. Alex scored at least 80% on his tests. Dr. Pepperberg thought he could do better, except for his mischievous "bad attitude" and well-developed sense of humor. Dr. Pepperberg's last endeavor with Alex before he suddenly died was teaching him to read. Many of the techniques she used to teach Alex new words, counting, and reading are now being used to teach children, especially those with learning problems. Because of Alex, it is recognized that children learn in a similar way to birds and other non-human animals.

I began communicating with mammals and birds very early in my life. My pet chickens, calves, horses, and dogs easily learned to do what I asked of them, understood English words and phrases, and responded to voice requests. Later in life, as a wildlife rehabilitator, I found each wild bird, mammal, or other animal was intelligently aware of its new and unfamiliar surroundings and quickly adapted to them. The injured ones definitely let me know they felt pain. Owls and raccoons actually sound like they are crying when they are hurt. Many of the animals showed obvious affection to siblings, to other animals of the same or different species, and to me.

One example of fondness shown by siblings was two fledgling American Robins. The affection between the two was obvious as they grew up. I received them as hatchlings and as fledglings I taught them to come when called while in a flight room learning to fly and eat by themselves. Once they were released, I called them to a certain tree, used as a rendezvous site to feed them. Until they had learned to procure their own food by watching adult robins catch worms and insects, the two fledglings had to be given food and water several times a day. All went well until the afternoon of the fourth day after release. When it was time for their early afternoon feeding, one was already at the rendezvous tree, making mournful chirping sounds. It was immediately obvious by the tone of the young robin's vocalizations that something was wrong. After a few minutes of searching, I found a circle of fledgling robin feathers, where a Sharp-shinned Hawk had eaten its prey. The remaining fledgling refused to eat. No matter how many times I called, it wouldn't come down for food. It just sat in the rendezvous tree and chirped mournfully for its sibling the rest of that day. The next morning, it was still sitting in the rendezvous tree, chirping in the same mournful tones. Late that afternoon, I finally persuaded it to come down to eat. By the next day, it had stopped making the strange chirping sounds and began following an adult male robin. It watched intently while he found and pulled worms from the ground, observed how he caught insects, and learned from the adult where the creek was to drink and bathe. After several days of instruction by the male robin, the young one no longer needed supplemental food and water. It continued to shadow the adult until they migrated. The male robin accepted the lone youngster and tutored it as if it were his own.

Scientific research and many years of interaction with and observation of animals of a large variety of species have produced undeniable evidence that vertebrates and invertebrate animals such as octopus have the ability to reason intelligently and express feelings and emotion. Many people still deny it, but it is becoming more difficult to maintain the outdated beliefs.

An invertebrate animal I interacted with for about a year was a lovely little brownish spider who had leg segments with brown and tan alternating stripes. Spidy, as I called her, had constructed a rather messy web in the upper left corner of the window above our kitchen sink. That was in the 1970s when we lived in our house one-half mile east of East Missoula.

Two or three times every day, I caught a fly or a lawn insect to place in her web. Spidy ran down the web, wrapped the insect in spider silk, then sucked out the juices from the insect's body. I always gave her something to eat when I was going to do the dishes so I could watch her while I worked. If I forgot to catch an insect and began working around the sink area, Spidy came out of her corner where she usually stayed unless eating, and down onto the web far enough for me to see her, apparently to get my attention. That reminded me to kill an insect and put it in the web, which Spidy immediately ran to, wrapped neatly, and ate while I worked and watched. In the winter, she had to be content with mealworms that had just shed their hard, outer skin and were soft and white. Spidy actually seemed to like the mealworms after she became used to eating them. I killed it by pinching its head before putting it in the web. Otherwise a mealworm wiggling around in the web would damage it.

During the summer, fall, and winter, Spidy shed her skin three times, each time emerging a bit larger but still the same color. I always found her shed skin on the window ledge below her web. I had begun feeding Spidy in June or July and continued every day for a year. The first week of the next June, we went to Yellowstone National Park for three days. I put several insects in Spidy's web early in the morning the day before we left. When we returned a beautiful shiny black spider came down from the corner to greet me, wanting to be fed. Her newly shed brown and tan skin was lying on the window ledge. The problem was, now a full-grown adult female, Spidy had a perfect red hourglass shape on her stomach. She was and always had been a Western Black Widow spider (*Latrodectus hesperus*). I hadn't known immature black widow spiders were brown and tan in color.

I didn't mind, because she was still the same Spidy who came down from her corner to be fed. I had no fear she was going to jump on me and bite me, as some people erroneously think they do. They only bite when someone puts their hand on them or they feel threatened when being squished under clothes or blankets. They certainly don't run around looking for someone to jump on and bite.

Needless to say, Bob was none too happy a black widow spider was living in our kitchen window. He wasn't afraid of her, but since she was a breeding age female, she would likely attract a few males into our house. After mating, she would lay eggs and produce many baby black widow spiders. Bob thought having several hundred black widow spiders living in our house with us might not be wise.

I checked with the University of Montana to see if anyone was studying black widow spiders. As it happened a professor was doing just that, but he was having a hard time getting some of his spiders to eat and act naturally in captivity. I told him about Spidy and how I had fed her almost every day for a year. He came to get her the next day. I asked him to report back to me how she did. When he picked her up with his forceps, he broke off one of her legs. He said it would grow back, but I wasn't happy about that. About a week after he took Spidy, he called to tell me she was doing well and was eating the insects he gave her. I doubt she missed me since she was still being fed, but I definitely missed her. She likely missed her window, as the professor kept his spiders in containers. I don't know if he ever published a paper on his black widow spiders.

Hopefully Spidy helped him find out what he wanted to know about them. She was definitely an interesting little arachnid.

Animals also demonstrate they have long memories that have nothing to do with instinct or genetic programming. Several of the stories in this book are about birds who came back to the people who raised and released them in order to obtain food and assistance after various periods of time on their own. The longest time I am aware of between when a bird left and when it returned was reported in an article by Dorinda Troutman in our local paper, *The Bitterroot Star* on March 26, 2006. In 1983, a couple found two newly hatched Canada Goose (*Branta canadensis*) goslings sitting on the midline of a highway. They couldn't locate the nest or parents, so they took the goslings home and raised them. After the young geese learned to fly, they flew around the neighborhood but returned home to be fed. Both came when called to eat grain or fresh grass out of the couple's hands. When the geese, both of whom appeared to be female, were a year old, they left in the spring and didn't return. In spring 2006, 22 years later, one of the then 23-year-old female geese returned to the couple's yard. The man went out and made the special call he had used when they were young. She walked right up to him and began eating fresh grass out of his hand as if she had never been away. Geese are known to live between 25 and 30 years. It is likely the goose found a mate and went with him each year to where they nested. Geese mate for life so possibly she lost her mate during the fall or winter hunting season. Being unattached, she was free to return the next spring to where she was raised. It is highly unlikely any other wild goose would respond to the man's special call, or walk up and eat grass out of his hand. Twenty-two years is a long time for a goose to remember the humans who raised her and where she was raised, but obviously she did.

Even more unusual was an example of people learning to communicate with an insect and vice versa. This event happened in January 2006, when a Western Tiger Swallowtail (*Papilio rutulus*) butterfly emerged from his cocoon inside a bank in Anaconda, Montana. Apparently, the caterpillar had crawled into the bank in late summer or fall 2005. Because it was in a warm environment, it emerged as a butterfly inside the bank in January. In Montana, that is midwinter, with very cold outside temperatures and no flowers on which to feed, so the butterfly couldn't be released outside.

The butterfly, christened Butterfly Bob by the bank employees, lived until March 10. Over two months is quite a long life for a butterfly inside a building. The reason Butterfly Bob lived so long was because the bank

350

employees fed him warm sugar water in what they called his "nesting box." At first, Butterfly Bob flew around in the bank and remained for long periods in the drive-through window where he could sit in the sun. Butterflies run on solar power, so he had to sun himself in order to fly. He made friends with many bank customers as well as employees who worked there. He landed on people and climbed from human finger to human finger as he was passed around. Eventually his wings became so deteriorated and tattered he could no longer fly.

That is when the real communication began. Bank employees quickly learned to observe Butterfly Bob's behavior. When he was in the drive-through window and flapped his wings, he wanted to go to his sugar water dish to "nectar," a word used to describe how butterflies eat by sucking nectar from flowers or, in Butterfly Bob's case, sugar water from a pan. They draw the liquid up through a tube called a proboscis, which is coiled under the butterfly's head when it is not being used. They unroll the proboscis to drink, using it like a straw. After Butterfly Bob drank all the sugar water he wanted, he flapped his wings again, meaning he wanted to go back to the sunny drive-through window. On Sundays, one of the bank employees went to the bank several times during daylight hours to carry Butterfly Bob to the feeding pan and back to the window.

Butterflies don't live forever and Butterfly Bob eventually died. After they heard he had died, many customers and others brought butterfly magnets, cards, glassware, and other memorabilia to the bank. One bank employee was quoted as saying "Butterfly Bob meant a lot to people."

Hopefully all those people will pay more attention to other wildlife, and may even connect with some of them in a similar way. All animals have the ability to reason and communicate, and they possess many other unique abilities, depending on their species and how their body is formed. Accepting this obvious truth makes the world so much more interesting and exciting, as those who connected to and communicated with Butterfly Bob found. If there are still those who will not accept the fact that non-human animals think, feel emotions, and communicate with other animals, it is their great loss. All who love and communicate with the human and non-human animals who share and enrich their lives will agree.

**Wolf call penetrates,
like an arrow, straight to the
core of one's spirit.**

CPSIA information can be obtained
at www.ICGtesting.com
Printed in the USA
LVHW081320170321
681760LV00034B/697